D1428913

The Wild Flowers of Ireland

The Habitat Guide

Declan Doogue and Carsten Krieger

Gill & Macmillan

Gill & Macmillan Ltd
Hume Avenue
Park West
Dublin 12
with associated companies throughout the world
www.gillmacmillan.ie

© Declan Doogue 2010
Photographs © Carsten Krieger 2010

ISBN 978 0717 1 46611

Design and print origination in Ireland by Design Image, Dublin
Printed by TBC

The paper used in this book is made from the wood pulp of managed forests. For every tree felled, at least one tree is planted, thereby renewing natural resources.

Any links to external websites should not be construed as an endorsement by Gill & Macmillan of the content or views of the linked materials.

A CIP catalogue for this book is available from the British Library.

5 4 3 2

Endpaper images © Carsten Krieger

Contents

Preface

Having led hundreds of outings for naturalists throughout Ireland, I have been constantly impressed by the interest in plants and habitat demonstrated by people who know and love their countryside and who recognise the diversity of plants and animals that give it so much of its character. Over the years, these encounters with local natural history groups have been rewarding and I have always wished that the sparks of interest so evident in the field could have been maintained. To a great extent the production of this book has been driven by the enthusiastic support I have received on these field outings. It is an acknowledgment of the dynamic that draws together in common purpose individuals from many different areas and backgrounds, all interested and willing to share their knowledge, understanding and insights. I have not yet led an outing where I did not learn something new and worthwhile from the attendees.

When I was first asked to lead outings with the Dublin Naturalists' Field Club over 40 years ago, I was overwhelmed by the body of formal facts and informal ecological knowledge so abundantly in evidence among its membership. To prepare for these trips I tried, therefore, to draw together various bits of information about the habits and habitats of the individual species and the extent to which their distributions at national and local level were influenced by environmental conditions. My favourite book at the time was the second edition of *Britain's Green Mantle* by Sir Arthur Tansley, which had just appeared. I frequently had recourse to it while preparing my outings and was able to plan my field trips following the ecological and environmental approaches outlined in that work. I still do. Tansley's book concluded with a postscript on the conservation of plants and habitat that anticipated many of the environmental changes that were to have such an effect on our native flora in subsequent years.

More recently Ireland has been given Julie Fossitt's *A Guide to Habitats in Ireland*, which provides a formal structure of habitat classification based on real Irish examples and establishes a concordance between different habitats in their Irish manifestation and comparable or equivalent habitats in Europe. This work has been of the greatest significance in providing a frame of reference and understanding for Irish ecologists and conservationists, who can integrate their discoveries and researches into a broader ecological and biogeographical schema.

Standard plant identification texts usually present information grouped on a taxonomic basis, where closely-related species are positioned near to each other on the page. This format is particularly useful when people are in a position to compare and contrast the different species of the same family or genus. However, plants occupy different spaces and habitats. It is more usual to find a mixture of different species from different plant families present at a single site. Similar related species may be found in other habitats. In preparing the accounts in this book I have attempted to convey a flavour of the main species present, coupling these with the more obvious ecological processes that operate, the pressures these habitats are under and, above all, the sense of plants in their place. In a world driven by an apparent need for change for its own sake, it is refreshing to encounter parts of the countryside where elements of natural and semi-natural habitat survive in sustainable, uncontrived conditions. These precious surviving natural spaces are templates, showing what needs to be done or not done to protect our wilder areas. Well-intentioned initiatives often result in actions that do things to the environment rather than for it! These significant areas also form natural reservoirs of native seeds for the time when the pressures on our natural habitats may become less severe.

When I came into natural history, botanists were just beginning to use the National Grid, which had begun to appear on the half-inch to the mile maps only a few years earlier. Since that time, far better maps have appeared and the entire country is now mapped on a scale of 1 to 50,000, with even more detailed maps available for some areas. The great IT developments, particularly in the area of Geographical Information Systems (GIS), have meant that people can now view copies of the original 6 and 25 inch to the mile maps and, at the click of a button, overlay on their computer screens the present-day aerial photographs of the same areas. Field naturalists with compact hand-held GPS devices can define their geographical position in Ireland to within a few metres. These devices have greatly improved the ability of field recorders to collect data and pass it on to others. Digital photography and storage have made it possible to record the presence of various species at a site and send these images on to others for identification and recording purposes. The newly-established National Biodiversity Data Centre has developed a number of important biological and environmental mapping initiatives and the State has become increasingly involved in biological recording, conservation assessment and various significant schemes to protect aspects of the Irish natural landscape.

Although data-handling procedures and presentation have improved beyond all imagination, the basic skills entailed in field botany have changed little over the years. Most of the plant species encountered by field botanists in the past still occur somewhere in Ireland but many of their colonies have been lost to economic progress. Identifying the whereabouts of these rare species and conveying this information to the appropriate authorities has become a matter of the greatest importance. Data, information and even knowledge will count for little without the formal transmission of that knowledge to those who have responsibility for the protection of our environment.

I hope that this book will go some way to alerting naturalists to the pleasures of field botany and the potential value of their observations to both the conservation movement and their local communities. It is important that individuals with that knowledge pass it on to as many others as possible. For those yet to begin the quest, this may be a first step.

A Note on Names

Plant names follow the third edition of the *New Flora of the British Isles* by Clive Stace, published in 2010. A number of familiar scientific names have been changed in that work, often resurrecting older but less well-known names. Where appropriate, the better-known name has been indicated, thus Lesser Celandine, *Ficaria verna (Ranunculus ficaria)*. A number of well-known and local popular Irish names have consciously been retained.

GRASSLANDS

Dry species-rich grasslands with Common Knapweed, Ox-eye Daisy, Devil's-bit Scabious, Eyebrights and Wild Carrot were once a widespread feature of lime-rich soils in the Irish lowlands. Many have now been converted to species-poor lush agricultural grassland.

Introduction

Plants in
their Place

There are over a thousand different species of flowering plant and fern growing in the wild in Ireland. Many of these are native to this island but others have arrived at various stages with the direct or indirect assistance of man. In recent years many additional species have shown signs of becoming established here, threatening both the existing native species and long-established arrivals.

Alterations in the distribution of species – plant and animal – give expression and advance warning of environmental changes, to our landscape, water quality and habitat diversity. These changes, though slight on a day-to-day basis, are unrelenting in their impact. A falling water table will result in the loss of many plants of damp lowland grasslands. Fluctuations in price-support mechanisms will affect the extent and character of farming at a local level. Factors such as these can completely change the flora of an area, converting common species to uncommon and rendering extinct some previously known local rarities.

To appreciate the impact of these changes it is necessary to understand the botanical evidence. The floristic data, particularly of rare species, built up mainly in the nineteenth century by a small group of naturalists formed a very useful source of reference on the condition of the environment at that time. In the light of further data generated in the twentieth century, it is now possible to appreciate the subsequent impact of environmental and habitat changes. This requires some knowledge of species, place and habitat. The discoveries of various naturalists, and particularly field botanists, give guidance as to where these plants may still be found. This book is a contribution to that process, trying to convey a sense of plants in their natural places and the significance of their occurrence there.

Learning the plants and particularly the uncommon or ecologically significant plants of an area can make an important contribution to their ongoing conservation. However, finding these plants can be difficult. Many are rare. They don't all grow together at the same time and in the same place. Luckily, there are usually a number of species associated strongly with individual habitat types. By visiting the same place at different times of the year, insights develop into the order in which species grow, flower and seed. Individual species will be seen to have their favoured patches within an area. Spotting these patterns and finding explanations for them is part of the art of field botany.

Getting the right name on a plant in the field is reward enough for many naturalists, but isolated items of data such as plant names can be joined up with environmental and geographical information to generate a more holistic overview of a particular site or habitat. Certain combinations of species can be expected to occur in different areas. In well-defined habitats such as shingle shores or deciduous woodlands a number of easily-found plant species grow, which characterise each of these areas. This book has grouped different combinations of the more obvious species into their preferred habitats. Mention is usually made of other rarer species that are often found in association with these commoner ones. Some grasses, sedges and rushes are included in the text. They are very useful indicators of habitat type but there are plenty of conspicuous and more easily-identified plants to begin with. It is by looking at the similarities and differences that we begin to appreciate and understand better the ecological workings of our familiar sites.

There is no need to travel long distances to look for exotic species. There are plenty growing in urban and suburban environments. Although more and more agricultural ground is now closed off to casual visitors, there are many areas still open to the public. Even within a site many factors – light, water, nutrients or grazing – operate in combination, allowing certain species to grow well in one spot and precluding their occurrence nearby. Use is now being made of computer-based predictive modelling to explain localised patterns of distribution and to anticipate the impacts of certain land-use alterations. These models will be very important in the future when applied to the present body of contemporary field data, which in time will become the new evidential baseline. Simple species lists, supported by photographs and GPS grid references, can become the new environmental benchmarks. These investigations do not have to be comprehensive. Simple recording, even photo-graphing the condition of a pond or a roadside verge on a particular date, can give future researchers essential data. Increased informed awareness on the part of the public and the State may go some way towards holding onto to a little of what remains of our natural biodiversity.

There is pattern to this diversity. Certain species occur regularly with others. On seeing a certain species in the field, experienced field botanists draw up a mental list of other species that might be expected in the same habitat. That experience can take many years to acquire but can be speeded up by contact with other field botanists. This is usually best done through the Naturalists' Field Clubs, especially those of Dublin and Belfast. These two clubs have been in existence for well over a century and in a sense are the inheritors and custodians of the natural history tradition in Ireland.

A little further into field botany and the beginner will start to discover rare plants growing exactly where the botanists of the nineteenth century first recorded them. Some of these may not have been recorded by anyone in the intervening period even in relatively well-botanised areas. Discoveries of this sort, of either national rarities or

RED VALERIAN

Red Valerian is a garden species brought originally from the Mediterranean region. It is now well naturalised on walls and beginning to spread into natural habitats.

MARSH MARIGOLD

Marsh Marigold is one of the largest of the late spring flowers. A native species, it is common in marshes and ditches and resembles a giant-flowered buttercup.

WOOD AVENS

Despite its name, Wood Avens can cope with less shaded conditions such as roadsides and trackways, especially where grazing is excluded.

local specialities, make it possible to envisage the terrain as it was when the records were originally made. Something has allowed these sites to retain the flora of older times. By studying these areas we are better equipped to appreciate the effects of both benign and malign recent land-use changes.

There are always instances of plants growing in the supposed 'wrong' place. When this happens, we are challenged to search for points of environmental similarity between apparently different habitats. The habitat classifications that have been developed over the years are very useful in guiding us to an understanding of environment, but they are not sacrosanct. Plants had taken up their positions in the landscape long before these human-centred classification systems had taken form. Plants such as Wallflower, Heath Speedwell, Marsh Marigold and Wood Avens did not acquire their names without good reason.

Physical processes mould the landscape, determining the type of soils and agriculture, the areas of habitation and the places where nature can still find expression. Knowing some of the plants that grow wild in the countryside, on the coast, on the banks of rivers and lakes and on the bogs and moorlands gives us insights into the processes that formed our landscape in the past and continue to mould it in the present. The future is never far away and the rate of loss for some habitats will continue to increase until there is little left to lose.

The Search for Plants

When we look back at the works of the botanists of former times we can only be amazed at their achievements. At the start of the nineteenth century transport was poor and very tiring. Communication by letter and parcel was prohibitively expensive. Field botany (the search for plants in their place) as an intellectual or even a recreational activity was virtually unknown to most people. Reliable botanical books written in English were only becoming available, mainly because of J.E. Smith's rendition into English of his own *Flora Britannica*. Most field botany and distribution studies were conducted by a small number of well-positioned academics and enthusiasts. On the other hand, some plants were very much easier to find then than now. There was far more natural habitat and access to the countryside was much easier. People were more prepared to walk long distances and by the end of the nineteenth century an extensive railway network criss-crossed the country. Fragments of these lost railway routes still survive and interestingly still provide habitats for plants that otherwise might not occur in certain areas.

Collecting Herbarium Specimens

Early botanists collected large numbers of rare specimens for preservation or identification purposes. Conservation was not generally an issue. It was often necessary to collect a specimen because it needed to be examined later under a microscope. Unidentified specimens could then be dried and forwarded to experts for their opinions.

Many species looked (and still look) disconcertingly similar. It was not always easy to identify them (or even see them as being different from each other) unless two or more specimens could be compared side by side in the field. This was easier said than done. The

FLY ORCHID

Fly Orchid has flowers that really do resemble a spectacular insect, and the lower lip (the labellum) is velvet brown with a shining blue patch. It occurs occasionally on dry limestone pavements and in wetter fenny ground in the Midlands.

BARREN STRAWBERRY (ABOVE) AND WILD STRAWBERRY (ABOVE RIGHT)

The fruits of Barren Strawberry never become the tasty edible roadside morsel of proper Wild Strawberry. Both occur on woodland margins and roadside verges. Barren Strawberry flowers earlier, has far fewer overlapping petals and can cope with shadier conditions.

plants had to be found in flower in more or less the same area and at the same time. Field botanists, however, could only be in one place at a time.

In the very early days of botany, herbalists acquired substantial volumes of named pressed reference specimens. Using these was a cumbersome and expensive process made much easier by the appearance of printed books and later by hand-coloured engravings. Plants could be identified in the field without the need in many cases to collect specimens. Even that necessity is

greatly reduced nowadays. With modern digital photography, high-quality close-up images can be created easily. Not only can these pictures convey a great deal of detail but can also show the position of the plant in relation to its habitat and broader landscape setting. This gives future seekers for the plant a reasonable chance to re-find it and to consider the impact of land-use or other changes that have taken place in the interim.

The collecting of specimens has gone very much out of favour recently. There is usually no

DANDELION

Naturalists begin their engagement with botany at an early age, blowing the heads of a Dandelion 'clock'. Each seed or achene is surmounted by a parachute (pappus), which carries the achene on the wind to new ground. Dandelions are thus superbly adapted to colonise new open ground such as flower beds and motorway verges.

valid excuse for uprooting a plant, particularly when its identity is known. It becomes more necessary when part of a specimen really does need to be examined under a microscope. If it represents a rare or significant discovery, then that specimen should be lodged in one of the main herbaria. Herbarium specimens, when properly prepared and annotated, form a body of reference material that other botanists can subsequently reassess. A botanist in a European state investigating a particular species, genus or family can request specimens on loan from the network of herbaria that covers the world. In this way, he can assemble in one spot all the available material, possibly collected over centuries from many different lands by many different botanists. He will also have the benefit of comments made by other botanists, usually written directly onto the herbarium sheets in those intervening years.

Fieldcraft

Field botany is something of an art. Although the objectives may have altered, the basic exercise has not changed much in the last two centuries. It can begin in gardens, flower beds and lawns, progressing to semi-public areas, coastal habitats, mountain and forest walks. There are plenty of new discoveries to be made and many local areas to explore, long before the need for extended searches in remote parts of the country.

Most field botanists have acquired their fieldcraft by going out with other botanists. This is by far the most effective method, which connects the newcomer to the tradition of plant recording that has been going on for three centuries in Ireland and much longer elsewhere. Tips and fieldcraft skills are acquired, learning where to find plants, which species give clues to the history or geography of a site or alert us to the possible presence of other rare species nearby. Patience and a willingness to poke about in waste ground and not be discouraged by the looks of inquisitive by-passers are important. A simple way to become familiar with the sites of some of the rarer plants is to acquire copies of the various county floras that have been produced for various Irish counties. These books give the localities and habitats for many rare plants. It is then a matter of going to the places indicated and using the habitat information provided, trying to re-find the sites for plants where they were discovered by previous workers. Many have been lost through habitat destruction. Many others have survived, especially on the coast, in mountainous areas, on lakeshores and natural woodland.

Field botany can be approached in different ways. For many, it is simply a way to see and name the various plants that stand out in the course of a walk. For others it is a matter of discovering the ways in which different combinations of species occur and then recognising that there is pattern to these combinations. Some people are absorbed by the need to protect our rarest and legally-protected species. Others are fascinated by the way in which many foreign species have recently become established in semi-wild situations, perhaps in response to altered climate patterns. We are fortunate in Ireland in that the discoveries of many rare native Irish plants made by Irish botanists were well catalogued and provide clear evidence of what species were once prominent in an area. Their disappearance tracks clearly the decline in our botanical heritage. The cost/benefit analysis of the loss of plant habitat against economic benefits seldom stands up.

Unlike other outdoor activities, field botany is very inexpensive. The only equipment necessary is a good quality hand lens and these usually come in magnifications from × 8 to × 20. The wider the lens, the easier it is to find the part of the flower you need to examine. The lower-powered magnification ones are usually easier to use. Position the specimen so that the sunlight rather than the shadow of your head falls on it. There are all sorts of useful gadgets now available, some of which are in effect high-power close-focus cameras, capable of creating very good optical images that can be digitally enlarged and transferred to a computer for further processing.

Another very useful item to have in the field is a plastic bag into which specimens may be collected. If a herbarium specimen is to be made, it should be chosen to show the parts that are most necessary for identification. If the spines of the fruits are for example, essential features for recognition, then they should appear on the specimen. Sometimes all that is needed is a small 'pinch' of a fruiting branch, especially when the botanist has gained sufficient experience to know which bit to collect. This will usually do little harm, especially to large perennial plants.

A brief note, included in the bag, stating where the specimen was collected, the type of habitat and the date, is usually necessary. Additional details such as the collector's name, the grid reference and the official name of the county or vice-county can be added. Usually voucher specimens or photographs are advisable if a botanist is considering submitting a note for publication to one of the scientific journals.

In no circumstances should plants that are known to be rare be picked, nor should their habitats be interfered with. This applies particularly to the list of legally-protected species, many of which are seriously threatened or endangered in their few surviving Irish habitats.

HAZEL

The female flowers of Hazel are among the first to appear in the year. They must be searched for from January on, tiny structures less than a centimetre in length, appearing to consist mainly of red protruding stigmas. If fertilised, these will produce hazel nuts later in the year. An inexpensive x 8 hand lens opens up an amazing vista for an enthusiastic naturalist.

The main aim in preparing a herbarium specimen is to dry the fresh plant under pressure so that it does not curl up. The specimen is placed between absorbent papers (newspaper) and some weight is applied from above, to squeeze out the water and transport it away from the specimen. The more rapidly the papers are changed, the better the chances of preserving the colours of the specimen. Some narrow-leaved species such as grasses and smaller sedges dry out very quickly. Other larger or more succulent species require several changes of paper before the plant is properly dried.

Recording Plants

Because plants are not mobile, it becomes possible to examine living specimens at close quarters. Field botanists usually have no problem getting down on the ground to examine a small plant or an interesting fragment of dune grassland. A group of field botanists will start by recording all the plants in the immediate vicinity. After a short while they will look further afield and move off determinedly towards a patch of differently-coloured vegetation in the distance. They will then head for a patch of scrub, a drain, an old ruined building or a roadside verge. The basic idea is to investigate many different small sites within larger tracts of land. In this way, an idea forms as to the number of species present but also the way in which individual species are distributed in slightly different conditions within the area under investigation.

In the past, botanists were prepared to walk for many hours in search of rarities and clearly found enough plants to make the effort worth their while. This practice continues to the present day and many spectacular finds are still occasionally made by field workers while visiting special habitats. However, most fieldwork nowadays concentrates on generating precise lists of species from small areas and often from very specific habitat types. In IT terms, these short lists can be easily maintained as separate data items that can be connected to supporting habitat information such as site, habitat, date or an OS grid reference. The records can later be merged for presentation as maps at different levels of resolution. More significantly, these amalgamated data items can be cross-referenced and compared in order to provide objective assessments of the state of our environment. In its most basic form, they can be used to illustrate the changing fortunes of individual species over time and to assess their current conservation status. In combination with other associated species from the same habitat type, they can demonstrate the extent to which the vegetation and species of various habitats have fared. In the process they can go some way towards identifying the factors that have caused these changes. Simple IT tools such as coincidence mapping (showing the occurrence of certain combinations of species) can be utilised as predictor tools to identify potential sites for species that have not been seen for many years. At a more utilitarian level, distributional data are also now used to model the impact of changing environmental conditions on water tables, air and water quality, agricultural pollution and land-use changes. A more recent development has involved the incorporation of some of the more significant distributional data into local authority databases, where the information they contain eventually may feed into local and national biodiversity plans and actions.

The Growth of Field Botany

Field botany is an unusual subject. It does not fit conveniently into the sciences, or into the arts. In an obituary notice of Alexander Goodman More, a major naturalist and keeper of the Natural History Museum in Dublin, who died in 1895, the Irish ornithologist R.M. Barrington wrote: 'He was not a scientist of the modern type.' He was making the point, which clearly needed to be made, even then, that standards of fieldcraft, the verification of records and the accuracy and custodianship of the biological records-base were significant tasks that required certain research insights. That was over a century ago and little has changed. For many students and non-students, field botany could become an enduring intellectual pleasure, combining aesthetics, observation, a little fieldcraft and the satisfaction of seeing the obvious, never before noticed. Even in Barrington's time, for many, botany was essentially a laboratory-based activity, far removed from the quest for and understanding of plants in the wild. And yet botanical lore had been an essential part of life for many years, if only at the purely utilitarian level. It formed part of the connection between people and countryside, a connection that has been weakened recently by the closing off of much of the countryside and the switch to urban living. The shift from a vernacular study driven by necessary self-interest (food, timber) and physical wellbeing (herbal medicine) to an intellectual or cultural pursuit began to take hold mainly from the eighteenth century. However, several important published works had brought field botany to the attention of a more general readership long before that.

Plant recording started late in Ireland, but has continued for almost 300 years. It existed long before that elsewhere, especially in Italy, Germany and Britain. Herbals, as actual published books, first began to appear in the fifteenth century although illustrated manuscripts existed long before that. The printed herbals of writers such as Leonhart Fuchs (1501–66) contain descriptions, mainly of medicinal plants, some of which had been abstracted from earlier commentators. However, some of the species accounts of Fuchs were connected to locations where he had encountered the plants in the wild. In time, recording the sites of occurrence of species (not only medicinal herbs) was to become an end in itself.

Many native Irish plants were certainly used as medicinal herbs. It is likely that various other medicinal and culinary plants were introduced by religious orders and the Anglo-Normans. By the early eighteenth century there was already a body of medicinal lore accumulated in book form by the herbal practitioners of the time. Publication in Ireland, however, lagged well behind. The first herbal for Ireland was not published until 1726. It was produced by Caleb Threlkeld, a dissenting minister from Cumberland. Threlkeld, who worked in Mark's Alley West off Francis Street in Dublin, collected plants and had a network of suppliers of medicinal herbs from all over Ireland. His flora, entitled *Synopsis Stirpium Hibernicarum*, was written (mostly) in English rather than Latin, which made it accessible to a greater readership. He quotes liberally from many learned sources (Greek, Latin and French) either agreeing or sometimes vehemently disagreeing with earlier authors, often for reasons that have nothing to do with botany.

Fuchsia

Fuchsia, named in honour of Leonhart Fuchs, an early botanist and herbalist, is another common garden plant that has been widely planted. It is one of the few deciduous shrubs able to endure the strong winds of the west coast of Ireland. It came originally from Chile and Argentina.

Hemp-agrimony

Caleb Threlkeld, one of the first herbalists to botanise in Ireland, recorded Hemp-agrimony sometime before 1726 near the banks of the River Liffey near Inchicore in Dublin, where it still flourishes.

Spring Gentian

Spring Gentian was one of the first species to be recorded in a formal botanical sense from Ireland. Its startling blue flowers are at their best in May, attracting many botanical visitors to the Burren.

WALL PENNYWORT (NAVELWORT)

Threlkeld found Wall Pennywort on the wall of a demolished church at Lucan, Co. Dublin in 1722. It continues to grow on old walls but is really a plant of rock exposures in lightly-shaded terrain.

He often recorded the locations where he, his helpers and other earlier researchers found these plants. Thus he speaks of Hemp-agrimony, *Eupatorium cannabinum*, growing 'In moist Rills, as under Inisacore-hill [i.e. Inchicore] near the Liffey Banks' or Spring Gentian, *Gentiana verna*, growing 'In the Mountains between Gort and Galloway'. On May Day 1722, he recorded his discovery of Navelwort or Wall Pennywort, *Umbilicus rupestris*, growing out of the wall of a demolished church at Lucan. He here combines four distinct elements – the name of the plant (and, therefore, the skill and knowledge entailed in its discovery and correct identification), the location of the discovery, the date and his personal association with the record. Some of these plants still grow where he or others found them almost three centuries ago. Many others have by now disappeared, mainly because most urban centres are much cleaner now than then. In some instances he also indicated the sort of habitat type in which he knew the plant to grow. Many of these ecological inclusions still make perfect sense to modern field botanists.

The book is of interest for another reason – it includes the first published list of Gaelic names, which were incorporated into the text using a recently-cut Gaelic type. Threlkeld's book does not have descriptions of the species, instead listing the virtues of the plant along with some associated anecdotal material. The person wanting to name an unknown species would have had to search elsewhere. The layout of the book is modelled closely on the books of the much more celebrated English botanist John Ray. It is arranged in alphabetical order using the long polynomials that were such a feature of herbals, which survived for many years. Our familiar Daisy was referred to at the time as 'BELLIS MINOR SYLVESTRIS SIMPLEX', a phrase that had been in use for many years before the *Synopsis*. Other contemporary botanists would have utilised other names for the same species.

Publishing was a very expensive business and illustrations were extremely costly. There are various instances where the original woodblocks used to illustrate certain herbals were sold on from publisher to publisher and re-used in texts by different authors years later. One way of dealing with this costly difficulty was by acquiring a *Hortus Siccus* – literally a collection of dried plant specimens, bound up in book form, which could be used as reference material by doctors, herbalists

DAISY

Daisy, originally encumbered with complicated phrase names such as *Bellis Minor Sylvestris Simplex* or *Bellis scapo nudo uniflora* had its name tidied up to the much more convenient *Bellis perennis* by Linnaeus.

GERMANDER SPEEDWELL

Germander Speedwell, *Veronica chamaedrys*, with its two conspicuous stamens and a solitary style would have been placed early in the system of classification developed by Linnaeus, who also popularised the binomial system of nomenclature.

and apothecaries. These volumes could be assembled by knowledgeable herbalists or purchased, ready-made, as sets of pressed named specimens by those studying medicine. A number of these volumes have survived to the present day.

Prior to this, herbal-botanists would have had great difficulty in naming many plants and equating them with species that had been described elsewhere. A botanist working in isolation in Siberia might not be expected to have easy access to the learning of the Italian botanists and herbalists who, as well as being in contact with one another, would also have had access, both linguistic and physical, to the libraries of the time. Then, and for many years before, botanists not only discovered new plants but also published original descriptions of them and gave them names. Other botanists working elsewhere might have discovered and described the same species but given it a different name. There might, therefore, be several names in use for the same species. This created many uncertainties as regards the correct identification of species, which would have had serious consequences for herbalists and their patients. This muddle needed to be sorted out.

The impetus for this rationalisation was provided by the Swedish botanist Carl Linnaeus, although other botanists had previously brought forward other systems of classification. Linnaeus, in an extraordinary feat of mental overview, made a number of major contributions to botanical studies. In a series of trips to various parts of northern Europe, visiting the gardens, herbaria and libraries of various institutions and working on preserved specimens in his own collections and those of others, he attempted to bring order to the world of plant identification and nomenclature. His major work, *Species Plantarum* (1753), initiated a system of naming plants that was to increase greatly the access of many people to the subject. An account of a species in this great work begins with the name that he adopted or proposed. Beneath this stands a brief but concise description of the species, along with the names that had been used by previous authors and comments on their geographical occurrence. The name Linnaeus gave was a shortened name, usually of two parts, the genus and the species. Thus the familiar Daisy became simply *Bellis perennis*. This was a great improvement from the various pre-existing awkward descriptive phrase-names such as *Bellis scapo nudo uniflora*, or *Bellis minor sylvestris simplex*. At a stroke he had simplified not only the naming system but had also pulled the earlier names under a single title, and attached the name to a brief but separate description. This is the basis upon which species are named to this day, though the process is by now far more regulated.

Linnaeus's *Species Plantarum* had itself become possible because, in 1737, 16 years earlier, he had produced his *Genera Plantarum*, which in turn had evolved from earlier works. In this he laid out the way that the genera of plants as they were then known to him were to be arranged. He devised a system of classification, which became known as the Linnean Sexual System, based on the numbers of the different organs in the flower – the number of stamens, then pistils. This is a central element in plant classification. The genus *Veronica* with its two stamens and single pistil belonged to the DIANDRIA, MONOGYNIA, under which were 22 other genera from very different modern plant families. Thus, plants with very different growth forms, leaves, stems, even habitats are connected by similarities in their flowering structures.

For all its artificiality, the system was relatively easy to work and was widely adopted by several generations of botanists. The species were arranged within the book in ascending arithmetical order of stamens. The user would begin by counting the stamens of an unknown specimen, then the pistils and so on. In this way a short list of genera and species would emerge. It was then a matter of working through the descriptions within the various genera to find the one that matched best. Linnaeus had developed a system that was future-proofed to cope with the anticipated discoveries which, as expected, flowed in as the botanical exploration of the known world increased.

The accounts of the Irish flora from the early nineteenth century were organised on this system and its use continued for some years. Its great practical utility was that it provided a method whereby botanists could arrive more reliably at the correct name for a plant. If the plant could be named, then it could be connected with other relevant pieces of knowledge. In this way it gradually became possible to build up a greater overview of the physical characteristics and geographical distribution of individual species. This led to an appreciation of the association of certain species with certain habitats and a later realisation that different habitat types, though superficially similar, hosted different combinations of species.

Although the Linnaean system of classification was effectively abandoned shortly after, in favour of more 'natural' arrangements, the binomial system of nomenclature coupled with the tidying up of the earlier names had a huge influence in promoting the study of plants in the field. Much of the earlier uncertainty of naming had been removed and there was a widespread regularisation of the way in which the names were applied. Many books on plant identification were produced. The quest for plants for their own sake became an acceptable outdoor and intellectual pursuit in an era when access to university education was not an option for most people. Field clubs began to appear where knowledge was shared and fieldcraft skills were acquired. They were in effect the open universities of their time. The era of the amateur naturalist had arrived. Various prominent botanists encouraged the search for plants and scientific journals published accounts of the quest for plants in different parts of Ireland by British and Irish botanists. The (Royal) Dublin Society and the

1970–1986
1987–1999
2000–2009

DARK-RED HELLEBORINE

Recording and mapping the geographical distributions of species are major features of most field botany. The maps indicate the presence of species at the level of the 10 km square. For rare species such as Dark-red Helleborine, information of this nature is vital in defining areas in need of special conservation measures.

Royal Irish Academy were very much involved in supporting these researches. The efforts made by many individuals resulted in the production of two major reviews of the state of knowledge of the Irish flora, *Cybele Hibernica*, by David Moore and A.G. More published in 1866 and revised by Nathaniel Colgan and Reginald Scully in a new edition in 1898. In both these works, Ireland is divided into 12 botanical regions and details of habitat, status and distribution are included for each species.

By the end of the nineteenth century the cumulative product of various studies at county level began to appear in print. The most convenient genre for publication became the 'County Flora', usually a substantial book that summarised the distributions of species at the level of the county. These books, modelled on various county and local floras produced in Britain, appeared for counties such as Dublin, Kerry, Donegal, and also for the north-east of Ireland, many of their authors having been inspired by the encouragement of A.G. More. The next great giant of Irish botanical exploration, Robert Lloyd Praeger, finding that the divisions of *Cybele Hibernica* were too large and encompassed too much topographical diversity, divided Ireland into 40 divisions ('vice-counties'), splitting the larger counties of Cork, Kerry, Galway, Mayo, Donegal and Tipperary into two or three more manageable divisions. He travelled throughout the country, concentrating on the less well-worked areas. His investigations provide a powerful snapshot of the state of the Irish flora at the start of the twentieth century. The data were presented in one of his major works, *Irish Topographical Botany*, which was published by the Royal Irish Academy in 1901. A summary of the distribution of each species was given with more detailed locality information for the rarer species.

More recently, computerisation has made the production of distribution maps, which show the broad geographical patterns of individual species using dots on maps, a relatively straightforward task. Each dot represents the occurrence of a species within a 10-km square of the Irish National Grid. However, modern biological distribution data often exists at a much finer level of resolution and most serious botanical recorders use hand-held GPS instruments to generate very precise grid references, at least for the rarer species.

The golden age of Irish botany occurred at the end of the nineteenth century, when the leaders of Irish field botany put in the sort of effort that we can only imagine nowadays. In the space of about 40 years they travelled most of the country and produced paper after paper on the distribution of Irish plants. Their researches provide the evidential basis for what we now know to have grown there. Nathaniel Colgan, for instance, produced his *Flora of the County Dublin* in 1904. It lists in detail the sites where he found the rarest plants and also reviews the records made by previous workers. We can now understand the botanical impact of many of the environmental changes that occurred since that time.

Rare plants are rare because the habitat conditions that they themselves require are rare. It has, therefore, become more and more difficult to find them. The environmental pounding that our countryside has taken in the last century has drastically reduced the amount of available habitat for large numbers of plants. Some species, once common, have now become rare. Some of our rarest Irish species are now approaching extinction, tracking the gradual decline in the structural diversity of the countryside. Two extremes are evident in the way in which much of the rural environment is managed. At one end of this polarity there is extreme exploitation, culminating in the creation of the great species-poor green desert of silage grassland that now covers most of fertile lowland Ireland. At the other end there is the increasing phenomenon of abandonment, where species-rich grassland is gradually reverting to bracken and rough scrub when grazing and subsidy is removed.

The search for plants in their natural surroundings is a straightforward activity, which can be taken at various levels. For some, that walk in the countryside admiring a few of the more obvious colourful species is quite enough. With time, smaller plants with less flashy colours come to notice. As the botanical searcher becomes more experienced, the species begin to reveal something of themselves and their whereabouts.

At a national or international level, we can see how the geography of individual species is determined by climate. The wetness of the west has resulted in the formation of great areas of blanket bog dominated by species seldom seen in the east. The much sunnier and drier south-east has a range

BRACKEN

As many upland areas are abandoned, Bracken reclaims the land, engulfing rough pasture, boundaries and even trackways.

of species that is virtually unknown in the north-west. These distribution patterns are well-known and reflect much broader patterns of oceanic and continental climatic influence. Occasionally, a colony of a species is found beyond its known range. A gravel pit somewhere in the Midlands holds a colony of a legally-protected open-ground species. A small woodland, apparently similar to

many others nearby, has a colony of a rare woodland orchid. Why they grow in one place and not in another is part of the challenge and interest of field botany.

At a more local level, we can see how these local distributions of plants tell us a great deal about the soils, hydrology and land-use history of an area. The inquiring walker-explorer will find that the covering of plants across most of our countryside provides a living testament of the land-use history, geography and geology that lie beneath. At a typical walking pace, broad ecological perspectives become visible – the extent of impeded drainage indicated by the rushy fields, the vista of Bracken re-invading abandoned upland grassland. At a slower pace, the explorer will recognise the presence of former habitation, signalled by the isolated clusters of Elder or Tea-tree persisting long after the homesteads where they once grew have been levelled. A lime-loving species gives way to a species of more acid ground where the covering of glacial till becomes thinner and bedrock protrudes. A walk through a sand dune system reveals the extent and impact of ground water in the dune slacks. These are some of the botanical expressions of local, small-scale diversity and part of the satisfaction of fieldwork lies in recognising these physical and biological differences and the way they relate to each other. Bit by bit, like elements in a giant jigsaw, the observer realises that

CROPLAND

Although many annual weeds were recorded from cornfields in the past, modern cereal management regimes give them little chance. A few can survive, especially those that can germinate after the crop has been cut.

there is pattern to the combinations of species that are encountered. Later still, the causes for some of the variation in species composition and the reasons for that pattern begin to clarify. The first step is to become familiar with the main eye-catching species. Each has a tale to tell. In time the patterns become clearer. The quest matures and becomes not so much a matter of seeing the wood for the trees, but of searching for the reasons for the existence of the wood itself.

The botanists of the past left us an amazing legacy of information that even today is only gradually being progressed into useful knowledge. Field workers in botany, from across the social divide, found common cause in the search for plants at a time when background, social or professional, greatly influenced the character of opportunities available to people. Their coming together, at least metaphorically (for they lived in different places at different times), created a body of evidence of the natural diversity of our countryside and has led profoundly to our belated appreciation of what remains of it.

Habitat, Community and Succession

A botanical visit to a sandhill system will yield a list of plant species typical of sandhills. A similar visit to an undamaged raised bog will produce a list of species characteristic of raised bogs. Few species will turn up on both lists. Even in similar conditions there may be little in the way of species overlap. Ling, *Calluna vulgaris*, Cross-leaved Heath, *Erica tetralix*, and Sundew, *Drosera rotundifolia*, will consistently occur closely together in raised bogs, but are unlikely to be encountered in an outer dune system. Similarly Marram, *Ammophila arenaria*, Sea Spurge, *Euphorbia paralias*, and Sea Holly, *Eryngium maritimum*, will occur in a sand dune system but we do not expect to see them in a raised bog or in any other inland habitats. When habitats are so different from each other, in terms of their soil, water regimes, salt tolerance and many other factors, the differences are expressed clearly by their lack of species in common. However, when certain habitats are not quite so dissimilar, a number of species emerge with the ability to flourish in each. Biting Stonecrop, *Sedum acre*, will grow in thin, stabilised sand dune grassland and partly-vegetated shingle ridges and will also occur inland in lime-rich gravel pits and on old walls. This species needs free-draining, lime-rich, sunny situations. It finds these and other more subtle environmental conditions present in these habitats. It will not do well, therefore, in a raised bog.

However, there are some species that can cope with what to our eyes are very different habitats. The raised bog specialist Ling will also be abundant on mountain blanket bogs. This is no surprise, but it can also turn up in wet areas in leached dune systems. Bell Heather, *Erica cinerea*, typically a species that dominates heathland, grows with great

ROUND-LEAVED SUNDEW

Round-leaved Sundew is a species of wet, acid peaty ground such as raised bogs, blanket bogs and damp areas in heathland. Its leaves are equipped with sticky hairs with which it traps small insects. It rarely occurs other than in these habitats.

SEA HOLLY

Sea Holly is confined to the coast, where it grows on sand dunes, and coarse sand on consolidated shingle ridges.

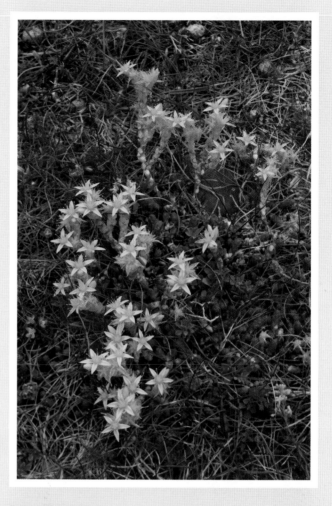

BITING STONECROP

Biting Stonecrop is at its most natural in thinly-grassed sand dune systems but has managed to spread inland onto sandy grassland and more obviously on roofs and gutters of old houses in country towns.

success on dry leached dunes. Species with the ability to live in many different habitats are at an immediate geographical advantage. Species with a narrower ecological amplitude can only function well within a limited range of habitats.

Good comprehensive species lists can be very useful aids in determining which habitat type a naturalist is examining. Such species lists are often prepared from small sample areas (generally a 2 m × 2 m square) and form the basis of a great deal of

habitat and community investigation. The smaller the sample, the easier it becomes to connect it to some environmental variable or combination of variables. Too large a sample allows in too much extra data, which cannot then be pinned tightly to particular environmental factors. The habitat combines many different factors that interact but not always continuously, at the same time or to the same degree. A wood may have more light falling on its floor in December than in August. The

WOODLAND

When trees die new light falls on ground that may have been in shade for many years.
Sometimes plants that have not been seen for years germinate, grow and flower in the
clearings.

Many microspecies of Bramble can rapidly invade abandoned heathy and acid ground.

upper parts of a salt marsh may be flooded for less than a week each year.

We speak loosely of 'habitat' when we often strictly intend the 'habitat type'. An individual species may be said to be typical of the salt marsh habitat, but that term is a type of shorthand for a range of interacting environmental variables that occur within the salt marsh formation. The combination of species and the relative proportions of each growing in the habitat constitute the vegetation. Vegetation classification (i.e. categorising the various combinations of co-occurring species) is a very complicated exercise. The species occurring in close proximity on a site are there because they share to some degree a set of environmental requirements, not because they are of necessity symbiotic (though there are some exceptions here).

The mixture of species present on a site is the outcome of the physical conditions, climate, management, distance from other colonies, opportunities for establishment, colonisation and many other factors. When plants are encountered growing in 'unusual' places, it reminds us that the conditions are unusual only from our perceptions of the boundaries of habitat.

There therefore emerges a selection of plants with varying degrees of affiliation to individual habitats. Their differing environmental requirements determine their success or lack of it in contrasting habitats. Species with broad tolerances within a certain habitat type may accordingly be widely distributed within it. Species with more specialised requirements will be much rarer within the larger habitat. In heathland a number of different species live together but in very different ways. Bell Heather, a fairly robust perennial species, may be widespread through heathy ground, but Small Cudweed, *Filago minima*, which is also a plant of heathy ground but a tiny non-competitive annual species, may only appear briefly on bare, open stony ground after a heathland fire and may disappear again as the taller vegetation recovers.

SCRUBLAND (ABOVE) AND BLACKTHORN (NEXT PAGE)

In certain circumstances a form of scrub woodland reappears following abandonment of rocky ground. Hawthorn, Blackthorn and Hazel reassert themselves, to be joined by taller trees in the absence of intense grazing.

The vegetation of many habitats is, therefore, in a state of alteration over time. The freshly-tilled field is gradually colonised by a succession of quickly-germinating annual species. These are succeeded by more enduring perennials, especially grasses, which are in turn followed by invasive scrub species like Elder and Brambles. Later, trees will appear and eventually shade out most of the previous species but in time create suitable conditions for woodland species. The maturing process from open ground to woodland may take centuries, but many transformations come about much faster. The aquatic vegetation of small, shallow open-water drains can change after a few summers to a choking scraw of dense, tall-growing, nutrient-demanding emergent grasses. In some natural habitats, especially on the coast, the successional clock is reset very often, sometimes

even within a year when the component parts of shingle ridges, fore-dunes and even sand dune systems are dismantled and reconstituted often by the actions of wind or tide. The process of germination, growth and re-establishment restarts.

At the other end of the succession timeline, things are very different. Deciduous woodland habitats are very stable once they have achieved the end point in a succession. They are the natural climax vegetation for most of Ireland when allowed to develop. But even here, in dense woodland, the process of succession can be reactivated. An old tree eventually dies, falls and decays. A huge influx of light falls on the formerly shaded soil. New plants spring up as the seeds of species not seen for years germinate in the new light.

Between these two extremes, other processes operate. The natural grasslands of the countryside are maintained in a species-poor condition by intensive grazing and silage production. As currently farmed, they will not become the forests that once grew in their place but which were felled many years ago. In recent years, the reverse is also taking place. Areas of economically-marginal rocky pasture, once able to sustain an open grassland flora, are now being abandoned, engulfed by Furze, Bracken and Blackthorn as these species gradually reclaim their former territories. Open grassland species, accustomed to a degree of bright sunshine, fall into shade and go into decline.

These are some of the components that go into the mix of determining which species will succeed and which will fail. When they are coupled with the impact of price-support mechanisms and the depletion of structural diversity, all result in alteration in species distribution and community composition. Rare species tend to get rarer. Some common species become more common. Invasive species may come and go and others become naturalised. These natural fluctuations and very unnatural alterations now stand contraposed in Ireland as elsewhere in the world.

Latin Names

Many naturalists are put off by so-called 'Latin' names. Ornithologists have always called a Robin a Robin rather than *Erithacus rubecula*. Entomologists would never refer to *Aglais urticae* as anything other than a Small Tortoiseshell Butterfly. All properly described species have scientific names, but most of these do not have 'real' genuine vernacular names. Colourful and conspicuous species are the exception. The Primrose, *Primula vulgaris*, and Cowslip, *Primula veris*, have acquired English popular names. In Ireland there is a wealth of well vouched-for Gaelic plant names, some of which have crept into Hiberno-English. Yellow Flag or Flaggers, *Iris pseudacorus*, can still be heard called Fellistrums. In many parts of Ireland the term 'Ragwort' is rarely used, being replaced by variants of Buachalán. The same species can have a wealth of local names throughout its geographical range. This is not a problem if everyone speaks the same

COWSLIP

On lime-rich grasslands in springtime, Cowslips (as their scientific name *Primula veris* indicates) thrive where grazing is light and the sward has not been 'improved'.

language and calls the species by the same name. However, popular vernacular names can be applied to very different organisms even within the same language area. To most Irish people, a 'Daddy Long Legs' is a large fly with six very long legs, usually encountered trapped inside a window. An American will apply the same name to a Harvestman, a relation of the spiders, equipped with eight legs and no wings. The need for a standardised system of naming was appreciated at a very early stage and has been maintained to the present day. The great advantage of the Latinised names is that botanists in Ireland, England and the rest of the world know that when they refer to *Iris pseudacorus*, they all know which species is intended. Furthermore, as if to emphasise the importance of taxonomic Latin, when a new plant is described for the first time, and its name published, that description must include a detailed statement of the characteristics of the new species written in Latin.

There are usually three parts to a name, the genus, the species and the name of the describer (or subsequent reviser of the name). Thus Cowslip, *Primula veris* L., belongs to the genus *Primula* of which there are a number of similar and related species including Primrose, *Primula vulgaris.* The abbreviation 'L.' after the name indicates that it was validly described by Linnaeus originally.

Scientific names may have derived from many sources and have been 'Latinised', i.e. they have been made to fit into the syntax and grammar of botanical Latin, irrespective of their original linguistic source. The initial name of the species or genus may have been a genuine vernacular term of long standing, often because the plant had a utilitarian purpose. These qualities may be reflected in the specific names – some were used as food (*edulis* = edible), as medicinal herbs (*officinalis* = used in medicine) or because of some conspicuous

YELLOW IRIS (YELLOW FLAG)

A wet field of Fellistrums (Feileastram) might also be called Flaggers, Yellow Flag, Yellow Iris and various other names. The scientific name *Iris pseudacorus* simplifies matters botanically but loses some of the vernacular culture.

BURNET ROSE

Burnet Rose has recently had its older name – *Rosa spinosissima* – restored. The stems and branches are covered with fine needle-sharp prickles that discourage ramblers and grazing livestock. As a result, a number of grazing-sensitive species can often find sanctuary where the rose has not grown to form dense low thickets.

characteristic such as the colour of their petals (*albus* = white, *luteus* = yellow). In many other cases the generic name may have been coined in honour of a botanist, e.g. *Rudbeckia*, *Linnaea* and *Fuchsia* after Olaus Rudbeck, Carl Linnaeus and Leonhart Fuchs respectively. The Latinised versions of place names can also be utilised. Various names derived from the Roman names for places – *carthaginiensis*, *londinensis*, *britannicus* – are fairly obvious but many others are unfamiliar to the modern reader. There are interesting survivals. Eboracium, the Roman name for York, crops up in the name of the Bramble, *Rubus eboracensis*, which would ring a bell with horse-racing fans who attend the Ebor Festival at York racecourse. There are also many specific epithets that describe parts of the plant. A plant organ may be kidney-shaped (reniform – *reniformis*), sickle-shaped (falcate – *falcatus*) or keeled (*carinatus*) and so on. For example, an older name (now revived) for Burnet Rose was *Rosa spinosissima*, which more than adequately conveys the true character of its prickles.

Many plants, especially the small and inconspicuous species, never had vernacular names and, therefore, many simply had to be invented. Even where there were authentic names, their usage had to be standardised. The Bluebells of Scotland refers to a species of *Campanula* and has nothing to do with the woodland plant of Ireland and England, *Hyacinthoides non-scripta*. Some of these contrived English names can be a rather off-putting. Robert Lloyd Praeger succinctly summarised it in his preface *to A Tourist's Flora of the West of Ireland* (1909): 'English names are added for the sake of those who find it easier to remember "Bristle-leaved Spike-rush" than *Scirpus setaceus*.' This remark was made of course when Latin was a much more prominent component of the school curriculum.

RAGWORT

Pulling 'Buacháláns' from pasture was a necessity for many years and under its official name, Ragwort, it even made it onto the list of noxious weeds.

HAREBELL

Harebell, *Campanula rotundifolia*, which was sometimes called Bluebell, is a relative of Canterbury Bells. The Bluebell, *Hyacinthoides non-scripta*, belongs to a very different family from the Harebell.

Another source of irritation rests in the way in which a habitat-related specific epithet sometimes seems to bear no relation to the environment in which we encounter the particular species. This usually happens when a plant was appropriately named to reflect its association with a particular habitat, e.g. *aquaticus* (or *aquatica*), *sylvaticus* (or *sylvatica*) to denote its affinity to wetland or woodland habitats. However, it does not follow that a species is confined to woodlands throughout its range. A species might be limited to sheltering woodlands in Central Europe, but when growing in the milder and more oceanic climate of the west of Ireland may be more common in open terrain. If we had active taxonomists in Ireland 300 years ago, the world might have been given more plant species with names like *hibernicus*.

Bluebell

Usually a woodland plant, Bluebell can also occur in more open situations, often where Bracken creates a low, shading canopy. Here it also occurs with other widespread woodland species such as Pignut, Primrose and Violet.

WATER MINT

Water Mint, *Mentha aquatica*, occurs in a variety of
wetland situations and is widely distributed
throughout Ireland.

Distribution, Biogeography and Conservation

Once botanical recording took on its relatively modern form, the study of the distribution of species then became a very important part of field botany. The process of finding, naming correctly and recording the results of fieldwork has carried on through the great debates on creation, evolution and, more recently, cladistics and molecular biology. At its simplest, these studies revealed that many species were not distributed evenly across Ireland. Many were widespread, but within their broadly-defined geographical ranges had patchy distributions that were clearly related to their habitat preferences. When more information was assembled, it then became possible to advance theories as to why certain species occurred where they did but failed elsewhere. These investigations were informed by an increasing appreciation of the impact of factors such as climate, soil formation, geomorphology and human-plant interactions. Researches of this type were to have great significance many years later in deciding which species and habitats were of conservation importance.

In tandem with other botanical survey work elsewhere in Europe, plant geographers had realised that a number of species occurred in the west of Ireland that were not known in Britain. These plants grew in naturally wild areas and did not have a reputation for invasiveness elsewhere in the world. On the European mainland some of these were known only from the Iberian Peninsula, the Atlantic coast of France and even the Mediterranean. Ireland was, therefore, seen as something of a geographical outpost for these species. The routes by which they had made their way into Ireland were not immediately evident.

Some, such as Large-flowered Butterwort, *Pinguicula grandiflora*, Kidney Saxifrage, *Saxifraga hirsuta*, St Patrick's-cabbage, *Saxifraga spathularis*, and Strawberry-tree, *Arbutus unedo*, were, therefore, of great geographical interest. Were the existing colonies the surviving remnants of species that were once much more widespread and had become rarer as environmental conditions altered? Or had they made their way into Ireland possibly via some route from the south-west?

IRISH SPURGE

Irish Spurge is frequent over much of south-west Ireland in sheltered situations – woodlands, river glens and even hedged roadsides. It is extremely rare in Britain and confined to south-west England.

Other species, such as Irish Spurge, *Euphorbia hyberna*, and Cornish Moneywort, *Sibthorpia europaea*, had broadly similar geographical distributions but did grow in Britain. Cornish Moneywort is a small creeping herb on damp, shady, acid soil widespread in the Dingle peninsula and nowhere else in Ireland, which next turns up in south-western Britain, especially in Cornwall and Devon. Irish Spurge is a large plant that is widespread in sheltered situations throughout much of Cork and Kerry but in Britain is limited to a few sites in the south-west.

There was also a remarkable group of heaths and heathers found to occur in the west of Ireland. The best known of these is St Dabeoc's Heath, *Daboecia cantabrica*, which is very obvious in rocky, heathy ground throughout the west. It is a large and colourful heath with bright magenta tubular flowers, now widely sold in garden centres. Three other heathers belong here also: Irish Heath, *Erica erigena*, is found in the edges of bogs and moorland in Galway and Mayo, Mackay's Heath, *Erica mackayana*, in Galway, Mayo and Donegal, and recently found in Kerry, neither of which are known in the wild in Britain, and Dorset Heath, *Erica ciliaris*, in Connemara, which as its name indicates occurs in Dorset and also in Devon and Cornwall.

An even more peculiar group of species was identified also in the west and north-west. This was a so-called American group. The most intriguing is a plant called Pipewort, *Eriocaulon aquaticum*. It grows on the margins of shallow pools in blanket bog from Cork to Donegal, appearing again in lakes on Skye and elsewhere in Scotland but nowhere else in Europe. It is, however, widely distributed in North America. A more colourful species with a similar distribution is Irish Lady's-tresses,

Spiranthes romanzoffiana. This is scattered in wet peaty ground often subject to flooding and largely exhibiting a western distribution from Cork to Lough Neagh but is possibly extending its range. It also occurs in Scotland and in a few English sites, but next appears in North America.

Within the context of Ireland alone, the revealed distributions of many of these species were shown to be strongly associated with areas of high rainfall and 'soft' days, which fitted in nicely with corresponding climate patterns in Britain and Europe. Research and debate still continues as to how and when these species got here. Traditional methods such as pollen analysis have shown that some of these species were present when the peat bogs were forming. Modern molecular research is now being employed to estimate the times of their arrival here and to examine their current status.

Another issue that has emerged from these geographical studies is the significant number of species which made it into Britain but which failed to get into Ireland before the rising post-glacial seas cut off access to the island. Most of these species had a strong southerly bias and others now have pronouncedly northern distributions and occur in the colder areas of upland Scotland. For its size, Ireland has a very diverse range of soils and topography, but we lack the high mountains of Scotland and the warm soils of the south of England. We are also further away from the European mainland, cut off by two stretches of water. This made and continues to make colonisation by natural means very difficult and is compounded by the heavily-managed character of our landscape.

The pattern has become very complicated in recent years by the arrival and establishment of a large number of invasive species. Many wild areas are being invaded by robust species that originally escaped from gardens and are now consolidating their ranges. The spread of very obvious species such as Rhododendron, *Rhododendron ponticum*, and Giant Hogweed, *Heracleum mantegazzianum*, and more recently Giant Rhubarb, *Gunnera tinctoria*, has been fairly well tracked but many other species are well established and clearly out-competing the native flora here.

Early studies showed that some native species were only found near the coast, on high ground, in lakes or rivers. These distributions were linked to the range of habitat types that a species was able to occupy. Some were closely associated with human habitation sites and others were only encountered in dark woods or the spray zone of sea cliffs. Other species were found in a wide range of habitats and, therefore, had wide distributions.

The development of computerised data-handling systems greatly altered the way in which fieldwork was conducted. The data that existed up to the 1950s was of very mixed quality. Although a species might have been found in every vice-county in Ireland, there were many instances where such a species might have been abundant in some areas and very rare or absent in others. To address the issues of biological distribution at a more precise level, other methods were devised.

Many field surveys were conducted throughout Britain and Ireland, mainly in the 1950s. These data were computerised, linked to older data that could be allocated a sufficiently precise grid reference (not always possible) and presented as a very substantial atlas showing the distribution of each species on a 10-km basis. At a glance the contemporary status of each species could be ascertained and the distributions compared in Britain and Ireland. It then became possible to envisage which combinations of environmental factors such as rainfall, soil type and elevation might have combined to bring about these distributions. Recently the entire project was revived and resulted in the production of *The New Atlas of the British & Irish Flora*. Most of the fieldwork for this project was conducted by volunteer botanists for the BSBI (Botanical Society of the British Isles).

In an inverse way, plant distribution has become a means to indicate the whereabouts of habitats. Field botanists now use combinations of locality data for older records, geographical information systems (GIS) and aerial photographs to predict likely sites for rare plants and habitats. Distribution data, when properly localised, provide a body of raw data with many other useful functions. The data, when utilised properly, can provide information on the changing state of the environment, and contribute to an understanding of the effects of water pollution or excessive grazing, of gradual drainage, peat removal or the abandonment of marginal land.

The various mapping projects also made it possible to determine which species were rare or common, widespread or of limited range, locally abundant or thinly scattered. By probing the data a little, it was possible to form an opinion as to whether a species was native or introduced, a casual contaminant in imported grain or a long-established weed of cultivation. These findings served to inform naturalists of the status of plants and their value as materials for interpreting the Irish landscape. These data became central in determining which species are most urgently in need of conservation at a local level. A species with a clear-cut distribution such as Irish Spurge can be very common at a number of sites within its range, less frequent as it reaches its geographical limits and may then re-appear elsewhere in Ireland, when and where a sufficient number of its environmental requirements are satisfied. A nice example is afforded by St Patrick's-cabbage. Within its main range (Cork to Donegal) it occurs commonly on acid rocks, even growing on trees and old walls. It grows on many of the offshore islands and can be seen abundantly around many of the tourist routes

BELL HEATHER

Detailed recording and mapping of the distribution of both common and rare species of flora has made it possible to target which species and habitats are most in need of conservation.

THRIFT

Thrift or Sea Pink thrives in windswept ground in the sea-spray zone, assisted in no small part by its cushion-forming habit and strong rooting system, which anchors it firmly in the soil.

GRASSLAND

Many of our Irish grasslands have by now lost most of their botanical interest. Much of the countryside was tilled at various stages in history. The natural grassland flora takes a long time to recover.

of Ireland through Connemara, Mayo and into Donegal. It flowers profusely in May and June and is a spectacular plant on many roadside rock exposures. It extends less conspicuously into east Munster, occurring in a number of fairly select sites in Waterford and Tipperary. The details of this interesting and archetypal 'Lusitanian' distribution had been fairly well worked out by the end of the nineteenth century but in 1924, while botanising on the west flank of Cloghernagh Mountain in the Baravore Corrie of Lugnaquilla, Arthur W. Stelfox and James P. Brunker found this species for the first time in the east of Ireland. The occurrence of a population of this species in this site, so detached from the nearest Waterford and Tipperary colonies, was of great biogeographical significance. Within the context of Ireland, the single isolated colony on Lugnaquilla tells us more and is arguably more important than any individual colony of similar size within the main range of the species. It is often the outliers, the populations that are at the edges of the range of a species, that tell us most about the *de facto* needs of a species and give us insights into the reasons for its current distribution. This simple one-species illustration indicates some of the difficulties involved in implementing conservation protection measures at a national level using national legislation. A species may be exceedingly rare in some part of Ireland and be of great biogeographical significance but may not enjoy national protection because it is sufficiently common elsewhere in the State.

In recent years a degree of protection has been achieved for our rarest species by means of the Flora Protection Order. This is a legal instrument that prohibits damaging the habitat of a number of species. The list of protected species is revised from time to time, and at present it contains about 70 species. Similar protection is afforded to a number of species in Northern Ireland.

A further measure of protection is by means of the formal recognition of sites worthy of conservation, the so-called Habitats Directive. A representative listing of a cross-section of the main Irish habitats of importance at European level has been developed. Many of these sites are currently being designated for protection and have management plans prepared for them. The great advantage of broad site-based conservation is that selected areas can be managed in their entirety. The combination of conditions, physical, environmental, economic and social, which prevailed many years ago cannot be reinstated or even replicated. For many species and habitats, the tipping point, the environmental cocktail necessary to keep certain species alive and well, has been reached. These environmental changes are not always obvious. People understandably become upset when favourite trees are felled, hedges grubbed out or quarry ponds used as rubbish tips. However, far more significant though less immediately obvious changes are underway. At an all-Ireland scale, the gradual lowering of the water table as the result of arterial drainage converts a fine orchid-rich marsh to an average species-poor pasture in a few years. Price-support mechanisms bring about the conversion of our colourful lime-rich grasslands in the lowlands of Ireland to expanses of rye-grass and white clover mixtures. Species once common in clear-water rivers have been replaced by pollution-tolerant, nutrient-demanding aquatics. The body of evidence provided by the species distribution maps is overwhelming. The abundance of open circles on many of these maps (denoting recently unconfirmed records) points tellingly to the ways in which the landscape has been aesthetically reduced and stripped of a significant part of its diversity. The palate that once held the 'Forty Shades of Green' is much more subdued now.

Weeds in Flower Beds

Most people first encounter nature at close quarters in their gardens, where a number of plants live quite successful existences in places where neither nature nor gardeners had ever intended them to grow. In creating suburban gardens, with their own mix of microhabitats, mankind has provided suitable ground for many species that might otherwise have a far more restricted distribution in Ireland. Flower beds, lawns, flower pots, even walls provide habitats for different plants, some unexpected, some unwanted, most unappreciated. The ordinary suburban garden includes various areas that have been colonised by a variety of wild and semi-wild plants. Some of these have been around for so long that they are often understandably considered to be wild even in Ireland. Collectively, most of these are dismissed as 'weeds' because they grow in places where gardeners wish they didn't. But in what sort of ground did these plants originally live before the era of the suburban garden? Where did they all come from? How did they get to Ireland? These plants are all wild somewhere in the world but over the years many have spread from their original natural homes to other places. The routes taken by some invasive species have been fairly well recorded. Others are now far more widespread in their newly-colonised territories than they ever were in their native habitats. Many have been around for so long as world-wide garden weeds that it is uncertain where their original homes were.

Some of these plants had evolved their own lifestyle characteristics, equipping them with an ability to colonise new ground far from their lands of origin. Each species has its own tale to tell and their modern colonising strategies and geographical distributions provide historical evidence of the ways and means by which they travelled to different parts of the world. Archaeologists have made great contributions to our understanding of the

FLOWER BEDS

Even the best-tended gardens offer opportunity for invasive species, usually short-lived weeds but also perennials. Open flower beds, gravel pathways, lawns and especially old walls all present suitable habitats for colonisation.

COMMON FUMITORY

Fumitory species are highly successful colonists of open ground, often springing up when the ground has been disturbed. Their seeds can lie dormant in the soil for years until they are brought to the surface, where they grow flower, set seed and may not be seen again for years.

SPEEDWELL

Some Speedwells have become widespread weeds of flower beds and gardens, having spread into Ireland from various natural habitats elsewhere in the world. They thrive in man-made habitats here.

native status or otherwise of many species by examining the preserved remains of plants (especially seeds) associated with ancient human habitation, where everything from buried soils to the preserved contents of the digestive tract of long-dead humans have furnished evidence of the presence of certain species at various eras in the archaeological record.

As the original wildwood was cleared and Neolithic man began to farm and plant, a number of previously wild species spread into the new, more open, tilled ground. Many of these plants have spread slowly across continents, sometimes as contaminants in seed or as followers of agriculture. Different phases of human expansion connected with the natural habitats of other potential weedy colonists. More recently these more natural and gradual colonisation processes have been accelerated by infrastructural developments and increased by world trade. Seeds of certain species are now distributed accidentally but rapidly from industrial-scale plant nurseries in the soil compost of ornamental plants and forwarded as undetected and unwanted passengers to the gardens of Ireland.

The arrival of these unintended visitors initiates an ongoing battle between gardener and botanical invaders, the former equipped with trowels, an array of plant poisons, bark mulch and low maintenance ground-covering undershrubs. The invaders, on the other hand, have the benefit of thousands of years of breeding strategies that have enabled them to spread, occupy and sustain themselves in newly-occupied territory for many years.

The species that spread either as contaminants in imported seed or were cultivated as culinary or medicinal herbs are collectively classified as archaeophytes, a group of plants (not necessarily related) associated with human habitation for many years and naturalised before 1500. In recent times some of these have been able to spread rapidly into suitable open ground where there is little in the way of competition from tougher grasses and other heavy vegetation. Many of these weedy species are annuals, dying at the end of the growing season. Many are heat demanding and germinate rapidly in moist warm conditions.

One of the most widespread and obvious weeds of contemporary Irish flower beds is Common Field-speedwell, *Veronica persica*, sometimes known as Persian Speedwell. Botanists in Ireland were unaware of this species growing here until the first half of the nineteenth century, after which it spread rapidly throughout the country. First found in Britain in 1825, it seems to have spread from south-west Asia. It has an extended flowering period (March to September) but in recent years has been seen flowering throughout the year. It can now be found not only in gardens but also on disturbed waste ground around cities and in arable fields. Why can a species like this survive even in crops of cereal fields where herbicide application can see off most cornfield weeds? One possible reason is that its seeds do not sprout all at once. Some seeds germinate well after the last herbicide application and can grow, flower, fruit and cast new seed among the stubble, long before the next round of cereal-sowing begins. It is this persistent seed bank that is central to its survival, and is a feature of a large number of plants collectively considered to be weeds.

A more long-established garden weed is Red Dead-nettle, *Lamium purpureum*. This is also quite common in cereal crops but does very well in flower beds and other waste ground. It has a square stem and an unusually-shaped flower that produces four neat little seeds in each calyx. Like Common Field-speedwell, is has a lengthy flowering season and sets seeds through most of the year. It was listed in Threlkeld's *Synopsis* as Neantog M(h)uire, recorded sometime before 1726 among rubbish under walls. That such an open-ground species had acquired an Irish name by that date indicates that it may have already been established for some considerable time.

Some species may have been genuine natives in this country but now behave differently. Thale Cress, *Arabidopsis thaliana*, is a case in point. Most of the nineteenth-century botanists considered this to be either a local or a rather rare species and so it was until the middle of the twentieth century, when it seems to have spread from many of its apparently native habitats into suburban gardens. The older records suggest that it was usually found on dry banks, rocks and walls. Today, it also occurs throughout lowland Ireland often, ironically, at the base of walls where gardeners have sprayed the more vigorous vegetation with weed killer.

SHEPHERD'S PURSE

Shepherd's Purse is one of the easiest garden weeds to identify. It has tiny white flowers like other close-related species but its fruits are very distinctive, being flattened into an almost triangular shape. Large plants produce thousands of seeds. In common with many other fast-growing annual species it thrives in the area at the base of walls that has been cleared by herbicides.

Three other Crucifers with very small white flowers grow commonly in gardens: Shepherd's Purse, *Capsella bursa-pastoris*, Hairy Bitter-cress, *Cardamine hirsuta*, and more recently, Wavy Bitter-cress, *Cardamine flexuosa*. The flowers of all four are very similar – small (less than 5 mm across), with four petals arranged in a cross shape – and all do well in the weed-killer zone. Shepherd's Purse is the easiest to identify, with flattened, heart-shaped fruits which, when opened, split into two equal parts, each containing many minute seeds. The fruits of the other two and Thale Cress are long and narrow. Gardeners pulling them out will find their hands sprayed with their tiny seeds as the dried out seed pods burst apart.

Wavy Bitter-cress is another excellent example of an undoubtedly native species that has managed to spread from its original natural habitats into suburbia, via the nursery and garden centre route. In Ireland it is a native species of damp trackways, especially in slightly wet woodlands. It has a zigzag or wavy stem, hence the name.

The renewed trend for flower and organic allotment gardening has given many other plants abundant opportunity to spread rapidly throughout the country. Indeed, it is often possible to predict the next colonising weeds of an area by making a casual inspection of the neglected sections of local garden centres.

Most weeds of the flower bed areas are annuals. They can get started and do their worst before the gardener can pull them out. Slower-growing perennials thrive on neglect and eventually take a bigger effort to remove. One group of annual plants that is very familiar is the bright red poppy, Common Poppy, *Papaver rhoeas*, and Long-headed Poppy, *Papaver dubium*. The poppy that usually springs up from dormant seed on newly-created motorway verges is Common

POPPIES

Where the ground has been turned over and has escaped spraying, various annual weeds predominate, at least in the short term. Poppies are particularly characteristic of this temporary habitat, especially on the margins of corn fields.

COMMON POPPY

The most conspicuous poppy over most of Ireland is Common Poppy, *Papaver rhoeas*. It has a smooth seed capsule and stems with protruding hairs.

SCARLET PIMPERNEL

Scarlet Pimpernel has spread from natural sandy ground habitats on the coast onto warm dry-ground situations inland.

LARGE BINDWEED

Large Bindweed, an introduced species, has spread onto waste ground, into neglected gardens and is usually encountered climbing over fences and railings. It is larger than the native species Hedge Bindweed and has inflated and overlapping bracts outside the unified corolla-tube that conceal the calyx. In our native species these bracts are flat and not overlapping.

Poppy. The simplest way to distinguish them is to check the hairs on their stems. In Common Poppy, the hairs stand out clearly from the stem while those on Long-headed Poppy lie flattened up against the stem and might be missed at first glance. The fruits of Common Poppy are only slightly taller than broad, in contrast to the Long-headed Poppy whose seed pods are about twice as long as wide. Long-headed Poppy has two subspecies that can be easily distinguished from each other. Snap off a flowering stem near the top and check the colour of the juice (latex). In one subspecies (subsp. *dubium*) the latex is white but in the other (subsp. *lecoqii*) it is yellow. The yellow-latex subspecies seems to be commoner on sandy soils that are richer in lime, while the subspecies with white latex occurs on a variety of soils.

There are two other much rarer red poppies in Ireland. Both have spines on their fruits (the commoner ones are smooth-fruited). Prickly Poppy, *Papaver argemone*, is the less rare one, occurring on sandy roadsides and tilled or disturbed soil near the coast in the south and south-east. The other, Rough Poppy, *Papaver hybridum*, was always rare in Ireland and is now a legally-protected species, seen recently in only a handful of sites.

Many weeds appear and disappear only to appear some years later. Scarlet Pimpernel, *Anagallis arvensis*, is a case in point. It is widespread in gardens throughout Ireland but its natural home appears to be sandy, often nutrient-rich ground near the sea. It has bright red petals and a low, much-branched growth form. Once established, it can produce hundreds of brightly-coloured flowers and seeds throughout the summer. It can be found on dry, sunny, sandy ground such as sandpits, associated with old ruins, especially where they are established on warm rock outcrops, and on disturbed roadsides and laneways where there is little competition from taller, rougher vegetation. That is a feature of many of our open ground weeds. They are not well adapted for life beneath the undergrowth. They require open sunny ground, typical of the environment in which they originally evolved. Once heavier, longer-lived vegetation closes in, as it does over time, these smaller annuals get shaded out, their seeds can't germinate in the cooler shade and after a while they seem to disappear. However, many of these weedy annual species have an ace up their sleeve – dormant seed. Some seeds can remain viable for many years in the soil. Over time, a significant proportion of the seeds die, but some can remain alive in a state of cold-storage for many years. When the soil is turned over, some of these seeds are brought nearer the surface to germinate and grow again.

Different species have taken hold in gardens in different parts of Ireland. The south and south-eastern parts of the country are much sunnier and have less rainfall. In contrast, the open ground of the north and north-west is often less sunny and is much wetter. These major climatic and environmental conditions change the pattern of invasive weeds that can be found occupying the best-kept gardens. Even within one suburban housing estate different patterns of species composition from garden to garden can be detected. Comparing the weeds of your flower bed with those of your nearest neighbours can be a fascinating and revealing exercise.

Lawns and Parks

For many gardeners, the lawn is their pride and joy. For others, it is an ongoing torment. A short walk along a street will show how different lawns reveal something about the soils, the history of the garden and the characteristics of their owners. Careful weeding out of unruly or non-conformist species coupled with weed killer and fertiliser application encourages grass. That is the plan. Very few plants can survive in a modern well-managed lawn. Lawnmowers (both human and instrument) don't allow most plants to grow properly. A large proportion of most tall-growing plants is situated well above where the mower cuts. Stems, leaves, flowers and fruits are easily cropped. On the other hand, low-growing plants that cling to the ground can tolerate quite a bit of mowing.

The well-tended lawn can, therefore, be something of a botanical desert. Even from the start, biodiversity is severely challenged. When a lawn is prepared from new, the ground is dug, soil sieved and grass seed is sown. Once the grass takes hold, most annual weed seeds, fond of warmth, are disinclined to germinate because of the onset of sudden and – from their perspective – drastic changes in the soil microclimate. Far less light falls on the soil. The ground gets cooler, damper and, in time, more compacted. A few short-lived species make brief appearances and get chopped fairly quickly. Perennial invaders, on the other hand, need more time to get properly established, time which the gardener it not inclined to give. Where drastic control measures are not employed, a lawn will gradually be colonised by a succession of species that can tolerate some mowing.

The Daisy, *Bellis perennis*, illustrates the point. The flowering head and thin leafless stem are the standard components of daisy chains. Only a small percentage of its biomass is contained in the stem and flowers. Cutting off the head makes very little difference to the rest of the plant because it has the ability to produce side-shoots and set up new plants.

RIBWORT PLANTAIN

Ribwort Plantain is a native plant of semi-natural grassland, including stabilised sand dunes and coastal grassland. It has spread with great success into lawns and parkland where its low-growing rosette-forming habit usually helps it to survive mowing. The individual flowers are tiny, usually only recognisable by the conspicuous anthers that bob in the wind on long filaments.

Over time these plants can form dense mats where few other species can grow. When mowing has been delayed, daisies flower abundantly. Another lawn-specialist, Ribwort Plantain, *Plantago lanceolata*, has the same general structure and can similarly throw up rapidly-growing flowering stems if not cut in time. It does not have much of a flower, producing a dark-brown head with protruding stamens with bobbing cream-coloured anthers.

White clover, *Trifolium repens*, is another such species. Its creeping habit enables it to spread and send out short runners to form new plants. It is often included in agricultural seed mixtures, especially for silage grassland where it is mixed with Rye-grass, *Lolium perenne*, to form a nutritious sward, good for making silage, but disastrous for biodiversity.

The real bane of the lawn-conscious gardener is Slender Speedwell, *Veronica filiformis*. This bright lilac-blue flowered species is a relatively recent arrival in Ireland, at least as an escape. It has the typical Speedwell flower, with four petals, two stamens and a protruding style. It forms spectacular drifts of colour in Irish lawns from April to June and then dies back to leave large bare patches where it took on the lawn grasses and won. It was introduced as an ornamental plant and has exacted retribution on gardeners ever since. First recorded as a serious escape in Britain in 1927, its natural home is in Anatolia (Turkey) and the Caucasus. It began to appear in Irish gardens shortly after, and is now established throughout Ireland and has even spread into semi-wild habitats. It seems to be spread from garden to garden by vegetative propagation, possibly transported on shared lawnmowers.

In time, some seriously neglected lawns begin to assume the biodiversity characteristics of roadside verges, as older lawns acquire species from the surrounding countryside. Sometimes species have survived from the original semi-natural grasslands that existed before the housing estates were built. Some lawns, especially those that have been lightly managed, have a springy feel when walked on. This is in part due to the amount of moss present in the lawn but also reflects the degree of trampling, compaction and earthworm activity. Where lawns have been developed on lime-rich soils and have not been too harshly treated by weed killers, species such as Cat's-ear, *Hypochoeris radicata*, Autumn Hawkbit, *Scorzoneroides (Leontodon) autumnalis*, and the more instantly-recognisable Bird's-foot Trefoil, *Lotus corniculatus*, will grow well.

Dandelions are the real specialists of garden lawns and urban waste ground and often do very well in unattended flower beds. They spread by means of feathered seeds and each dandelion head ('clock') can produce hundreds of them. If not weeded out, they can fruit and spread rapidly into flower beds, where they can be even more successful. They have long, strong tap-roots, which means that they can survive even very severe

RED CLOVER

Though a native plant, most of the Red Clover we see nowadays is derived from cultivated stock, usually in large agricultural forms.

CAT'S-EAR

Cat's-ear is widespread in grasslands, including lawns and pastures. Most of its leaves are at ground level and the flowering stems do not get the chance to develop properly. When it escapes grazing and mowing it can become a substantial and colourful plant.

mowing. There are over 200 different microspecies of dandelion in Britain and Ireland. In Ireland, a large number are only known from waste ground and are fairly obvious recent introductions. However, there are many other native microspecies that are closely associated with different habitat types such as sandhills, marshlands, roadside verges and old long-established grasslands.

In amenity grassland, a widespread feature of parks, golf courses and open spaces associated with public buildings, weeding by hand is not an option. These artificial prairies are usually managed by a combination of frequent mowing and large-scale selective herbicide applications. The search for interesting plants in these areas is best directed to places where the ride-on mower cannot go – edges of walls, dips and drains and the base of trees, especially where roots are exposed. Many public parks now have small areas set aside where the natural flora of an area is allowed to express itself, and species such as Self-heal, *Prunella vulgaris*, Red Clover, *Trifolium pratense*, Lesser Trefoil, *Trifolium dubium*, Yarrow, *Achillea millefolium*, and various grasses all do well here. Where parkland grassland has been sympathetically managed and was formed on lime-rich soils, there are even occasional instances where very attractive species such as Cowslips, *Primula veris*, Pyramidal Orchid, *Anacamptis pyramidalis*, and Scarlet Pimpernel, *Anagallis arvensis*, thrive. These have survived from the days when grass cover was thinner and much richer in species. They create a vivid, colourful and lasting colour contrast to the more uniform greenness of the heavily-managed areas. Their persistence testifies to the endurance of some species, when grassland is managed for sustainable, more natural diversity, a diversity that can be maintained without resort to the quick-fix deception of a packet of so-called 'wild-flower' seed mixture.

PYRAMIDAL ORCHID (LEFT)

When lime-rich grasslands have not been cut they can produce an abundance of interesting species. Pyramidal Orchid, usually characteristic of grasslands near the sea, can also appear in lawns, especially in the semi-natural grassland of business parks and large institutional buildings where the original pastures have been retained and not reseeded.

Urban Waste Ground

Over the years, urban centres have acquired their own distinctive selection of plant species. These 'Survivals and New Arrivals' have become established here through importation, intended or otherwise, and cultivation, and also include a number of genuinely native species that may have spread by natural methods from the countryside. Some have survived from a time when there was far more open agricultural ground in our towns and cities. In their different ways these species track the changes in commercial life of Ireland over the centuries. The older centres of many towns have many species that are absent from the newer areas. These differences are partly due to the structural and physical differences between the old and new sectors. In cities and towns the natural and colonising species fight it out or reach an accommodation with each other, competing for resources and living space just as so many other species do in very different natural habitats. They have arrived equipped with inherited ecological preferences, which enable them to thrive in some places and cause them to fail in others. Botanical colonists of various sorts have been so successful in some urban areas that there are now paradoxically more species living in a semi-wild state there than in areas of equivalent size in the nearby countryside.

The great natural colonist of abandoned urban wasteland is the Sycamore, *Acer pseudoplatanus*. It is not native to Ireland but is very capable of producing great numbers of viable seeds. These germinate readily and if left unattended an area can easily become a sort of linear woodland in a short number of years. Small streams running through old towns always have a few extra species, sometimes many more, where seeds wash up on the banks and take root on the retaining walls. Old railway lines have species that seldom occur elsewhere. Part of the fascination of urban plant geography is trying to puzzle out why certain areas are so suitable for some plants and so unsuitable for others. Local studies may identify the ecological factors that favour certain species but prevent them from spreading beyond the areas they occupied a century ago. The more varied and diverse the structural attributes of an area, the greater the range of habitats that exist to allow various plants to become established. Species have various devices that help them to spread and many of these capabilities are evident in the range of species that has come to live in our built-up areas.

In ecological terms, towns and cities are very different from their surrounding countrysides. The buildings, set close together, form an environment that includes the adjoining paths, lanes and roadsides. Towns are usually warmer. The heat released from buildings warms up the immediate area, creating a 'heat island' effect. This in turn favours warmth-demanding species, many of which come from much hotter lands. Towns have more hard surfaces, such as roofs, roads, driveways and car parks. As a result, rainwater runs off and is usually directed into piped drains and sewers, quickly leaving the area where it falls. Some small sheltered areas may seldom get rain. The alignment of buildings often creates great inequalities in the way in which rainfall, sunlight and heat are distributed. This is most evident on frosty days. Roads that run east–west remain frozen much longer than those that run north–south. Incongruous melted patches in otherwise frozen roads indicate the presence of underground pipes bringing warmer water from factories and boilers. The narrow frost-free zone on the footpath close to the base of walls shows where reflecting heat

caused water on the path to evaporate or where the rain-shadow cast by the wall kept the ground dry in the first case. This narrow stretch – often fouled by dogs and avoided by pedestrians – is where moss grows in winter and spring, giving winter annuals a chance to get established.

Urban centres are prime targets for invasion by neophytes (plants that were first introduced after 1500). During phases of urban decline and renewal there are numerous opportunities for newly-arriving species to get established. Lots of

SYCAMORE

Though not a native species, Sycamore can become established very rapidly in waste ground in cities, where it can form small thickets in neglected areas.

open disturbed ground, loose soil and builders' rubble provide plenty of suitable dry, free-draining ground for these new arrivals, many of which grow in similar open warm ground in their original natural homes. Most of the species that hitch a lift on the garden-centre and nursery distribution network had already done so in Britain decades earlier. In recent years many of these species have come into Ireland directly from the European mainland. Some of the new colonists can, in time, be expected to become established. There have been many historical sources of introduction and gardening has given many new species a head start. Major building episodes of the past 20 years (housing, motorways, shopping centres and civic buildings) have brought many new opportunist species into the country. Others were here in small quantities, barely hanging on and have since spread throughout the country. 'Cut and fill' operations bring huge lorry loads of earth from one area to another, complete with seeds and viable roots. Soil clinging to the huge tyres and tracks of earth-

COMMON GROUNDSEL

Disturbed open ground is ideal for species that can germinate and grow fast. Having an annual lifestyle helps. Many common garden weeds can complete their life cycle in a couple of months. Soil transported on the tracks and tyres of earth-moving machinery can bring species into areas where they are rarely seen.

moving machinery is moved *en bloc* across several counties in a couple of hours and deposited in some new area, bringing seeds of species to places where they never grew.

Suburban walls in established areas have been sprayed or marked by generations of territorially-conscious dogs. Older buildings have been sprayed for centuries. These visits constantly enrich the soil at the base of the wall, resulting in a localised nutrient build-up. This can be seen in the distribution of a few nutrient-tolerant lichens growing on the corner walls of suburbia. A series of coloured bands of different species of algae and lichens indicate the subtle relationship of plant succession on vertically-aligned nutrient gradients with more obvious influences such as the height of the local dogs! This colonisation process can also be seen on chimneys and on the apex of roofs where a few species of grey and yellow lichens flourish in the bird droppings zone.

The zone at the bottom of the wall is, therefore, a rather unusual habitat. It is warm (at least on one side), nutrient-rich and connected to the soil below where not sealed off with cement. Suburban paths and tracks are usually not shaded by trees, at least not on the public side. Hedges are planted close to the inner side of the outer wall, and plants that get started opportunistically on the other side can send down roots to the soil. A simple examination of most wall-bases will show that some species (usually the smaller, shallow-rooted ones) are simply living in the join of the wall and path or in the untrampled areas of mossy growth. Others, usually with deeper-probing roots, are able to insinuate themselves down between the gaps at the base of the wall.

The species composition varies from town to town. However, differences in the species-mix even along a single street illustrate the differing environmental requirements of individual species. In general, annual species do best on shallow soils where they do not need to go head-to-head with the perennials that ultimately will need access to deeper soils. There are a few annual or biennial herbaceous species that are very typical of this wall-base habitat. These include Wall Barley, *Hordeum murinum*, and Hedge Mustard, *Sisymbrium officinale*. Wall Barley is a regular component of tracksides in the older parts of Dublin City. Its heads are equipped with long awns with spines like agricultural barley. They are sometimes used as darts by schoolboys because the awns can cling annoyingly to jumpers and coats. As its name suggests, it was known to Linnaeus and his predecessors because of its association with walls even in the Europe of the 1700s. It had obviously made the move long before that. In Dublin, Threlkeld found it 'Upon the sides of the Highway, and on the Walls leading to Bagatrath [Dublin South City]'. For many years Wall Barley was mainly a Dublin-based species but recently it has spread to several other towns well away from the east coast, accidentally by human agency.

Hedge Mustard is a much more widespread species, throughout Ireland. As its name suggests it can grow in hedges, but it usually prefers sunnier situations. It may be native, but its distribution is strongly biased in favour of urban areas and it is well known to grow better on warmer, nutrient-rich soils. In late summer the stems of the plant die, snap off and the entire twiggy ball can roll around on streets and waste ground, scattering its seeds. Another closely-related specialist of this zone, but a more recent arrival, is Eastern Rocket, *Sisymbrium orientale*. Originally a native of east and south-east Europe and the Near East, it has spread throughout Europe, arriving in Ireland at the end of the nineteenth century, apparently as a contaminant with imported grain. Many other grain-truck species arrived and persisted for some years, their colonies being topped up with new seed scattered from grain trucks supplying the breweries and mills of Ireland. Containerisation soon put an end to this. As a result, a number of these species are seldom seen now and when they do surface they are clearly casual (non-persistent) in their occurrence. However, various towns and cities in Ireland now have viable self-sustaining colonies of Eastern Rocket, especially in back lanes in the older areas.

Another species from the same genus is London Rocket, *Sisymbrium irio*. This was widespread in the past around a few of the larger towns but has almost disappeared from most of its old haunts, although it has turned up in recent years in old parts of Dublin city and Loughshinny Harbour in areas where it had been recorded in the past. This suggests that some colonies are able to sustain themselves despite all the changes that have taken place as older streets are tidied up.

It helps greatly if the seeds that a plant produces have a long soil-life. One such well-known example is Annual Mercury, *Mecurialis annua*. It is commonly found around Dublin and Cork and less commonly around Kilkenny and a few isolated colonies elsewhere. Its (dead) seeds are known from archaeological digs in Viking York and it had clearly managed to become an urban species in this part of the world many years ago.

The back-lane habitat, which was such an important feature of the older suburbs, is still a useful area in which to search for plants. These lanes often run behind Georgian and Victorian buildings now set in flats. The surfaces of the lanes have remained unrepaired for long periods and bring the botanical explorer into a labyrinthine network of lock-up garages and small industry where unusual plants persist on the margins of seldom-visited green lanes, sometimes even near the centres of large cities. In many respects they resemble rutted farm tracks from bygone times and it comes as little surprise that some of the plants of a different era can hang on in such places. There is little here in the way of modern tarmacadam, cement or weed killers to see off these plants. Real (non-athletic) cinder tracks can still be found. Broken drainpipes and leaky underground piping diversify the habitat. Where heavy vehicles pass along the trackways, the soil beneath becomes very compacted, drainage is impeded and small pools form in winter. Even in summertime, temporary puddles retain water for a few extra days, giving some species an extra chance to germinate. Discarded domestic rubbish can survive, persist and undergo a protracted decomposition here much longer than it can when in the public view. Tidying officialdom finds other places to tidy. But the dogs still do their business and elevated nutrient levels are still maintained.

Oxford Ragwort, *Senecio squalidus*, is a good example of a species that has spread spectacularly into cities. It was brought into the Oxford Botanic Gardens in the seventeenth century and escaped onto the walls of the town and spread, particularly on the railways throughout Britain. It reached Ireland sometime before 1839 and spread from Cork by the railways to all the main towns and, in recent years, further afield. It has even been found to hybridise with our local groundsel to form plants that look like biggish versions of our Common Groundsel, *Senecio vulgaris*, but with ray florets. At first glance, Oxford Ragwort resembles an ordinary ragwort but that species rarely grows as successfully as this on railway sidings. It has bright yellow flowers and the inflorescence is much more spread out in contrast to Common Ragwort, which has a dense flat-topped inflorescence.

Another relatively recent arrival is Buddleia or Butterfly Bush, *Buddleja davidii*. It is a native of China and was brought to this part of the world as a garden plant at the end of the nineteenth century. Within a very short time it was very well established on all sorts of urban waste ground, particularly rubble, edges of car parks and collapsing buildings. Habitats of this type were abundant in the Ireland of the mid-twentieth century and Buddleia spread throughout the island. In recent times high development costs in urban areas have reduced the time-window when substantial land parcels can be allowed to lie fallow. As a result, many of the species that used to take several years to get properly established now fail to get started. Shiny new modular office blocks don't yet have enough grit-filled nooks and crannies where these larger species can take hold and cling on. Even so, various other shorter-lived species, such as the thistles, can gain a rapid toehold on this untidy, rubbly ground in the short term.

Long ago, a number of plants established themselves on old walls and now form a body of living evidence of domestic life in earlier times. Castles, abbeys, hospitals and other institutions had gardens where plants were grown for food and medicine. Some of these plants can still be found associated with old ruins, clinging, if not to the walls themselves, at least to the broader curtilage or former boundaries of the site. Nowadays the lands surrounding these buildings have either been tidied, built on, landscaped, grazed up to the walls, used as cattle sheds or tilled. Finding some of these old plants can be a bit of a challenge but there are often plants scattered here and there behind a wall or safely out of reach of cattle or landscapers. A fairly regular survivor is a small-flowered, yellow-flowered poppy with bright yellow latex – Greater Celandine, *Chelidonium majus*. (It has nothing to

Spear Thistle

Spear Thistle is the largest of the thistles normally encountered on waste ground in cities and in the countryside. The large heads consist of many separate flowers, each of which will produce a parachute seed in late summer.

WHITE DEAD-NETTLE

The leaves of White Dead-nettle do not sting and its flowers are a bright feature in late spring. It is usually found associated with old buildings and roadsides and is seldom encountered in natural habitats.

do with Lesser Celandine, which is a member of the Buttercup family.) In the past it was used as a herbal remedy for a wide variety of afflictions and survives around old Norman ruins, along with a suite of other species that is seldom encountered elsewhere. It sometimes turns up around old farm buildings, some of which are founded the site of much older buildings.

Many of these plants were deliberately cultivated as medicinal herbs. Others were grown to liven up the taste and variety of medieval food, which cannot have been very exciting. The most widespread potherb was probably Alexanders, *Smyrnium olusatrum*. In the south and east, this species is very common, often growing far from habitation. It can live on sea cliffs and roadside banks and can compete very successfully with natural vegetation. It flowers very early in the year, and produces dense heads of yellowish-green flowers. In late summer the almost-black fruits appear. It might be mistaken for a native species in these coastal areas. It is much rarer inland, where it is more clearly confined to towns, villages, old isolated buildings and ruins, indicating areas of more ancient habitation and cultivation. Other old food plants can often be found where it grows, such as Good King Henry, *Chenopodium bonus-henricus*. It was often grown as a vegetable and there were many records for it in nineteenth-century botanical literature. It is much rarer now but still turns up, usually near old farmsteads and castles. It is species such as this that hover on the archaeophyte/neophyte cusp (AD 1500) in Ireland. It is by now difficult to be sure when they arrived and more difficult still to be sure when they began to persist.

Some of these species clearly did very well in medieval times around cities when there was far more dirt and rubbish lying about. Some were actually native species, usually from coastal areas, that had managed to spread inland. Many of these still persist more or less regularly in natural areas near the sea. Some are particularly common in bird colonies where their appetite for manure is more than liberally satisfied in the guano-colonies of nesting seagulls. Slender Thistle, *Carduus tenuiflorus*, Henbane, *Hyoscyamus niger*, and Bristly Oxtongue, *Picris echoides*, can often turn up in such situations inland, usually flourishing briefly on the sites of excavated soil such as undisturbed building foundations. Other species are often concentrated around these sites of medieval habitation, including White Dead-nettle, *Lamium album*, Hemlock, *Conium maculatum*, Mugwort, *Artemisia vulgaris*, Black Horehound, *Ballota nigra*, and Greater Celandine. All are nutrient-demanding species and, therefore, are still occasionally found near abandoned silage pits and cattle-feeding areas. In the past, cattle were kept much closer to habitation, even in cities, and their dung, when not recycled as farmyard manure, would have raised the nitrogen level of the soil immediately surrounding the domestic buildings.

One of the best-known invaders to have spread into towns was Pineapple Weed, *Matricaria discoidea*. It was first spotted in Ireland in Carrickmines, Co. Dublin, in 1894, but within a short period of time spread to many rural parts of Ireland. The species is native to northern Asia and may have spread initially into north-west America then eastward across North America, arriving in Europe in the mid-nineteenth century and into Ireland via poultry feed. It is more than thoroughly established in Ireland, frequenting farm tracks and lanes, forming self-sustaining colonies wherever there are open, slightly damp, nutrient-rich areas. The popular name comes from the cluster of minute yellow flowers similar to those at the centre

PINEAPPLE WEED

Pineapple Weed arrived in Ireland towards the end of
the nineteenth century and spread rapidly throughout
the island. It has clusters of flowers formed into dense
yellow heads resembling those in the centre of a Daisy.
They release a fruity scent when squeezed.

of a Daisy. When crushed, they release a sweet scent similar to pineapple. It has fine, deeply-divided leaves as has its close relative, Scented Mayweed, *Matricaria recutita*, which is an occasional casual on dry sunny waste ground. Its dried flower heads are sold as chamomile tea. Like Pineapple Weed, it has a sweet scent. The yellow centre to the flower head has a distinct ring of white ray-florets similar to Daisy. Another species that may have travelled a similar route from America is Lesser Swine's Cress, *Lepidium didymum* (*Coronopus didymus*). It was not recorded here until 1819 in Cork but was subsequently found around many coastal towns. It has a distinctive unpleasant smell. In recent years it has spread throughout the south and east of the island and appears to be still increasing its range.

Another pavement and shady back-lane specialist is Mossy Pearlwort, *Sagina procumbens*. It forms dense mats of small, very narrow leaves that cling to the ground and which, when matted together, really do make it look like a moss. It can also grow in shady flower beds and lawns, but is most spectacularly successful on the garden paths of older houses. The flowers are very inconspicuous, producing distinct sepals but at best rudimentary petals. Unusually for a species that does so well in urban situations, it also occurs in more open ground in natural wetland habitats such as marshes and fens. Another species from the wild is Small-leaved Knotweed, *Polygonum arenastrum*, which grows naturally on sandy, gravelly seashores. This species is extremely tolerant of trampling and once established, especially in cracks in pavements, can persist for many years.

People taking up field botany are sometimes dismayed by the number of different species that belong to the Carrot family. Many of these were formerly cultivated. However, they have many distinct features, particularly the fruits, which can be ribbed or smooth, covered with prickles or spines, flat or curved. The leaves are often highly scented and it comes as no surprise that Parsley,

WILD CARROT

The complex heads of many members of the Carrot family are composed of hundreds or even thousands of separate flowers. Many familiar edible plants belong here, including Parsnip, Carrot, Lovage, Dill and Parsley. The family also includes a number of very poisonous species.

Fennel, Parsnip, Carrot, Angelica, Coriander, Lovage, Dill, Cumin and Rock Samphire all belong to this family. Most of these were introduced into Ireland although Rock Samphire, *Crithmum maritimum*, occurs wild around the coast. A number of these also occur as formerly-cultivated herbs and some are known to have persisted in the same sites for over a century. Parsley, *Petroselenium crispum*, was discovered by Nathaniel Colgan, apparently naturalised, on a bank by the Martello Tower in Skerries, Co. Dublin, in 1902 and there it still grows, on rocks and even on the walls of nearby old buildings, large and luxuriant.

Many species apparently widespread throughout Ireland are, on closer examination, often found only near older habitation. Farms, villages, castles and town streets were far smellier in medieval times than today. Lots of species with high nitrogen demands made their way into the towns from a variety of wild areas, and lingered for many years after. This can still be seen around the Irish countryside. An abandoned silage pit, a rotting bale of straw in a ditch, a neglected cattle feeder – all provide lots of decaying nourishment for these plants. When these nutrient-rich features are associated with rubble and waste ground, the structural diversity of a site increases and so does its flora.

To find remnants of this former set of plants it is best to search in older small towns. Seek out graveyards, old railway stations, anywhere that a bit of open stony or rubbly ground is still accessible. These places are increasingly being fenced off because of concerns about public safety and insurance liability but they are well worth the effort as they can often produce species that have not been seen for many years. Some of the best hunting grounds are where soil has been disturbed, such as the site of an abandoned building project. Seed that has been buried and dormant for years is brought to the surface and germinates. When three, four or more species put in an appearance all on one site and are clearly associated with the recently-piled up soil, then the botanical hunter is onto a good thing. If these areas are not built on fairly quickly, the plants may flower and set seed, giving their colonies a new lease of life, possibly for a few more decades.

In time, many of these sites become grassed-over as perennial species take hold and shade out the short-lived annuals and non-assertive perennials. Ground of this sort, therefore, needs to be continually disturbed in order to maintain this aspect of a flora that has been gradually getting rarer. Managing these habitats for nature conservation is not easy. The dormant seed bank does not last indefinitely. Little by little, the percentage of buried viable seeds of these species decreases. That is, in part, why they are now so rare.

ROSEBAY WILLOWHERB (LEFT)

Rosebay Willowherb is one of the major colonists of all sorts of waste ground, even spreading onto cut-over raised bogs and clear-felled conifer plantations. Though originally a native of upland rocky and scree habitats, new colonies became established through the twentieth century and the species has now spread aggressively throughout the country.

Urban Willowherbs

The great urban invader is Rosebay Willowherb, *Chamerion angustifolum* (formerly *Epilobium angustifolium*). It spread rapidly onto building sites in Britain after World War II when so many towns and cities were bombed. The species spread onto the charred rubble and railway sidings, acquiring the name 'Fireweed' along the way. For many years it was a native plant of upland rocky situations in Ireland. The editors of *Cybele Hibernica 2* (1898) considered it to be rare and very local. They gave a long list of locations from where it had been recorded, mostly wild, rocky places and cliffs. Discussion continues as to whether the modern urban colonies derived from these native centres or whether some newer more aggressive strain became dominant in lowland areas. It can become a very large plant, which can produce many thousands of seeds, each carried on the wind by a small parachute. When it gets established on waste ground in cities it can out-compete many smaller species. In Ireland it is also now found in extreme abundance where conifer plantations have been clear-felled. It also invaded the drying out edges of raised bogs.

Other smaller willowherbs also do very well in the city. The most common species for many years around towns was Broad-leaved Willowherb, *Epilobium montanum*. This is widespread throughout Ireland, where it is also common in hedgerows and woodland margins. About 30 years ago another species, American Willowherb, *Epilobium ciliatum*, began to spread and was found at wall-bases all around the main cities within a short period of time. Since then, not only has it spread throughout Ireland but it now frequently forms hybrids with native species, especially Broad-leaved Willowherb. Within the past decade another species, Square-stalked Willowherb, *Epilobium tetragonum*, has taken hold around towns. Like other invasive species, it has a long history of occurring as a casual. Various willowherb species are well known to hybridise and it may be the case in a few years' time that many of the existing populations of native species will be diluted by genes from these recent arrivals. There is one other willowherb, Small-flowered Willowherb, *Epilobium roseum*, which is seldom seen nowadays. Its flowers are very different in colour (almost white when they open, then becoming streaked with rose-pink) and the leaves are clearly stalked and more strongly ribbed. It still turns up occasionally, often in areas where it has been recorded in the past but not seen for many years. It prefers damp, open, shaded ground that remains relatively unvegetated. Therefore, it can persist in areas that are occasionally sprayed with weed killers. There are few habitats where it can grow in the wild where these combinations of circumstances prevail. Damp, open, shaded ground will become covered over by grasses such as Creeping Bent, *Agrostis stolonifera*, and Creeping Buttercup, *Ranunculus repens*. Small-flowered Willowherb is one of those species that may just possibly be native in Ireland or an archaeophyte or both. Time doesn't always tell.

Old Walls and Ruins

The Irish landscape is liberally and conspicuously sprinkled with old ruins. The walls of castles, churches, large estates, civic buildings and the retaining walls of railway embankments and other buildings have over time been colonised by a number of plant species, some of which seldom live elsewhere in Ireland. The existence of popular English names such as Wallflower, Pellitory-of-the-wall and Wall Pepper exemplify the success with which some of these species have exploited the built environment. Buildings are completely artificial structures. Therefore, the question arises as to where these colonising species lived before these walls were built. Some species were either deliberately or accidentally introduced by man into the country, usually for medicinal or ornamental reasons, within the past 1,000 years and have become established or persist on walls. Another group of genuinely native Irish species made their own way, spreading from natural and usually rocky habitats within the Irish countryside onto the new buildings of the time. In both cases there were enough points of environmental similarity between the plants' original natural habitats and the buildings of the Irish countryside to make it possible for them to extend their ranges and find new homes. In a sense an ongoing botanical battle between the native and newcomer was being fought on the fabric of these old buildings. This struggle comes complete with issues such as natural succession, colonisation, displacement, local extermination and sheer opportunism. The conflict continues to this day and can be observed in most older towns and cities.

Old walls, or at least those from Christian and early Norman times onwards, were usually formed of cut stone, hewn from rock outcrops and from other areas where natural bedrock came close to the surface. Their stone blocks were held together with primitive lime-based cement, which disintegrated over time. Grit, sand and dust gradually accumulated in the spaces between the cut stones and a thin soil began to form. The stones

IVY-LEAVED TOADFLAX

Ivy-leaved Toadflax, a small relative of the Snapdragons, was introduced as a garden plant and has become established on many shaded walls, especially those of churchyards and old estates. Its roots penetrate down into the cooler and moister recesses between the stonework, allowing it to cope with dry conditions that would kill many other plants here. See also p. 78.

themselves functioned as a sort of storage heater, warming up by day and retaining heat well into the evening. These small areas were very much warmer and drier than the surrounding wooded or grassy countryside. Even in places where the rocks themselves are predominantly acid, the lime-rich mortar allowed lime-loving species to spread into areas where they would not otherwise live. In these relatively-favourable conditions, some species were able to spread much further north and west into cooler and wetter areas. At a local level a number of plants were enabled to grow in areas where there was no suitable ground for rock-dwelling species.

The wall itself has many ecological characteristics of significance to the potential botanical colonist. Factors such as the alignment of the wall to sun, rainfall and wind, the nature of the capping (if any) and the amount of shade cast by other buildings or trees all combine to influence its ecology. Depending on these factors, the amount of water that can fall and be retained on different parts of the wall varies widely. As a result, the microclimate and soil conditions on the top of a wall are often very different from those on its side. Only the most drought-tolerant species can survive on the top of a wall. Where there are vertical elements built into the top of the wall, a thin soil can build up more easily. Most of the water that falls on the top of the wall eventually makes its way down through the spaces between the cut stones, carrying grit, sand and nutrients from decaying plant matter and bird droppings. Some of the crevices can be quite moist and provide habitat for many of our native ferns. The thicker the wall, the deeper some of these crevices become. In these circumstances, larger and usually deep-rooting species can take a strong grip on the stones and damper soil within the wall, with disastrous results for smaller, less aggressive species and even for the wall itself.

Short-lived Annuals

Living conditions on the top of a wall are very different from those at the side. Rain runs off rapidly because there is so little soil to retain water. The underlying stone can get very hot and dry. Sometimes a little skin of vegetation forms on the top of cut stone walls, especially those made of limestone. Some of this layer of soil and grit is held together by a mat of drought-tolerant mosses. This provides an interesting habitat for a number of plants with very different life cycles and survival strategies. These plants are classified collectively as winter annuals. They germinate in autumn and produce small basal leaf-rosettes. Then, once the days warm up, they put on a burst of growth, flower, set seeds and die in a couple of months. These seeds remain dormant until the following autumn. The main plants that grow in this way are Spring Whitlow-grass, *Erophila verna*, Rue-leaved Saxifrage, *Saxifraga tridactylites*, Wall Speedwell, *Veronica arvensis*, and Lesser Chickweed, *Stellaria pallida*. Search for these species in spring. By summer you will find only withered stems. All of these also grow in natural habitats near the coast whence they have made their way inland by a variety of routes.

Succulents

Water, therefore, becomes vital to the ecology of a wall and its plants. Soil in a garden can hold onto water. This is not the case on walls so plants need to have a number of attributes to get through the summer drought. Although species from very different geographical backgrounds can take hold, they do so on different parts of the wall. In Ireland, Wall Pepper, *Sedum acre*, grows naturally in stable dune grassland. It is well adapted to drought conditions, having thick, fleshy leaves that soak up and retain rainwater. It has spread from these natural habitats, and is now a conspicuous feature of many old walls. It grows on both the thin skin of earth that forms on the tops of walls and on asbestos and corrugated iron roofs. It can often be seen spilling out over clogged-up roof gutters. It produces great spreads of bright yellow flowers in early summer. The name Wall Pepper comes from the fact that its younger leaves, when chewed, have a strong peppery taste (not recommended) – hence its other popular name, Biting Stonecrop. A close relative of Wall Pepper is White Stonecrop, *Sedum album*. This is a much more recent invader, having been brought into the country as a garden plant, and has spread to old walls. As long ago as 1902, it was noted by Nathaniel Colgan growing on the summit of Knockachree Hill, Dalkey, Co. Dublin. It is now beginning to spread onto natural rocky habitats near the sea, where it even displaces Biting Stonecrop and another native stonecrop, English Stonecrop, *Sedum anglicum*. English Stonecrop can also grow on walls but usually those that are formed of acid rocks such as granite or mica schist. Other members of the Stonecrop family also do quite well on walls. The creeping decumbent stems of Reflexed Stonecrop, *Sedum rupestre*, form a great reddish-leaved mat on tops of walls, and the flowering stems produce large heads of bright yellow flowers. This is usually found fairly close to houses and seems to be commoner now on walls than in gardens and shows signs of spreading into rocky places near the sea. The House-leek, *Sempervivum tectorum*, was formerly grown on walls and roofs to ward off lightning strikes. It still persists on abandoned farm buildings.

In areas where the rocks are sufficiently acid, Navelwort, *Umbilicus rupestris*, is fairly frequent. It has large, round fleshy leaves and tall spikes of pale yellowish-green flowers and grows best in sheltered areas of acid rock exposures that occur in deep river valleys and wooded mountain glens. It occurs throughout Ireland, but mainly in areas of higher rainfall. It becomes very rare in the centre, where there are few places that are sufficiently sheltered, rocky and acid.

NAVELWORT (WALL PENNYWORT)

Navelwort, usually a species of exposed rocks in sheltered situations, has spread onto many old walls, where it is usually commonest on the more shaded sides.

ENGLISH STONECROP

English Stonecrop, typically found on dry open rock exposures, has spread onto many nearby stone walls, where it finds sufficient points of environmental similarity between its natural and man-made habitats. It has dense clusters of fleshy leaves that soak up rainwater. For plants of this type, the succulent strategy is essential, especially on dry-stone walls where there is very little soil to retain water.

PELLITORY-OF-THE-WALL

Pellitory-of-the-wall did not acquire its traditional name without good reason. Although it grows apparently as a native on dry rocky and stony ground near the sea, in many inland parts of Ireland it is only known on old stone walls.

Old Invaders

One of the most obvious plants of old buildings is Wallflower, *Erysimum cherii*. It has been around for many years but is not native to Ireland. It is believed to have come originally from the eastern Mediterranean. The colour-form that has become naturalised on old castle walls is usually a dull yellowish or brownish-flowered plant, very different from the flashy modern cultivars. However, some of these modern inventions have also reverted to their ancestral lifestyle and become established on waste ground around cities. Some old towns are festooned with this species in late spring but others are now suspiciously without it. In recent years there has been a tendency to clean up many of the old walls of these towns and in the process colonies of lichens and mosses that have taken centuries to develop have been wiped out by a few days' determined scrubbing. Repointing decaying cement, spraying weeds and general 'tidying' all have their effect. A quick glance up the

RUSTY-BACK FERN (ABOVE) AND HART'S-TONGUE FERN (ABOVE RIGHT)

Ferns have spread with great success onto walls in towns and cities from natural or wild habitats. Rusty-back Fern, abundant in open rocky limestone ground, has successfully taken up residence on many old mortared walls. Hart's-tongue Fern, commonly found in hedges and shaded lime-rich woodland, has also spread onto many old walls and can even manage in the centre of cities provided there is sufficient shade and a water supply such as a dripping drainpipe.

walls of an old castle can often show how far weed killer was sprayed. In the higher parts, the leaves and flowers of Wallflowers, Pellitory-of-the-wall and a number of fern species flourish. They form a striking visual contrast with the broken stems and poisoned leaves of their dead and dying siblings at the base of the wall.

Pellitory-of-the-wall, *Parietaria judaica*, is probably native in Ireland, especially on rocky ground near the sea. It has certainly spread with great success onto old walls and is now beginning to appear in the older suburbs, often at the bottom of walls where there are much higher levels of nitrogen. It is a perennial species and is well able to occupy many of the crevices in which it becomes established, in the process fending off colonisation by other species. Its distribution in Ireland and Britain is that of a sun-loving species and it is certainly commonest in the south and east. It is now frequently associated with the walls of old

IVY-LEAVED TOADFLAX

When examined closely, the flowers of Ivy-leaved
Toadflax are seen to resemble tiny Snapdragons. In
common with many other introduced species from
warmer climates, it has found walls to be a very
suitable analogue of its natural more rocky habitats.

abbeys and it may have been used as a medicinal herb, reputedly for urinary complaints. Threlkeld praised it, remarking that it was cooling, opening, cleansing, and good against 'Stone, Gravel, and stoppage of Urine'. It may, therefore, be an example of a native species that has been deliberately introduced into other parts of the country from its original native populations and now survives on walls and other stonework where conditions are warmer.

Ferns on Walls

In contrast to the so-called higher plants, walls – even from relatively recently (nineteenth century onwards) – have been colonised by a large number of native ferns that would normally be encountered naturally on rock outcrops such as the Burren and in Fermanagh. They don't need as much soil to get started but prefer their future homes to be well shaded and moist. These ferns spread by means of tiny air-borne spores, which waft about in their millions.

Over the years Wall-rue, *Asplenium ruta-muraria*, Maidenhair Spleenwort, *Asplenium trichomanes*, Rusty-back Fern, *Ceterach officinarum*, and various Polypody ferns have become firmly established, particularly on limestone walls. Black Spleenwort, *Asplenium adiantum-nigrum*, occurs on walls constructed from more acid stone. All these species produce spores, which are contained in clusters of sori. In some species they are so densely crowded on the undersides of the fronds that it seems as if the entire underside is clothed with a dense reddish-brown fur. In the generally softer Irish climate, even Hart's-tongue Fern can do well on walls, having spread from woodlands and hedge banks nearby. However, it is usually the case in the drier parts of Ireland that these species do better on the cooler and shadier sides of walls.

The supporting stonework and parapets of road bridges, railway viaducts and even the occasional canal aqueduct provide habitat for a number of ferns that seldom make it into urban areas. Brittle Bladder-fern, *Cystopteris fragilis*, can often be found on bridges in the uplands and has spread into the Midlands where, for instance, it has persisted on a leaking canal aqueduct for over a century. Many of the more remote bridges, especially those on higher ground, benefit from years of neglect and have acquired a number of rock-dwelling plants over time. They have often been built from the local rock. This in turn provides bare surfaces suitable for colonisation. They are seldom sprayed with weed killers and are usually sufficiently distant from towns to have avoided invasion by the garden species that are taking over so many of the urban walls.

The rusting drainpipe often introduces an additional element of diversity in urban habitats. Some town walls, even those of the inner city, have a trickle of water, concentrated on a central area by leaky guttering. These areas can usually be spotted, even on dry days, by the mosses and algae that grow on the walls. If these dripping areas are on the cooler or shaded sides of buildings they may often even support some of the ferns of hedgerows and woodland margins such as Male-fern, *Dryopteris filix-mas*, and Soft Shield-fern, *Polystichum setiferum*.

Ivy

At an early stage, Ivy poses little threat to the smaller plants of a wall but once established it will shade out almost all the other smaller species that have come to live there.

New Invaders

The numerous species that were introduced into gardens in the eighteenth and nineteenth centuries were imported from a variety of sources. In common with some of the earlier colonisers, these species did not have to spread naturally into Ireland but were instead being given a free lift into the country by gardeners. Their seeds, however, did not remain in gardens and soon found enough other places to grow to be very successful at expanding into the analogues of their natural habitats and by now some are threatening to oust both the natural and the 'old' invaders.

One of the main invasive species of walls nowadays is Red Valerian, *Centranthus ruber*. It is a robust plant, getting up to 80 cm high, with flowers that are usually pink though they can be red or white. This has become very successful in recent years and is now ousting many other wall plants. It puts up plenty of leaf, which shades out most of the smaller plants of arid conditions. It is exceptionally common on walls near railways and is now spreading onto sunny rocks near the coast. It came originally from the Mediterranean region but has become naturalised in all sorts of warm, dry ground now and is even showing signs of spreading onto sand dunes and natural rock exposures. Because it can do so well on walls it is beginning to damage the winter annual communities and generally reduces the local biodiversity of an area. It has a deep rooting system, which can soak up whatever water is available. Because it can become quite large and can produce quite a lot of leaf, it can create a very different microclimate at the point where its stems enter the crevices of the walls. The environment here is much more shaded and moister, utterly different from the sunny, extremely dry conditions favoured by the winter and short-lived spring annuals. They can't last long when in competition with this relatively new arrival.

A more recent introduction, Ivy-leaved Toadflax, *Cymbalaria muralis*, first began to make its appearance in Ireland in the mid-nineteenth century and even then was showing a proclivity for old walls and never seen far from gardens or houses. Since then it has spread throughout the island. At first glance it does not look like a potentially successful candidate for life on a stone wall. The leaves are very soft and slightly fleshy and look as if they would not do well in sunny situations. In fact, it is usually most vigorously opportunistic on slightly shaded damp old churchyard walls. When it was first introduced, it must have been quite a novelty, with its small lilac-coloured (rarely white) flowers with a yellow spot at the mouth of the corolla tube, the entire flower looking like a miniature snapdragon. The stems are creeping and can root in cracks and gaps between the stones where moisture is retained longer. It is native in the southern Alps, what was western Yugoslavia and Italy.

Snapdragon itself, *Antirrhinum majus*, is still a common feature of old walls and seems to form self-sustaining colonies although it can often be damaged by frost. It is also a native of south-west Europe.

Another well-established garden escape of recent times is Yellow Corydalis, *Pseudofumaria lutea*. This is another colourful trailer and climber from the southern Alps and is already getting a firm toehold on all sorts of walls.

Ivy can be something of a mixed blessing for wall vegetation. At the initial stages of growth it provides a vegetative network, holding together whatever soil has accumulated along with its suite of colonising species. However, once it gets going there are few species that can compete with it. The invasive Red Valerian can put up a bit of a fight as can Butterfly Bush, *Buddleja davidii*, and some older walls will have small trees such as elder or ash poking out above the ivy. However, most species simply don't have the competitive ability to survive on walls once ivy has taken hold. When it does get a grip it can do quite a bit of damage to walls, especially when the main stems begin to force the stonework apart. It is best not to let it take hold. The natural colonies of winter annuals, ferns and long-established invaders have enough to cope with.

Roadside Verges

R oadside verges are often the most natural parts of the original semi-wild landscape to have survived, especially in the lowlands. The dispersed traditional pattern of habitation in Ireland has resulted in large numbers of small roads running through the more fertile parts of the countryside. It is an entirely different matter in the vast thinly-populated boglands and moorland areas. This amazing network of roads and trails carries a surprising number of plant species in the narrow strip between the hard surface of the road and the adjoining hedge or wall. It is, in effect, an undesignated nature reserve, open to all. Many rare plants were recorded from roadside verges in the past and some still persist. Affectionately known as 'The Long Acre', this narrow grassy band, often less than a metre wide, still gives us some idea of the potential natural vegetation of an area. It retains elements of the local flora that have virtually disappeared from the hinterland.

Because of the way they are managed, roadside verges constitute a very different environment from the neighbouring farmed land even if they are not a cohesive habitat type in themselves. These verges are usually not grazed, which makes a huge difference to the flora. The taller vegetation and species, which would otherwise be eaten back to the base by cattle and sheep, can flower, seed and reproduce here. Occasional mowing of the verge checks the growth of scrub and trees encroaching from the hedgerow. Most roads have a verge on each side, allowing a slightly different flora to develop on opposite sides of the road. This is most evident where roads are aligned in an east–west direction rather than north–south as the amount of sunshine falling on the roadsides will vary considerably depending on their orientation. Many roadside verges include a drain, which may be part of larger networks of interlinked drain systems. Where they are piped, the waters are not available and make no great difference to the local flora. However, when the drains are open, wetland plants spread into areas that are otherwise too dry, increasing local biodiversity.

COW PARSLEY

Cow Parsley is the most conspicuous plant on most of our roadside verges. It flourishes from late spring onward and eventually overwhelms most of the smaller species that grow here. As the year progresses, it is succeeded by Hogweed and other robust species.

COMMON KNAPWEED

Common Knapweed is a widespread and common plant of semi-natural grasslands, which has spread with great success onto roadside verges. Its colourful flowers often signal the presence of other less common species of lime-rich grassland that still survive on the sides of our roads and trackways.

Roadside verges may be banked or on the flat. The immediate soil and its properties exert a major influence on the composition of the flora. The soil is or at least was usually very similar to that of the adjoining fields. However, over time a number of changes have taken place, epitomised by the gradual enrichment of the roadside verges as a result of excessive agricultural run-off. Fertiliser passes from the fields into water systems and hence into roadside drains. Some species are well positioned to benefit from this. These are mainly relatively large species with high nutrient demands. They thrive in this environment, where there is no grazing pressure and an abundance of nourishment. Two species, Cow Parsley, *Anthriscus sylvestris*, and Hogweed, *Heracleum sphondylium*, flower in spring and early summer, and each produces great quantities of leaf and reduces the supply of vernal light to smaller species. However, many other species, especially the taller and robust later-flowering ones, can cope with this and a sort of roadside timeline is established through the year. Early in the year, low, fast-growing plants like Lesser Celandine, *Ficaria verna* (*Ranunculus ficaria*), and Ivy-leaved Speedwell, *Veronica hederifolia*, appear with the spring, to be engulfed by taller vegetation as the year progresses. Where roadside verges are cut more frequently, the flora usually fares better, because sun-loving perennial herbaceous species are more likely to get a look-in. A number of these are rosette-forming species and can cover the ground with their leaves, discouraging competition.

Sunny banks are environmentally different from the flat verges. Being on a slope, the aspect of the land is different, tilted to the sun and concentrating the sun's rays. Roadside banks do not occur randomly in the landscape. Usually the undulating post-glacial landscape has retained many small sand and gravel ridges. Similarly, down-cutting streams have altered land contours at local level. Rather than make roads over these small hills, the road builders of an earlier era either followed the contours of the land when they could or cut through them when they had to. Cutting through the ridges created exposures in the soil and sometimes even in the underlying bedrock along many roadsides. These areas were subsequently colonised by whatever could spread from the adjoining countryside. Modern cuts such as these can be seen on a large scale in the course of motorway construction. New roads can either run on the flat, or on an earthen platform where the road passes through low-lying areas. However, where it goes through a glacial ridge there is usually a large, open, V-shaped cut in the landscape, where remnants of the local vegetation can become established. Some motorway verges even show seepage lines where ground water, issuing slowly along a line a metre or two above the road, can support wetland species such as Glaucous Sedge, *Carex flacca*, and Common Spotted-orchid, *Dactylorhiza fuchsii*. These exposed areas present on a large scale what must have been happening all around the country hundreds of years ago. Many major road developments are unfortunately planted up, covering the newly-exposed verges and rock exposures with nursery-derived trees and shrubs, thus squandering the opportunity to allow the local flora to recover. Where this has not happened, an interesting sequence of colonisation takes place. Initially, there is a great splurge of annual species such as poppies, usually the widespread Common Poppy, *Papaver rhoeas*. These species have survived as dormant seed for many years and spring up in great numbers in the short term. Depending on which species are present in the dormant seed bank, the area may become fairly rapidly colonised by many other species, some of which may no longer be locally common. Where major roadworks have cut through these gravel ridges, rare species such as Blue Fleabane, *Erigeron acer*, and Bee Orchid, *Ophrys apifera*, appear and persist for a number of years. At first this may seem an unusual habitat but these species occur naturally in lime-rich gravelly conditions where the vegetation is thinner. In the normal course of events they often appear in sand pits as part of a succession sequence, where they hold on until the heavier encroaching plants make conditions impossibly competitive.

BIRD'S-FOOT TREFOIL

The densely-flowering Bird's-foot Trefoil marks the presence of lime-rich dry grassland conditions. Though commonest and at its most natural in dune grassland, it has spread onto many roadside verges.

When the bank is high above the ambient ground surface it usually releases rainwater faster and is also somewhat removed from the effects of local ground water. As a result, the upper sections of the banks are not repeatedly flushed with

agricultural run-off. The areas whose soils were initially nutrient-poor have managed to remain so. The plants of these areas have a better chance in the absence of the usual nutrient-guzzlers.

In the lowlands the most instantly-recognisable roadside verge vegetation comprises a group of species that typically come from lime-rich grasslands. These bands of vegetation often stand out because of their colourful combinations of yellow and blue flowers, visible from some distance. Three or four of these species show up very well on roadside verges in early summer. Common Knapweed, *Centaurea nigra*, with a strong purple flower head is a regularly-occurring species on many of the verges in limestone soil areas and it is often joined by Field Scabious, *Knautia arvensis*, with flattened clusters of sky-blue flowers. These two species are perennial and herbaceous. Therefore, when they are cut back they simply grow up again the following year. Where they grow usually other species with similar environmental requirements also occur. Earlier in the year Cowslips, *Primula veris*, are often part of this group as is Ox-eye Daisy, *Leucanthemum vulgare*, and, on slightly sandier ground, Rough Hawkbit, *Leontodon hispidus*, in late summer. Agrimony, *Agrimonia eupatoria*, Bird's-foot Trefoil, *Lotus corniculatus*, Lady's Bedstraw, *Galium verum*, all appear at various stages and introduce various shades of yellow into the roadside colour scheme. Some of these species, especially the low-growing ones, have held on in lightly-grazed areas, but cannot cope with heavy

AGRIMONY

The tall stems of Agrimony, which can be almost a metre high, produce yellow flowers that open along the stem gradually through the summer. Because of its growth form it is often trimmed by roadside verge grass-cutting operations.

LADY'S BEDSTRAW

Lady's Bedstraw, typically a plant of lime-rich rocky grasslands and sand dunes, has managed to spread or persist on many thinly-vegetated roadside verges where growing conditions are right – sufficient lime on the soil, little mowing and, if possible, a sunny dry bank.

grazing, re-seeding, ploughing, trampling and soil compaction. Cowslip often occurs with a dry-ground buttercup, Bulbous Buttercup, *Ranunculus bulbosus*. Along with other species these can extend their ranges onto higher, more acid ground. Both occur commonly in sand dune systems but can often follow the lime-rich glacial drift quite high into the mountains.

Roadside verges in certain parts of the country are, however, in relatively good condition, especially in areas where the surrounding countryside has been managed less intensively. Roadsides in areas where there is a shallow covering of soil, where the land has not been deeply ploughed and where herbicides are not applied recklessly are often quite good for plants. Roadsides throughout the Burren are well known for their great displays of colour in late spring but verges in many other parts of the west and especially on the limestone are always worth examining. Here the contrast between the grazed and ungrazed areas is not as evident, especially in the traditional sheep-grazed areas, where roadsides are still grazed by straying farm animals. As a result, Blackthorn, *Prunus spinosa*, and other invasive species are kept in check. Many nationally-rare species can grow on relatively unmown roadsides throughout the west and on hilly ground elsewhere. There is a very conspicuous counterpart of the commoner knapweed, which is particularly obvious in these areas. This is Greater Knapweed, *Centaurea scabiosa*, a much bigger plant, with larger flower heads, many of which are surrounded by much longer flowers, making the head appear even larger. Similarly, a larger counterpart of our widespread Agrimony, Fragrant Agrimony, *Agrimonia procera*, is a notable feature of roadside verges on more neutral to slightly acidic soils throughout Ireland. In high summer two large St John's-worts become

very obvious on uncut roadside verges. Perforate St John's-wort, *Hypericum perforatum*, is widespread throughout the more lime-rich areas and has also spread onto railway lines. Imperforate St John's-wort, *Hypericum maculatum*, is slightly rarer nationally and can grow on more lime-deficient roadside soils.

A drive along a series of rising roads from the more lime-rich soils onto higher ground provides an easy overview of the way in which the flora changes. These changes relate to the depth and disposition of the glacial drift that covers much of the lowlands and fringes the lower sides of many of our mountains. It can have varying proportions of lime-rich or lime-poor material and may have been subsequently leached. The most obvious plant to show up the extreme contrast in soil type is Foxglove, *Digitalis purpurea*, and many other smaller and less conspicuous acid-ground species can be expected nearby. Sheep's-bit, *Jasione montana*, Sheep's Sorrel, *Rumex acetosella*, Wood Sage, *Teucrium scorodonia*, Smith's Pepperwort, *Lepidium heterophyllum*, and Slender St John's-wort, *Hypericum pulchrum*, all show up on roadside verges and banks, on more acid soils. The zone where the lime-loving and hating species overlap on roadsides is a fascinating area. On higher ground the verges become wilder and more characteristic of heathland with Ling, *Calluna vulgaris*, and Bell Heather, *Erica cinerea*, revealing the presence of very shallow, acid soils. The transition from one zone to the next, though gradual, is not necessarily evenly paced. Isolated pockets of drift material sometimes reworked by natural processes allow some species to appear on roadsides in equally unlikely-looking places. There are areas in the Wicklow Mountains and elsewhere where species usually considered to be typical of limestone soils occur on very dry, acid gravels.

On naturally moist nutrient-rich lowland soils or those that have been flushed by drains, a group of plants more typically from fertile wetland areas grow, often in great abundance, even though they may not occur in neighbouring fields. Great Willowherb, *Epilobium hirsutum*, and its smaller

Meadowsweet has spread from wetlands into roadside drains. In many instances the wetlands have now disappeared because of those drains.

relation, Hoary Willowherb, *Epilobium parviflorum*, are often luxuriant in these areas, as are Meadowsweet, *Filipendula ulmaria*, Angelica, *Angelica sylvestris*, and Hemp-agrimony, *Eupatorium cannabinum*. These roadside drains are also linked up, taking surplus water from higher ground and conveying it by the fall of the land into more clearly-defined streams and rivers. In various parts of Ireland, great stands of the Giant Horsetail, *Equisetum telmateia*, appear on roadsides and usually a spring or recently-emerged stream can be found nearby, often indicating the presence of other good habitats locally.

In a sense the generic roadside serves as a sort of cross-section of the countryside, like a giant transect, accessible and informative, pointing to areas that might otherwise be overlooked. Where it has not been poisoned, cut or flailed into botanical oblivion it has often retained the species of the local landscape long after they have been wiped out from the immediate vicinity.

Warning: Roadsides, especially those in undulating terrain, are extremely dangerous areas for pedestrians. Motorists have no inkling that botanists may be working on roadsides, particularly in areas where pedestrians seldom walk. Where possible, fieldwork should be conducted in cul-de-sacs, quiet roads with unimpeded visibility and at times of the day when there is little traffic. Sections of roadside that have been by-passed by road improvement schemes are often secure places to examine the flora, as are tracks leading to isolated houses. Be careful where you park your car and be prepared for offers of help or to be asked your business – often!

GREATER KNAPWEED

The spectacular heads of Greater Knapweed contrast strikingly with its far more widespread relative Common Knapweed (see p. 84). Greater Knapweed was once far more widely recorded on roadside verges. It can still be seen in quantity on many lightly-grazed roadsides in parts of the limestone areas of the west. In the east it is now mainly a plant of railway embankments and ungrazed grassland on low sea cliffs.

Marram Grass

Marram Grass is the main botanical agent responsible for the growth of coastal dunes. When inundated by sand it continues to grow, causing more sand to accumulate around its stems. In the meantime its dense network of roots consolidates the sand below that would otherwise blow away.

Sand Dunes

The type of beach beloved by sunbathers usually forms where sea shores shelve gently. Exposed sands dry out at low tide and are blown inland by sea breezes. Where the onshore winds meet some obstruction the sand is dropped and gradually forms little piles. There is a limit to how high these small sandhills can get. A drift of sand accumulating behind a swept-up drift log will only grow so high. However, if the obstruction is itself living and growing, the sand will continue to gather higher and higher, around and through it. This process may be observed around most of our sandy shores. Tufts of grass and other vegetation grow out on the shoreline and sand gathers initially in the lee of the plants. Shoreline grasses grow up through the accumulating sand and gradually the little sandhill gets higher. The vegetation slows the wind and any further blown sand is deposited in the wind shadow of the embryonic dune. Dunes grow relatively fast at first, but slow down as they mature. They can form on land, accumulating directly on pre-existing shores or can develop as part of sand-shingle ridge formation processes, growing as linear features parallel to the shore but separated for most of their length from the mainland. The latter dunes are often the most natural, because their growing tips are furthest away from the points of visitor access. In these areas, natural processes of growth are most evident and it is here that colonisation and succession by coastal plants can most clearly be seen. The direction taken by these dunes depends on the local topography, the direction of the winds at different times of year and the supply of sand. However, even the most heavily-used dunes can exhibit many of these natural processes.

Many local authorities have implemented beach conservation measures, where areas of foreshore are corralled off, particularly from motorised traffic, allowing loose sand to accumulate and giving the

Prickly Saltwort is an annual species and one of the few that can cope with the severe environment of the sandy foreshore. To survive here a species needs to cope with repeated sand-blasting, high levels of salt and inundation by high tides. Its prickly leaf tips may discourage trampling by human visitors.

natural vegetation a chance to grow. They also provide relatively safe areas for beach users.

The outermost dunes are very mobile. The wind shear effect is considerable and many plants trying to get established are constantly exposed to abrasion by sand. Anyone who has walked into the wind on a sea shore in winter can testify to this. Very few species can live out here. Nutrient input comes from drifted seaweeds and other sea-borne organic debris. Salt levels from the sea and spray are very high, diluted only by rainfall. Powdered sea-shells elevate the levels of lime. The shoreline flora consists of nutrient-hungry species such as Spear-leaved Orache, *Atriplex prostrata*, and Sea Sandwort, *Honkenya peploides*, especially where the matrix is stiffened by the presence of a little shingle. A small plant with cylindrical fleshy leaves with an extremely sharp point grows out here also. This is Prickly Saltwort, *Salsola kali*. There are two other plants completely at home here, Sea Rocket, *Cakile maritima*, and Sand Couch-grass, *Elytrigia juncea*. Sometimes small dunes begin to build up here but spring tides usually wash away most of these and restart the process of colonisation. To complete their life cycle in the available time-frame, plants have to mature quickly. Sea Rocket is the most obvious species. It has four white or pale mauve petals and produces a seed pod with one or two large seeds. It also has very fleshy, succulent leaves, a feature it shares with many other plants from salt-rich environments. It is widespread around the coasts of Ireland. Once it and other annual species die off, the sand that accumulated around their stems will blow away. However, other more long-lived species can get started here and will continue to grow long after the annual species have died off.

SEA ROCKET

Sea Rocket is one of the plants that contribute to the initial formations of sand dunes. It belongs to the Cruciferae and is a fast-growing, usually annual, flesh-leaved species growing best in and above the upper drift-line. It can cope with sand inundation and, if not trampled, each of the 4-petalled flowers produces several large fruits in summer.

Growing with Sea Rocket but slightly further up the shore is Sand Couch-grass. On sunny days its leaves are rolled inward – a water retention measure shared with other sand dune grasses. Its fruiting heads are very distinctive, as the individual spikelets snap off if they are pressed downwards against the direction of growth. Sand Couch-grass can grow up through the accreting sand and contributes to a general rising of the outer shoreline, at least in the period between the spring tides. In many cases this zone is now being invaded by a much larger grass, Lyme-grass, *Leymus arenarius*, which has large blue-green open flat leaves. On account of its fast-growing properties, Lyme-grass was frequently planted as a sand binder. In recent years it has started to spread rapidly and now forms substantial stands on some of our shores. Where these individual stands coalesce, they form a strong matted wall of vegetation, scoured on the outer side by the higher tides. Drifting and wind-blown seaweeds and other organic materials are often trapped by its robust tussocks, enriching the sandy soil trapped by its roots. Within this mass a number of common

PERENNIAL SOW-THISTLE

The large heads of Perennial Sow-thistle are often found in the lee of the outer dunes along with other species that have become familiar weeds of cultivation.

SEA BINDWEED

The beautiful large flowers of Sea Bindweed are a spectacular feature of undamaged sand dune systems. Although it sometimes grows on open coarser sand it is usually found a little in from the strandline, generally among low-growing Marram.

SEA HOLLY

Sea Holly also grows on sandy and shingle shores but is very sensitive to visitor pressure. It has strong spiny leaves but the stems break readily. It may be in decline. On more remote, little-used sandy shores the plants are impressively large and produce abundant flower-heads.

species grow, particularly Creeping Thistle, *Cirsium arvense*, Perennial Sow-thistle, *Sonchus arvensis*, and Cat's-ear, *Hypochoeris radicata*. Lyme-grass continues to spread and consolidate its existing colonies and looks set in some areas to oust or severely limit the natural gradation in topography and vegetation from open mobile dunes to the next natural zone, the Marram Dunes.

Marram Grass, *Ammophila arenaria*, is a remarkable species. In common with other plants of dune systems, it can grow up through the inundating sands, often forming very high dunes. On occasions, particularly after severe winter storms, when the outer dunes have been stripped by wave action, the exposed rooting system of Marram is evident. Beneath the protruding leaves and green stems extends a huge network of 'roots' that were once much nearer the surface, when the dune was building up. These rooting systems can be several metres long and wide and in effect not only direct nutrients and water to the plant but also form physical networks that hold the entire dune together. This species is the main driving force in the formation of larger dunes. A number of plants can grow here among the Marram tussocks, especially those from the foreshore. However, once it becomes tall and therefore less influenced by normal wave action other species can become established. Sea Spurge, *Euphorbia paralias*, Sea Bindweed, *Calystegia soldanella*, and Sea Holly, *Eryngium maritimum*, are regular members of this

DANDELION

The Dandelions of sand dune systems are very different from those of our roadside verges. These are usually much smaller native species unlike the large-leaved (micro)species that are so prominent in spring.

group, especially in the lee of the main dunes. The attractive pink flowers of Sea Bindweed are unmistakable and where it grows it can form large colonies and extend seaward into the Sand Couch-grass zone. Sea Spurge is a close relative of the Poinsettia. At first glance they may not appear to have much in common, but if you ignore the bright red flashy bracts of the Christmas pot plant

and examine instead the central parts of the flower, their structural similarities will become evident. The stems exude a white juice, a feature it shares with many other members of the Spurge family. Sea Holly is now becoming rarer on heavily-trampled dunes, but is a spectacular feature of many of our less accessible sea shores. One of the rarest of Irish plants is also known from this zone. Cottonweed, *Otanthus maritimus*, is a native from two small areas in Wexford, where it grows on sandy ground over shingle. Its occurrence here is of great interest because it is now thought to have died out in all its former sites in the south of Britain.

Further in on the flatter lower ground various forms of dune grassland develop. These systems are often held in place by another remarkable plant, Sand Sedge, *Carex arenaria*. This species sends out runners (rhizomes) in all directions and these take root and create new plants. The ensuing network of rhizomes can often be spotted in dune systems, where straight lines of new plants can be seen radiating out from a central point. It grows rapidly where stabilised dunes have lost their covering of vegetation and it is, therefore, very significant in repairing damaged dunes. This far in from the sea, the salt input is very much reduced and other plants typical of more stable conditions begin to appear. Many of these are typical of inland grasslands – Cat's-ear, Ragwort, *Senecio jacobea*, and dandelions, *Taraxacum officinale* agg. Many of the dandelions growing here are not ones that generally grow in

COMMON DODDER

Dodder is a declining parasitic species usually now seen in sand dune systems where its red twining stems feed in various host plants, often Lady's Bedstraw, but also on Bird's-foot Trefoil and Thyme.

RESTHARROW

The sticky leaves of Common Restharrow are covered with minute glandular hairs and the entire plant gives off an unpleasant scent when rubbed. In contrast the flowers are elegant and classic examples of the Pea family. It is found in older areas within the dune system, especially where a little erosion has occurred. Common Restharrow also gets inland on good-quality gravel ridges and sandy exposures.

gardens. The true sand dune dandelions usually have very divided leaves, are smaller and their fruits are reddish-brown unlike the darker brown of most of the inland species.

To appreciate the diversity of flora in these stable dune systems it is necessary to get down on hands and knees. A number of tiny species occur here. The most amazing ones are probably Early Forget-me-not, *Myosotis ramosissima*, Common Cornsalad, *Valerianella locusta*, and Wall Speedwell, *Veronica arvensis*. Each may be less than 2 cm tall and produce minute blue flowers, the Forget-me-not having a distinct yellow 'eye'. In other habitats these species can grow much taller. However, more obvious species such as Lady's Bedstraw, *Galium verum*, and Birds'-foot Trefoil, *Lotus corniculatus*, are much easier to see. In slightly more open places, Common Restharrow, *Ononis repens*, is conspicuous and Mouse-eared-hawkweed, *Pilosella officinarum*, can cover some of the driest ground with dense mats of leaves and stems. In all these areas there is evidence of dune vegetation dying back and restarting. On the crests of these low hills conditions are often quite arid. In summer, especially on the sunnier south-facing slopes, the vegetation begins to wilt. If there are high levels of visitor usage, these delicate communities are regularly trampled by pedestrians and the network of plant material that holds the dunes together begins to fail, resulting in the partial disintegration of the dunes. Some species such as Biting Stonecrop, *Sedum acre*, are drought specialists, evidenced by their fleshy leaves. There is a very noticeable moss here also, Sand-hill Screw-moss, *Tortula ruralis*, which in dry sunny weather looks brown and withered. However, if a little water is sprinkled on the leaves, they will revive within a minute and reassume the green appearance they have in damper weather. The

PYRAMIDIAL ORCHID

Dune grassland can be amazingly rich in species. Pyramidal Orchid and Kidney Vetch are regular and obvious elements of this but a closer look will reveal a variety of grasses and low-growing species such as Thyme.

alternative short-cycle annuals are also well geared to cope here, growing rapidly in early spring and completing their life cycles from seed to seed in a few months. Some of these fast-growing annuals germinate in or close to mats of this and other mosses. They are often joined by a very distinctive little grass, Sand Cat's-tail, *Phleum arenarium*.

KIDNEY VETCH

In early summer the dunes are often brightened by an abundance of flowers of Kidney Vetch. The flower structure indicates its relationship to Furze, Lupins and Sweet Peas.

Other commonly-encountered species in this area include Wild Pansy, *Viola tricolor*, Kidney Vetch, *Anthyllis vulneraria*, Common Centaury, *Centaurium erythraea*, Common Stork's-bill, *Erodium cicutarium*, Common Milkwort, *Polygala vulgaris*, Pyramidal Orchid, *Anacamptis pyramidalis*, Green-winged Orchid, *Anacamptis morio* (until recently *Orchis morio*), and Hop Trefoil, *Trifolium campestre*. These occur in various combinations depending on the amount of

vegetation cover, its stability, water supply and exposure to wind and sun.

In more stable systems, a number of lighter grasses begin to become more plentiful and with them a variety of very colourful species appear commonly. The Harebell, *Campanula rotundifolia*, Cowslip, *Primula veris*, Bulbous Buttercup, *Ranunculus bulbosus*, Field Wood-rush, *Luzula campestris*, and Lesser Meadow-rue, *Thalictrum minus*, are often to be found. All of these are often encountered in other non-dune habitats. Harebell occurs commonly on thin grassland in rocky ground both near the sea and also on much higher ground, especially in the Burren. Cowslip is a regular member of lime-rich grasslands and Lesser Meadow-rue occurs inland in rocky grassland on lakeshores, especially in the Midlands, albeit as a different subspecies.

A few rare species do best in dunes, though they are not confined to this habitat. Hound's-tongue, *Cynoglossum officinale*, is one such species that can often be seen in quantity in the lee of dunes and then scattered further in from the sea where it grows by open pockets of sand. It is a large coarse-leaved plant, getting up to a metre tall in sheltered situations. It has dull reddish-purple flowers and very unusual spiny fruits that can cling to clothing and are hence dispersed to other areas. Its distribution to some extent is echoed by another member of the same family (Boraginaceae). The tall spikes of blue flowers and spiny leaves of

CENTAURY

Common Centaury grows commonly on good-quality dunes, where it thrives in company with Thyme, various Eyebrights and a selection of short-lived winter annuals that have passed their best and gone to seed by the time the Centaury comes into flower.

VIPER'S-BUGLOSS

Viper's-bugloss can be a metre or more tall. Its dense flowering stems are particularly attractive to bees in high summer.

CARLINE THISTLE

Carline Thistle has a flower that appears to be 'everlasting' as the heads remain intact well into autumn. It is usually found in older sand dune systems and abundantly on dry soils over limestone bedrock. Less commonly it is encountered on esker gravel ridges, where it usually occurs in company with other rare species.

Viper's-bugloss, *Echium vulgare,* are instantly recognisable. In summer this species is visited by large numbers of bees and other insects. Both of these species are occasional in open gravelly ground in the east and were once more widespread inland. Although both are far commoner by the sea, they can grow on open sunny sandy ground inland. Viper's-bugloss is often spread along roadsides in sand taken from gravel deposits near the sea. The gravel trucks shed a certain amount of sand and included seeds and the distribution of this species follows their route. However, most of the plants that get started fail to establish permanent new colonies. Hound's-tongue is reputedly unpleasant-tasting to cattle, which may account for its occasional survival in a few sites.

In time, a good deal of lime-rich material is washed out of the soil-sand mix by rain (leaching) and some dunes can become acid. Botanists familiar with lime-rich dunes are often fascinated to encounter dune systems covered by acid-ground species such as Bell Heather, *Erica cinerea*, or Ling, *Calluna vulgaris*. Where dunes have been extensively leached they are often colonised by lichens, mainly from the genus *Cladonia*. These dunes are sometimes classified as 'grey' dunes, because of the colour of the lichens. This feature often occurs where dunes have been grazed over long periods by rabbits. Similarly leached or eroding dunes are locally dominated by Wild Thyme, *Thymus praecox*, even in apparently lime-rich dune systems. Over time, some dunes become engulfed by Bracken, *Pteridium aquilinum*, obscuring the original contours of the land, especially where there is sufficient ground water. The presence of Bracken can allow a number of shade-demanding species to take hold under its expanding fronds.

However, where dunes have been heavily leached, species more typical of heathland make their appearance. These include Heath Dog-violet, *Viola canina*, Heath Speedwell, *Veronica officinalis*, and even in sheltered areas, Common Dog-violet, *Viola riviniana*. In time these older dunes become colonised by Burnet Rose, *Rosa spinosissima*. This is usually the first rose to flower in late spring and has showy cream-coloured flowers. These produce dark red fruits in early summer. As it is covered with dense spines, it is a difficult plant to walk through and also discourages grazing by cattle and horses. As a result, where it has survived, many species that might otherwise have been eaten or trampled are able to find some protection. Carline Thistle, *Carlina vulgaris*, can also occur here in dry, thin dune grassland, often indicating where other interesting plants are also to be found.

Further inland the immediate impact of the sea lessens. Sand inundation (and hence salt) is much reduced. On lower, more level ground water supply is better. Most of the outer dune species disappear, although they may reappear occasionally when dunes collapse. Some deeper-rooted species of wet ground may appear – Angelica, *Angelica sylvestris*, often appears in incongruous situations, as does Hogweed, *Heracleum sphondylium*. These are species that would be encountered on most roadside verges, especially those with open drains. Marram Grass may still be found but rarely growing as vigorously as it does in the outer dunes.

It must be remembered that within a dune system there are many processes in train, and the landscape carries clues to events that may have occurred many years before. Dunes that were once outer dunes are over time superseded by other newer ones. This process is evidenced by long parallel sandhill systems aligned with the shoreline. Within the dunes, old sandhills may have disintegrated, having lost their cohesion when the vegetation network that held them together died back. Sometimes older dunes show signs of former blow-outs where weaknesses in the vegetation cover were exploited by the wind, tearing out the sides of the hills. These weaknesses can be initiated by excessive trampling or by fires caused by smouldering cigarette butts or disposable barbecues left behind, unquenched.

Sand dunes, especially in their outer regions, are constantly recreating themselves, as part of the annual cycle. In wetter areas such as dune slacks, willows and other scrub species may become established where the sandy ground gives way to more humus-rich soils. Here Brambles, *Rubus fruticosus* agg., Blackthorn, *Prunus spinosa*, Furze,

Ulex europaeus, and Hawthorn, *Crataegus monogyna*, can get a start. One introduced woody shrub species now threatens to cause great damage to our dunes. Sea Buckthorn, *Hippophae rhamnoides*, was planted as a sand binder, brought into Ireland to combat dune erosion. It did this quite effectively, but then carried on colonising ground where it was never intended to grow. It casts a shadow on a wild flora adapted to live in bright sunny conditions. Very few species can survive in its shade. Those that do are usually nutrient-demanding species such as nettles and docks. Various other tree species have been planted in dunes. Sycamore was often planted for shelter around summer houses and has survived long after the houses have fallen into decay. In some areas, various species of pine have been planted. These give a degree of physical stability to some mobile dune systems and have the advantage of providing a light shade when they are not planted too densely together. A number of unusual orchids and other rare species have managed to become established in these areas and add to the natural diversity at a local level.

FORE-DUNES

The zone just in front of the main dunes includes species that must cope with poor nutrition, drought, disturbance by beach visitors, inundation by sand and exposure to salt-laden sea spray and high tides driven higher by low atmospheric pressure and onshore winds. As if this was not enough, the plants of this zone, including Sea Rocket and Sand Couch, are now in competition with the spreading Lyme-grass, whose large, flat, blue-green leaves are an increasing feature of many sandy shores.

Salt Marshes

Salt marshes form where incoming tides deposit sand and silt in relatively calm water conditions. They develop mainly in the lee of peninsular sand spits or on the fringes of estuaries. The plants and vegetation that grow in these areas are well adapted to cope with highly-saline environments. A type of salt marsh vegetation can also form in sheltered bays and on rocky shores where the force of the waves is broken by the presence of offshore reefs. Salt marshes often appear as flat forbidding areas, difficult to visit, exposed to wind and rain. A good deal of domestic rubbish washed into rivers comes to rest here, trapped or embedded in the sticky muds, giving these areas an unsightly appearance. The fine silty material that underlies salt marshes, some of which originated on dry land and was washed into rivers and then re-deposited near their mouths, has been sorted by the sea. Wind-blown sand was also carried onto salt marshes. Depending on the direction of the onshore winds, the sloping character of the shore and the supply of sand, salt marshes can be wide or narrow. They do not form on wave-battered coasts or where there is a powerful tidal scour. However, certain types of salt marsh develop on platforms of submerged shingle. This process can often be seen when the vegetation of a salt marsh dies back to expose the pebbly layer beneath.

Salt marshes are inundated twice each day by the tides, which are highest in spring and autumn. The silty material they carry in is laid down evenly, conforming to the slope of the underlying shore. Because of this, they can flood very rapidly. However, some areas at the top of the salt marsh may be covered briefly for only a few days every year. The strong pressures exerted by this daily inundation bring about a distinct zonation in the vegetation. The silty material that forms the physical basis of salt marshes is eventually bound together by the roots of dense mats of colonising vegetation, but in the lowest parts of the marsh, conditions are very different.

Salt marshes

The wet soft mud flats at the lower end of salt marshes are not very suitable for most land plants but important feeding areas for birds. Many of these areas have now been invaded by the Cord-grass *Spartina* that has engulfed thousands of hectares of estuarine mud around the Irish coast.

Mud Flats

In the lowest parts of the salt marsh the silty mud is more or less permanently wet. The slightest rise in tide levels will flood these areas. This is quite a dangerous place to walk. Very few plants can survive here. Those that do must be able to endure extended periods of inundation by saltwater and also maintain a roothold in a substrate that is loose, slimy and poorly supplied with stones.

The specialists in this zone are the Eel-wracks of the genus *Zostera*, of which there are currently two species recognised from Ireland, each occurring at slightly different levels on the shore. They are very slippery and resemble long, stringy greenish seaweed and are only exposed to the air for a few hours every day. The long, narrow leaves have little supporting structure and flop on the mud when the tide recedes. Eel grasses are seldom seen growing *in situ* – the areas where they live are usually very slippery and difficult to examine. Their fragments are usually washed up on sea shores and shingle ridges after storms. Where they grow naturally there are usually no other flowering plants. Eel grass is the food plant of choice for overwintering Brent Geese.

Lower Salt Marsh

A little higher up the shore, but still below the zone where the main mass of broad-leaved plants begins to appear, is the Glasswort or *Salicornia* zone. A number of different Glasswort species live in salt marshes and they also exhibit zonation patterns related to inundation. Some of the lowermost-living species have fat, stubby, succulent

GLASSWORT

Glassworts belonging to various species occupy different niches in upper and lower salt marshes. Their fleshy and succulent stems enable them to grow in salty conditions that most other plants would find impossible.

CORD-GRASS (*SPARTINA*)

Where *Spartina* has not invaded there is now very little room for other plants. Occasionally *Zostera* species occur here but are more often seen washed up by the incoming tides.

stems. Those higher up have stems that look like knobbly fingers. One or two species can even grow on rocks and sea walls in the intertidal zone, where they are only briefly covered by seawater in the course of a normal day. Glassworts cope with the high salt levels by a mechanism termed osmosis – a process that reduces the amount of saltwater entering the tissues of the plant to a non-toxic level. Sea Blite, *Suadea maritima*, another fleshy species, also occurs here but can extend through to the top of most of our salt marshes.

The ecology of these low-lying muddy areas has been greatly damaged and altered, mainly by the invasion of Common Cord-grass, *Spartina anglica*, in the twentieth century. This grass arose through hybridisation and was planted to consolidate and accelerate salt marsh reclamation measures (i.e. to convert the muddy land to pasture). Colonies were planted around the coasts of Britain and Ireland and have spread further to many sites, carried by currents and waves. Once this species became locally established, it formed huge dense mats of vegetation, raising the ambient surface of the marsh to a higher level as floating vegetable matter was trapped between its stems. Many of our coastal mudflats – and our natural biodiversity – have been completely engulfed by this grass.

On slightly higher ground, inundation is reduced and other broad-leaved plants can grow. Drainage is better, the soil is more aerated and a different range of plants can take hold. The impact of salt is lessened because of the reduced levels of flooding by the sea and the increased influence of freshwater from ground sources or from rain. Different species of plant have differing levels of tolerance of these environmental stresses and are distributed accordingly. Their positions can overlap, intermingle or apparently intrude into other areas,

SALT MARSH VEGETATION

Sea Aster, a member of the Daisy family, is often very common in the upper parts of salt marshes and can also spread onto some sheltered but sea-sprayed cliffs. Sea Plantain can similarly occupy the upper parts of salt marshes, often forming dense clumps apparently in competition with Thrift.

often due to the presence of deep channels that allow seawater to enter these marshes in advance of the main tidal movements. Depending on the time of year, the upper reach of the tide may be extended by quite a distance, but the sea that floods quite rapidly can retreat just as fast.

There is usually a fairly distinct line of demarcation between this vegetated zone and the lower muddy areas. However, within the vegetated areas there is a good deal of variation. Depending on the length of the gradient from the muddy edge to the upper tidal limits, a number of conspicuous and easily-recognised species occur, including Sea Aster, *Aster tripolium*, Sea Arrow-grass, *Triglochin maritima*, and Sea Plantain, *Plantago maritima*. A densely-matted grass with very narrow leaves and very obvious runners covering the ground is Common Saltmarsh-grass, *Puccinellia maritima*. At their lower levels, typical salt marshes usually have Lax-flowered Sea-lavender, *Limonium humile*, and

SEA-LAVENDERS

Two main species of Sea Lavender occur in Ireland. Lax-flowered Sea-lavender occurs in the lower parts of salt marshes and has spreading branches with spaced out flower clusters. Rock Sea-lavender occurs higher up on the marsh and well into the spray zone on cliffs, rocks and even sea-piers. It has more densely-packed flowering branches, which are usually held more erectly.

SEA PURSLANE

Sea Purslane often grows on the margins of creeks and inlets within the salt marsh. It can thus reveal the routes by which the incoming sea can penetrate rapidly into the marsh in advance of the main tide.

Sea Purslane, *Atriplex portulacoides*. Both these species are regularly inundated by even medium tides. The flowers and flowering branches of Lax-flowered Sea-lavender are more spread out than its relative, Rock Sea-lavender, *Limonium binervosum*, which is usually found in and above the spray zone on rocky shores. The stands of Sea Purslane, which can often be 50 cm high, cover parts of the marsh with dwarf shrubby vegetation. From a distance, natural drainage lines dissecting the marsh can be seen, fringed by this species, which penetrates further up into the marsh along the sides of these water-courses. Visitors to salt marshes often find their route cut off by the rising tide, which has rapidly worked its way back up through the deeper creeks. This feature also enables other plants typical of the lower parts of the marsh to spread into the upper regions. As a result, it is often difficult to find a convincing line of demarcation between the different vegetation types.

Middle and Upper Salt Marsh

However, in the upper sectors the vegetation away from the drains consists mainly of dense low mats of Thrift, *Armeria maritima*, Sea Milkwort, *Glaux maritima*, and – toward the upper levels – two much taller coastal rushes, Saltmarsh Rush, *Juncus gerardii*, and Sea Rush, *Juncus maritimus*. Sometimes these rushes occur in substantial robust colonies, often in slightly different areas within the upper parts of the marsh. Around the high tide mark, where vegetable debris accumulates and decomposes, Common Scurvy-grass, *Cochlearia officinalis*, Sea Aster and both Sea Plantain and Sea Arrow-grass grow with much greater vigour than they did further down the salt marsh. Indeed, after certain high tides, the drift line flotsam consists of thousands of detached and decaying leaves of Sea Purslane. Other nutrient-demanding species here include a formidable mixture of *Atriplex* species, Sea Beet, *Beta vulgaris* ssp. *maritima*, and large stands of Scutch, *Elytrigia repens*.

Where these upper areas are irrigated by percolating freshwater, a number of otherwise rare species occur, provided they are not crowded out by their more robust neighbours. This habitat is

THRIFT

In certain favoured situations the upper stretches of salt marsh can comprise dense mats of Thrift to the virtual exclusion of all other species.

SEA MILKWORT

Sea Milkwort grows well in the upper parts of salt marshes and can also occur on damp shingle and even in sandy areas occasionally inundated by the sea.

Common Scurvy-grass, clearly not a grass but a member of the Cruciferae, occurs in the upper parts of salt marshes, especially in the drift-line.

rare and it has a number of species which, being very much confined to it, are rare also. The Strawberry-headed Clover, *Trifolium fragiferum*, is a good example. In early summer it resembles a low-growing, pink-flowered, round-headed clover. Later, as it goes into fruit, the calyx-lobes begin to inflate and for a few weeks the fruiting heads are conspicuous features of lightly-grazed grassland. Where freshwater passes down onto salt marsh vegetation, Parsley Water-dropwort, *Oenanthe lachenalii*, often occurs. This is a tall member of the Umbelliferae and can form substantial and conspicuous stands in ungrazed areas, along with

nearby colonies of Common Reed, *Phragmites communis*. On the other hand, Strawberry-headed Clover can endure a certain amount of light grazing, especially by horses. There are several coastal wetlands where Sea Arrow-grass and its close relative and non-saline counterpart, Marsh Arrow-grass, *Triglochin palustris*, grow near to each other, the former confined to the saltier ground, the other tracking the course of moving freshwater as it seeps and winds its way onto the salt marsh.

Sometimes the vegetation of salt marshes dies off in patches, particularly where seawater stands in low-lying areas. In periods of extended strong

In the drift-line a few nutrient-demanding species, such as Spear-leaved Orache, flourish. They thrive on the decomposed vegetable debris cast up by the highest tides and also spread into similar situations inland, such as manure heaps and abandoned silage pits.

sunshine, the water evaporates, salt levels rise and injure the vegetation. This pattern repeats itself. Gradually the plant cover disappears and a depression develops in the marsh, often revealing the substratum upon which the marsh was formed. Sometimes these depressions coalesce and form large, bare areas termed salt-pans. A colonisation sequence may then restart, with Glassworts coming back on the bare lowest-lying silt.

At the uppermost levels in the salt marsh, there are a number of species that are only inundated by the highest tides. Although they are usually confined to salt marshes they are unable to survive lower down the salinity and inundation gradients. Some of these species can sometimes be found in seaside towns, on piers and sea walls. There are now many recorded instances where some of these species have spread inland in Britain on salt-treated roads. These tendencies are increasingly noted in Ireland now. Because the highest levels of the marsh usually represent the uppermost levels of inundation, pedestrians and offroad motorists usually traverse these areas, skirting the wet ground and avoiding the agricultural land higher up. Vegetation is less typical here and is often dominated by grasses and more nutrient-demanding broad-leaved species, such as Spear-leaved Orache, *Atriplex prostrata*.

At this level in the typical salt marsh, most of the really salt-tolerant species have fallen away. However, where saltwater lingers on low-lying ground, especially after high spring tides, bare patches of mud appear, often in intermittently-flooded agricultural grassland. The persisting saltwater inhibits the growth of many inland species, leaving bare muddy areas open for colonisation by a few specialists. In summer, salt levels can be very high here as a result of evaporation. The most colourful species is Lesser Sea-spurrey, *Spergularia marina*, and this often grows with another *Puccinellia* species, Reflexed Saltmarsh-grass, *Puccinellia distans*. It can be recognised by the way in which the stalks of the spikelets are directed slightly downwards (deflexed). Some ordinary wetland plants of inland

COMMON REED

The area between the open sea and dry land is muddy, especially in estuarine situations, but most of the growing areas are occupied by a limited range of grasses. Common Reed often indicates areas where freshwater has percolated onto the upper parts of the marsh.

Dune Slacks

Dune slacks are habitats with wetland vegetation that occur in low-lying areas within sand dune systems. Ground water levels are close to the surface, even in summer. In winter, small temporary pools may form and persist into late spring. The character of the vegetation relates to the duration of inundation, to under-soil fluctuations in the water table, to the chemical nature of the sand and to local issues such as drainage, grazing by sheep, cattle, horses and rabbits as well as recreational use (or abuse) in more heavily-used dune systems. Dune slacks are highly-colourful features in the landscape, containing many attractive species of flowering plant. Their flora contrasts strikingly with that of the surrounding dunes. In common with many other habitat types, they go through a maturing process, sometimes starting out even as bare wet sandy ground that gradually becomes colonised by a sequence of ever larger species as the habitat evolves.

When water lingers on a site for longer than normal, it sets back the early spring vegetation, temporarily retarding the growth of heavier grasses. It sets the scene for a number of species that are not particularly water-demanding but are poor competitors. These species flourish in the thinly-vegetated areas when the waters recede. In this way, depending on the intensity and duration of flooding, the colonisation process can be restarted each year in some areas. It is often possible to detect in late spring a line of vegetable fragments, such as small twigs and detached leaves, scattered in a line corresponding to the so-called 'high-water mark', showing the upper levels of recent flooding, sometimes augmented when the sea breaks through the dunes. When this happens, not only are the winter floods prolonged, but species that are less salt-tolerant are also set back. Occasionally the extent of saline conditions is indicated by the presence of Sea Milkwort, *Glaux maritima*, and Sea Rush, *Juncus maritimus*. Sea Rush, being deep-rooted, can endure drier, less favourable conditions. Sea Milkwort fares better in thinner, wetter vegetation. Two species of Spike-rush, Common Spike-rush, *Eleocharis palustris*, and Slender Spike-rush, *Eleocharis uniglumis*, can both grow where water lingers for longer periods. In some areas a gradation can be seen from freshwater influences (*E. palustris*) to more brackish conditions (*E. uniglumis*).

COMMON REED

The area between the open sea and dry land is muddy, especially in estuarine situations, but most of the growing areas are occupied by a limited range of grasses. Common Reed often indicates areas where freshwater has percolated onto the upper parts of the marsh.

SILVERWEED (ABOVE AND BELOW)

Silverweed, a relative of the Strawberry, has long, divided leaves covered with silvery hairs. It produces 'runners' that form new plants, which can cover large areas of the upper salt marsh.

bare-mud conditions can grow here also. Celery-leaved Crowfoot, *Ranunculus sceleratus*, Silverweed, *Potentilla anserina*, and Marsh Foxtail, *Alopecuros geniculatus*, spread rapidly over bare mud, outpaced only by Creeping Bent, *Agrostis stolonifera*.

The grassy areas that occur at the tops of salt marshes are often grazed by livestock, at least in summer. Many ingenious measures have been devised by coastal farmers to reduce the impact of the highest tides, including the erection of sea walls. These can be formidable structures of cut-stone or more modest earthen banks, fringing the estuaries. Because these banks are usually covered with vegetation and are often partly worn away, they may not be recognised for what they are. Their positioning on the estuarine landscape indicates the craft and knowledge of local farmers and landowners of earlier generations. There is often a mechanism in place – in essence, a sluice gate – to release freshwater from streams and land drains that would otherwise gather and flood the land but prevent saltwater getting into farmland. In some areas, pumping stations have been installed to remove water from low-lying land behind the sea walls.

Saltwater does, however, get in, even if only along the drainage channels. Depending on the effectiveness of the sluice gates, the vegetation can vary greatly from season to season and from year to year. When high incoming seas meet large volumes of river-borne freshwater following long periods of rain, serious flooding often occurs. Supplementary drainage works and larger more robust sluice gates have ended much of the natural variation and fluctuations in water levels that formerly took place in the inner areas. As temporary pools disappear, biodiversity plummets.

Sometimes patches of salt marsh vegetation appear apparently far from any contact with the sea. Usually these (generally low-lying) areas can be found to be connected via a network of drains to the tops of salt marshes. Water gets in here, especially at the spring tides and a few species such as Sea Aster and Sea Club-rush, *Bulboschoenus maritimus*, show the upper extent of saline influence.

Particularly interesting formations occur when salt marshes adjoin sandy shores, especially on very gently sloping shores when the transition is gradual. This sometimes occurs on sheltered bays where dune systems have extended across an inlet and a salt marsh has formed in its lee. Where the dune system is still growing, usually near its tip, great stretches of sand are then exposed. These areas support species that are typical of the highest levels of the salt marsh or even the spray zone of rocky shores and can become abundant here. The salty sand in these areas is also silty and a dry crust often forms on the surface. Pedestrians walking through this sand leave crisp, well-defined footprints as they would in snow. These habitats are unusual in the limited numbers of species they can support but are all the more interesting because of that. They present a developing landscape in a very natural state. In these situations great colonies of Rock Sea-lavender have sometimes formed, colouring the entire area a bright blue in late summer.

Where these sandy salt marshes are in turn connected to ordinary 'dry' land they may reveal other processes. When ground water rises and percolates onto these sandy salt marshes, habitats resembling bare dune slacks can form. These often have species that are untypical of the locality but act as indicators of the presence of different environmental conditions. The white flowers of Knotted Pearlwort, *Sagina nodosa*, for example, can be found in these situations along with a number of rare species of moss that might otherwise be overlooked, pointing out the whereabouts of freshwater seepage areas in these intermediate zones.

There is another situation where plants typical of the salt marsh are to be found, usually on rocky shores where shell sand and gravel have accumulated, often sheltered by rocks on shores and usually perched at or below the normal high tide mark. They occur where the rocky shores rise steeply and where there is little opportunity for natural extended vegetation gradients to become evident. The entire sequence can be compressed into a few metres, vertically and horizontally. These pockets of sand and broken shells are usually held together by dense stands of Common Saltmarsh-grass, Saltmarsh Rush, Sea Milkwort and sedges such as Long-bracted Sedge, *Carex extensa*, and Distant Sedge, *Carex distans*, in the area just above high tide mark. All of these are typical of the mid and upper sections of salt marsh. In a few instances they also have Salt-marsh Flat-grass, *Blysmus rufus*, a species that is much commoner in northern salt marshes. Sometimes freshwater percolates onto these areas, keeping the roots irrigated and to some extent diluting the seawater that sometimes lodges in depressions and becomes highly saline in hot summers. Shingle shore species can often grow here, such as Silverweed and Autumn Hawkbit, *Scorzoneroides autumnalis* (in one of its many subspecies). However, these areas of trapped salt marsh can occur on rock platforms at several levels at one site, with Lax-flowered Sea-lavender, and even Glassworts, plants of the lower levels of salt marshes, present nearest the waves. Indeed, in the west of Ireland. Lax-flowered Sea-lavender can grow in the thinnest bands of coastal vegetation, often at the head of sheltered bays, along with Common Saltmarsh-grass and very few other species.

Dune Slacks

Dune slacks are habitats with wetland vegetation that occur in low-lying areas within sand dune systems. Ground water levels are close to the surface, even in summer. In winter, small temporary pools may form and persist into late spring. The character of the vegetation relates to the duration of inundation, to under-soil fluctuations in the water table, to the chemical nature of the sand and to local issues such as drainage, grazing by sheep, cattle, horses and rabbits as well as recreational use (or abuse) in more heavily-used dune systems. Dune slacks are highly-colourful features in the landscape, containing many attractive species of flowering plant. Their flora contrasts strikingly with that of the surrounding dunes. In common with many other habitat types, they go through a maturing process, sometimes starting out even as bare wet sandy ground that gradually becomes colonised by a sequence of ever larger species as the habitat evolves.

When water lingers on a site for longer than normal, it sets back the early spring vegetation, temporarily retarding the growth of heavier grasses. It sets the scene for a number of species that are not particularly water-demanding but are poor competitors. These species flourish in the thinly-vegetated areas when the waters recede. In this way, depending on the intensity and duration of flooding, the colonisation process can be restarted each year in some areas. It is often possible to detect in late spring a line of vegetable fragments, such as small twigs and detached leaves, scattered in a line corresponding to the so-called 'high-water mark', showing the upper levels of recent flooding, sometimes augmented when the sea breaks through the dunes. When this happens, not only are the winter floods prolonged, but species that are less salt-tolerant are also set back. Occasionally the extent of saline conditions is indicated by the presence of Sea Milkwort, *Glaux maritima*, and Sea Rush, *Juncus maritimus*. Sea Rush, being deep-rooted, can endure drier, less favourable conditions. Sea Milkwort fares better in thinner, wetter vegetation. Two species of Spike-rush, Common Spike-rush, *Eleocharis palustris*, and Slender Spike-rush, *Eleocharis uniglumis*, can both grow where water lingers for longer periods. In some areas a gradation can be seen from freshwater influences (*E. palustris*) to more brackish conditions (*E. uniglumis*).

KNOTTED PEARLWORT

Knotted Pearlwort is often to be seen on thinly-vegetated areas within dune slacks. It indicates where water has lain or the presence of springs or less well-defined seepage features.

DEVIL'S-BIT SCABIOUS

Devil's-bit Scabious is a common feature of dune slacks. It flowers relatively late in the season and can cover the slacks with its bluish flowers. Its presence usually defines neatly the effective boundaries of the slack.

A number of fairly delicate-looking species can thrive in these less salty areas. One of the most characteristic is Knotted Pearlwort, *Sagina nodosa*. This is usually a species of open ground in fens but is perfectly at home here and sometimes indicates areas where there may be some slight upwelling of ground water at certain times of the year. Bog Pimpernel, *Anagallis tenella*, can also occur in areas where there is some evidence of weak natural springs seeping out over thin vegetation. Sometimes these areas may be engulfed by rapidly-accreting blown sand. When these areas are covered, plant life, deprived of light, becomes virtually impossible. Dunes and small loose hills of sand are, however, mobile. As they move on, they can leave behind open areas close to the water table. In other instances dunes can literally break down ('blow-outs'), to expose lower wetter soils and gravel as their sands are transported by the winds, and colonisation reactivates.

As colonisation continues, other more permanent species gradually take hold. They are mostly perennial and gradually out-compete the annual communities in less heavily-flooded ground. Heavier grasses are particularly obvious at this stage, especially Creeping Bent, *Agrostis stolonifera*, and they can be joined in some places by other short-lived annuals. Creeping Bent sends out long stolons (creeping stems) that can cover large areas in a very short period of time. As long as the ground remains open, various other species can gain a temporary toehold.

Eventually these pioneering plants give way to a more herbaceous and mixed vegetation, with many colourful species, especially some of our most attractive orchids. Many of the species found in these areas are often typical of various wetlands in the Irish Midlands and the ecological differences that can be observed here reflect patterns that are evident in wetland systems inland. The species that

MARSH HELLEBORINE

Marsh Helleborine is one of the classic dune-slack species. When it occurs it can be present in huge numbers. It also grows inland in good-quality lime-rich wetlands.

(LEFT TO RIGHT): WATER MINT, FLEABANE AND COMMON TWAYBLADE

The flora of dune slacks is shared with many species from other wetland habitats. Water Mint and Fleabane are widespread in marsh ground. Common Twayblade is rarer and prefers more clearly lime-rich habitats, but can also occur in woodland settings.

indicate lime-rich conditions include Marsh Helleborine, *Epipactis palustris*, Variegated Horsetail, *Equisetum variegatum*, Common Marsh-bedstraw, *Galium palustre*, Devil's-bit Scabious, *Succisa pratensis*, Marsh Pennywort, *Hydrocotyle vulgaris*, Water Mint, *Mentha aquatica*, Marsh Horsetail, *Equisetum palustre*, Glaucous Sedge, *Carex flacca*, Common Fleabane, *Pulicaria dysenterica*, Grass of Parnassus, *Parnassia palustris*, Lesser Clubmoss, *Selaginella selaginoides*, Common Twayblade, *Neottia ovata*, Fragrant Orchid, *Gymnadenia conopsea*, Black Bog-rush, *Schoenus nigricans*, and Butterwort, *Pinguicula vulgaris*. Many of these species are typical of the fens and ungrazed fenny-lakeshores of the central plain. There is one orchid that is very obvious to dune slacks and appears in late spring. It

is part of the Early Marsh-orchid group, *Dactylorhiza incarnata* ssp. *coccinea*. This occurs in an unusual shade of dull crimson and there can literally be hundreds of flowering stems within a few square metres.

Indeed most of the species of dune slacks are not true halophytes despite their proximity to the sea though some species may be slightly salt-tolerant. If the sand is lime-rich, certain characteristic species will be widespread in dune slacks. Slacks may have formed where the surrounding sand is either heavily leached or derived from acid rocks, and then the vegetation will be more acid in character. These slightly poorer or less-lime rich conditions are indicated by the presence of Common Sedge, *Carex nigra*, Greater Bird's-foot Trefoil, *Lotus pedunculatus*, Silverweed,

GRASS OF PARNASSUS

Grass of Parnassus is one of the main dune-slack species that also occurs in lime-rich wetlands inland. It has a very small leaf that is easily overlooked in early summer but the simple flowering stems, each with a single blossom, appear later and are unmistakable.

Potentilla anserina, Cuckoo Flower, *Cardamine pratensis*, and Lesser Spearwort, *Ranunculus flammula*. In some areas nationally-declining species such as Adder's-tongue, *Ophioglossum vulgatum*, and Moonwort, *Botrychium lunaria*, can grow, especially where grazing is slight. In these situations the maritime (or at least the saline) influence is not apparent in the flora and the species are fairly typical of inland marshy grassland.

In ground that is more or less permanently damp, even in summer, the soil is densely compacted, held together by the roots of rushes and other sturdy species and very different from the looser, drier sandy material that can often blow away in periods of drought. In these areas, the soil is noticeably nutrient-rich and humus has usually formed. It is interesting to compare the effect that minor variations in topography can exert on the vegetation. Different species have different ranges of tolerance. Some only occur near the lowest, wettest level. Others occur right up to its highest point. However, there is usually a fairly clear line of demarcation between the lusher and usually darker green vegetation of the slack and the paler, thinner

FRAGRANT ORCHID

Fragrant Orchid grows well in dune
slacks and wet lime-rich grasslands.
The flowers are truly fragrant. It has
become very rare in recent years in
the east of Ireland and cannot now
be found in many of its old sites.

vegetation of the surrounding low dunes. However, even within the slack, minor vertical differences (as little as 10 cm) – and hence proximity to ground water – can be reflected in abrupt differences in the flora.

As the habitat matures further, various small woody species become established. The main colonists in Ireland are Creeping Willow, *Salix repens*, Grey Willow, *Salix cinerea*, and Alder, *Alnus glutinosa*. On some of the more acid dune slacks these may be joined by Eared Willow, *Salix aurita*. Creeping Willow is one of the species that can tolerate inundation by blown sand and grows up through it. In this way it contributes to the filling in of these dune slacks. However, even in these later stages of a dune slack's life there are a number of unusual species that can occur: the spectacular Yellow Bird's-nest, *Hypopitys monotropa*, grows on decaying leaf-humus and various species of Wintergreen, including Round-leaved Wintergreen, *Pyrola rotundifolia*, have been found in similar circumstances.

Where these systems have been heavily grazed and their waters used for cattle pools, dense rings of Creeping Willow are often the only obvious surviving botanical feature to indicate the former existence of dune slacks. The presence of scrub indicates that grazing levels were once low enough to allow trees to become established. These trees and creeping willow provide some protection from cattle grazing for some species and often indicate the sites of former open water. These areas sometimes provide habitat for relatively common taller, nutrient-demanding wetland species such as Great Willowherb, *Epilobium hirsutum*, Hoary Willowherb, *Epilobium parviflorum*, and Meadowsweet, *Filipendula ulmaria*.

Many dune slack systems have recently come under pressure from a variety of threats. Their major problem is the ongoing abstraction of ground water. This lowers the water table, reduces the degree and duration of flooding and increases the distance between the roots of a plant and the available water. Taller species with larger rooting

CUCKOO FLOWER

One of the first plants to flower in spring in dune slacks is Cuckoo Flower. It can grow in many different types of wetland and therefore has a much wider distribution than many of the lime-rich wetland group of plants.

systems can extend downwards to reach water, but other smaller and more delicate species cannot and, therefore, die. Water abstraction, driven by a variety of factors such as golf course irrigation, holiday homes and drinking areas for cattle, has greatly diminished the conservation value of these important areas. Sand accretion is a factor in some areas. Where there is a surplus of sand entering a dune slack system, certain low-growing species are inundated by blown sand. Some of these can grow up through the sand but the relative level of the

ground surface increases and consequently the distance from growing area to ground water increases. More recently, dune slacks and nearby sand dunes have been badly damaged by scramblers and quad-bikers.

Dune systems that have not been directly fertilised, at least in their outer areas, have maintained their botanical interest. However, open water is scarce in dune systems. Cattle pools are often excavated at the lowest points in dune slacks. Not only does this result in the further loss of water in already challenged areas, but the physical attrition caused by the cattle being concentrated in the one area, combined with their dung, has drastically altered these rare habitats. Areas of spectacular interest with many rare species have been converted and reduced to large stands of nettles and docks – species that indicate the extent to which the ground has become polluted with nutrients. Open water, where it exists into the summer, is often covered with dense algal growth. There is little in the way of lush grazing in these areas. Cattle fodder has to be supplied. Positioning cattle feeders in these areas makes a bad situation even worse.

The continued presence of surviving undamaged dune slacks goes a great way towards maintaining diversity in the landscape. They provide conditions where wetland plants can prosper in an otherwise very dry countryside, thus enhancing natural diversity. Even minor but permanent lowering of the water table gradually reduces that diversity. More major violations of these small areas can eliminate many species from considerable sections of the Irish landscape.

Shingle Shores

TEASEL

The interface zone between the top of the shingle ridge and thinly-vegetated waste or agricultural land lying just behind can provide habitat for all sorts of adventives. Teasel, though often casual in its occurrences, has proved very persistent in some sites, where it may be native.

Shingle shores develop where coarse gravel, pebbles and larger stones accumulate on relatively gently-sloping coasts. Some of these materials have been tossed about by the tides, ever higher and higher, until they are deposited far up the shore by the highest tides. Some ridges, especially on the west coast, have been deposited even further inland, cast up by high seas driven on by storm winds many years ago. Sometimes stones that are driven inland are either retained by earlier ridges or are too heavy to be dragged back into the sea by the backwash. These stony ridges are occasionally formed so far inland that they are now rarely disturbed by even the highest seas and have become colonised by typical inland vegetation.

In some places these pebble accumulations have formed ridges that run parallel to the coast. As they grow they have formed gravel barriers offshore across the mouths of low-lying land that would otherwise be flooded by the sea. The areas behind these ridges can become lagoons or salt marshes. Sand dune systems can form along their spines. Depending on the mix of sand and gravel, they can form robust features that can absorb a good deal of the sea's energy. Their pebbles can shift a little under the force of an incoming wave and, as the water is released again, the mixture is reshuffled. This force-distributing feature is often employed in coastal protection works, where caged versions of the shingle, known as gabions, are strategically positioned on eroding coastlines.

Shingle ridges are not secure places for plants. Because the pebbles and stones are so mobile there is little chance for soil to form in these areas, let alone for plants to take root and grow.

Water retention is virtually non-existent in the upper layers. The continual abrasion, rolling and washing of the stones by the sea, grinds most would-be colonisers to pieces long before they can mature. Yet somehow a number of plants live here, some of which are rarely encountered elsewhere. The dominant influences here are the mobility of the substrate, the availability of nutrients and the supply of water. The less disturbed the substrate, the more likely it is that plants will become established.

A second feature of relevance to plants on shingle shores is the size and distribution of the particles themselves. Considerable sorting by size and weight is carried out by the movements of the waves. A sheltered cove will often contain coarse sand sifted by the sea and deposited in parts of the shore where wave action is reduced. Conversely at the base of headlands, there may be large rolled stones, grinding away, partly trapped by rocky promontories. In time these stones will wear, becoming smaller and more mobile as they turn to rounded pebbles or are eventually reduced to sand that escapes, at least temporarily, from the sea, blown inland by onshore winds or washed on to the next cove. Pebbles and sand roll in at an angle to the shore, driven by the direction of the incoming waves, but roll back straight down the shore. This process goes on continually and results in the gradual movement along the coast of various mobile particles. In some areas lateral groynes have been positioned at right angles to the shore in order to reduce coastal erosion.

SHINGLE SHORELINE (ABOVE) AND ROCK SAMPHIRE (LEFT)

Few plants can survive on the lower parts of shingle ridges. Constant abrasion of stems, leaves and even seeds by the movement of wave-washed pebbles prevents any plants from becoming established. Higher up the shore there is less disturbance and species such as Rock Samphire (left) can establish a root-hold in more stable conditions.

HERB-ROBERT

Herb-Robert, typically a plant of hedgerows and associated roadside verges, can also thrive in more open conditions. Two additional subspecies are sometimes recognised – one grows well on limestone pavement and a second on coastal shingle.

At various points along a shingly shore there can be anything from coarse sand, gravels of various particle sizes to heavier pebbles and stones. Depending on the slope of the shore and the position and occurrence of obstructing features such as exposed bedrock, sea walls and promontories, these materials can occur in mixtures, or sometimes as stretches of pure coarse gravel. In some instances the shingle is augmented with broken sea-shells, which bring additional calcareous material into an area and this can influence the flora that comes to live on the shore. In places, small amounts of sandy material accumulates between the pebbles and forms continuous vertical connections between the dry upper and wetter lower layers. Particle size, therefore, becomes crucial to water supply. Capillary action can only work properly when there are sufficiently small spaces for ground water to move upwards.

The question arises as to how these plants could have become established in the first instance and then maintained themselves in such inhospitable ground. There are, in fact, a number of significant sources of nutrient input into these systems. For years coastal tillage farmers have appreciated the value of seaweed as manure, even to the point of disputing traditional rights to harvest it. Deep matted ribbons of seaweed are cast up by the waves and aligned along many of our shores, especially after high spring tides. Here they begin to decompose and gradually form a slimy nutrient-rich jelly that slips down between the pebbles. This substance then becomes mixed with sand and forms a sort of primitive soil.

There are other sources of nutrient, especially near large sea-bird colonies during the nesting season. The waste matter of sea birds (guano) finds its way back onto the shores and, in addition, the raw decomposing remains of dead birds, fish and other marine life wind up in these seaweed drift-lines and become incorporated into the layers below. Domestic sewage can also contribute to the nutrient input of these shores depending on the flow of offshore currents.

The scouring effect of the sea lower down the shore ensures that very little soil can ever form there. However, through the year, some of the higher sections of the shore are relatively untouched by the regular daily movement of the tides. These areas are usually sufficiently high up the shore to avoid all but the most drastic disturbances brought on by untypical and severe currents, waves and wind. Fast-growing plants are at an advantage here. Weather permitting, they can germinate, grow and fruit before the winter storms destroy their habitat and re-start the colonisation process. Different species have built-in strategies that allow them to cope with these circumstances.

In some instances, depending on recent storm history, some of these bands of seaweed and other matter are so dense and positioned on the shore in such a way that they dry out and form an organic crust, dry on top, wet beneath. Some fast-growing species that can cope with a very raw, partly decomposed organic-rich substrate can thrive here as they do also inland, on abandoned, decaying silage, rotting hay-stacks and even on thatched roofs as they slide into decay. The main species here is Spear-leaved Orache, *Atriplex prostrata*. Along with Annual Sea Blite, *Suadea maritima*, it can form distinct lines on the shore, above the reach of most tides, especially in late summer, long after the seaweed has disappeared. Another rarer species from the seaweed line, Babington's Orache, *Atriplex glabriuscula*, does not usually spread inland. Some shingle-shore species are also therophytes (plants that like warm, dry conditions) and it can get quite warm and humid in the

Sea Blite

Sea Blite, being an annual, and a species of sandy foreshores, can grow quickly on shingle ridges above the reach of most tides.

Sea Campion

Sea Campion has a strong rooting system that can anchor the plant firmly in the upper parts of the shingle shore close to the drift-line, where seaweeds and other plant materials decay to form a natural vegetable manure.

interstitial spaces given the combined effects of the sun on the pebbles and the heat released by decomposing vegetation.

Some longer-lived plants can be found growing in situations where their seeds clearly could not have germinated. They may have become established when the particular section of shore was sandier, or where a layer of this vegetable manure puree lay nearer the surface, giving the new roots the opportunity to grow downward and literally consolidate their position before becoming covered later by stones and pebbles. Combinations

of onshore winds and high waves coming in at unusual angles can change the distribution and character of the shore shingle overnight.

At a mid-level on the shore living conditions are not so stressful. These areas are usually characterised by the mixture of sand and pebbles and often form behind some of the lower crests or ridges of the shore. There can be several parallel ridges, representing separate storm and deposition events. These ridges can sometimes be reworked to form overlapping newer ridges following subsequent wave action from different directions.

SEA BEET

Sea Beet also thrives in and above the drift-line. Seaweed may be the main source of available nutrient in these areas, but it has a robust deep-rooting system that can get to more stable buried soil beneath the stony shingle.

A perennial species that does particularly well in these more stable areas is Sea Campion, *Silene uniflora*. It can survive inundation by coarse sand and grows up through it when necessary. It forms a dense leafy cushion and has a long root that can get down through the stones to damper ground. It produces dense masses of white flowers in early summer, looking like an overgrown alpine plant. It is often joined by another very robust perennial, Curled Dock, *Rumex crispus*. This is a widespread species throughout Ireland, but there is a well-known subspecies (ssp. *littoreus*) on shingle shores with conspicuous pale 'seeds' in place of the usual brown ones. It has an extremely sturdy root, which is normally buried in the shingle. Sometimes, after a severe battering by the sea, these roots are exposed and are left looking like a coarse, giant carrot still hanging on by the tips, even though the surrounding matrix of pebbles and gravel has been completely swept away. Another stalwart of this zone is Sea Beet, *Beta vulgaris* ssp. *maritima*. It too can tolerate a good deal of erosion of the substrate that immediately surrounds its substantial and robust rooting system.

The mid-level zone is where the most spectacular shingle shore species occur. The most colourful of these is Yellow Horned Poppy, *Glaucium flavum*. It has bright yellow flowers and huge long seed pods and hairy, almost bristly, greyish leaves. There are large colonies of this species on suitable shores all along the south and east coast and occasionally elsewhere. This species and a few others have a reputation for being somewhat fleeting in their occurrences on our shores. This may in part be due to the movements of the shingle itself along with its included seeds. Given the right combinations of circumstances

SEA SANDWORT

Sea Sandwort performs a useful function in consolidating sand and gravel in the upper parts of shingle ridges. When larger pebbles and stones are washed in, it can grow up through them. The leaves form a very distinctive cruciform pattern when viewed from above.

these seeds can be brought close to the surface to germinate. Another species that was once prominent in these areas is Henbane, *Hyoscyamus niger*. It was widely recorded around the coast in the past, and it is still established in a number of these coastal shingle areas.

One species that has not been so successful, even allowing for the lottery cycle of germination and establishment that takes place on shingle shores, is Oyster Plant, *Mertensia maritima*. Oyster Plant was first discovered in Ireland by William Sherard, thus making it one of the first Irish plants to be recorded. He found it 'On the Meuragh of Wicklow' – the gravel ridge that now carries the railway line south from Kilcoole, Newcastle and the Murrough of Wicklow Town. This shingle ridge has grown there to the sea side of the coastal marshes, which it physically protects from the sea. Oyster Plant was recorded on many shingle shores around the Irish coast in the nineteenth century. However, by the time of publication of *Cybele 2* (1898), it had become apparent that many of the colonies from the more southern parts of its range had apparently died out. The authors presciently commented that it was 'Rapidly decreasing in Ireland with many of our maritime species, perhaps through changes in the form or level of the shore-line'. It is now known mainly from shores in the north of Ireland. Another species, Ray's Knotweed, *Polygonum oxyspermum* ssp. *raii*, may have been undergoing similar losses, but it is not as conspicuous a species and its real distribution needs to be monitored carefully, as it may give insights into the different processes that are driving these changes.

YELLOW HORNED-POPPY

Yellow Horned-poppy is one of the
most spectacular shingle-ridge
species. It normally grows at the
top of the shore above the highest
tides. The numbers of maturing
plants from year to year may vary
widely. Depending on the impact
of winter storms and the
disposition of the sand and gravel
mix, seeds may be brought to
suitable germination points or not.

Another very large plant of this zone is Sea Kale, *Crambe maritima*. This has large curly cabbage-like leaves and the plants can be a metre wide and often almost as high. It has become very rare of late in Ireland. As well as being a native species it was also cultivated for food. Surviving plants from gardens were sometimes found around coastal towns where it may have reverted to its ancestral habits and habitat. Like Yellow Horned-poppy, it can appear and disappear, to reappear many years later. It is a large robust perennial, and produces large numbers of flowers, fruits and seeds, which is just as well because the attrition rate for its seeds must be extremely high.

Higher up the shore there is less movement and smaller species can do better. In these areas the more obvious sand and gravel mix is often held together on the surface by the dense fleshy stems and leaves of Sea Sandwort, *Honckenya peploides*.

SEA ROCKET

Sea Rocket is usually a plant of embryonic dunes but can also manage on shingle shores, where it usually occupies the seaweed-rich drift-line as it often does on sandy foreshores.

Individual plants can be quite large and deep-rooted but able to cope with some movement of the finer shingle. Its leaves are arranged in an amazingly regular cruciform pattern, best seen if a stem is examined head on. The flowers are a pale greenish-white and it produces large fruits in summer. It often grows with a distinctive grass more typically found on outer sand dunes. This is Sand Couch, *Elytrigia juncea*, which produces creeping stems and roots that bind the sand particles strongly together and go a long way to providing a preliminary grip for other species. Sea Rocket, *Cakile maritima*, and Sea Holly, *Eryngium maritimum*, can also do well here in sheltered pockets of consolidated sand, reinforced by buried pebbles. Another regularly-occurring species is Sea Mayweed, *Tripleurospermum maritimum*, with flowers like a giant daisy and finely-divided, strongly-smelling leaves that form a dense mound.

One of the most spectacular species from the sandy stable shingle crests is Sea Bindweed, *Calystegia soldanella*, although this is often also found in dune systems. It has small kidney-shaped leaves and huge, pink, trumpet-shaped flowers. These habitats can sometimes intergrade with those of Rock Samphire, *Crithmum maritimum*, which, like several of these plants, survives often on the crest of the gravel ridge, just out of reach of the roughest seas. However, the differences in the vegetation communities are not always clear-cut and they often overlap or grade off as the habitats themselves intermingle.

The roots of plants that can grow sufficiently far up the shore

BITTERSWEET (WOODY NIGHTSHADE)

Bittersweet grows well, often trailing across shingle on the upper sections of the shore. It frequently occurs where freshwater issues onto the lower shore, but is not visible because it is covered by deep layers of stones and pebbles.

have the benefit of sand that has accumulated beneath the more stable pebbles, but the amount of proper soil that can form in these areas is limited. All the plants that grow here have to be able to cope with high levels of salt, both in the seawater and driven in as sea spray. The longer the non salt-loving plants are inundated by saltwater, the lower their chances of survival. Many species have to be able to cope with long episodes of drought, because of the poor water-retaining characteristics of the upper pebbles, and, therefore, have to have roots that can reach the wet soil lower down.

Freshwater from rain and dew accumulates in sufficient quantity to give some of these plants a reasonable chance of survival. There are very few plants on shingle ridges that are common in salt marshes where inundation by the sea is much more frequent. Some species, especially some more typical of inland habitats, have the ability to find freshwater running off the land as hidden streams buried under the shingle. These include plants better known from other habitats, but often in slightly different genetic strains or forms. The main one is Woody Nightshade or Bittersweet, *Solanum*

COMMON CLEAVERS

Cleavers, better known as Sticky-back because of the minute prickles that cover its stems, often occurs in profusion on the upper parts of shingle ridges, where it forms dense patches between the larger stones.

dulcamara var. *marinum*, but we also have fleshy-leaved forms of Cleavers, *Galium aparine*, and Herb-Robert, *Geranium robertianum*. Woody Nightshade is a plant of riverbanks, wet ditches and emergent lakeside vegetation. On shingle shores its scrambling stems grow up through the larger stones that may not have been there to the same extent when the plant originally took root. The ability of Silverweed, *Potentilla anserina*, to produce long runners also enables it to spread from a single initial growing point, up, through and across the shingle-sand mixture, where its network of creeping, rooting stems holds the looser wind-blown sands together. The presence of hidden water may also explain the occurrence of some wetland horsetails that are sometimes encountered growing up incongruously through what looks like the remains of broken-down dry-stone walls. Horsetails are deep-rooted and long-lasting plants, often spreading by persistent clones that may have become established many years previously. A number of marshland plants can also grow here,

including Yellow Flag, *Iris pseudacorus*, on many western shores and even Greater Skull-cap, *Scutellaria galericulata*, normally a plant of stony lake-margins, on the shingle of the Copeland Islands off the Co. Down coast.

On the higher parts of shingle shores a few drought-resistant species do very well. The most colourful is probably Biting Stonecrop, *Sedum acre*, the plant so common in sand dunes and on inland walls, with its large, fleshy, succulent leaves that soak up whatever water is available when it rains. Wild Carrot, *Daucus carota*, does something similar and, in combination with a few other species, can produce a passable imitation of a midland gravel-pit flora, provided there is sufficient lime in the soil.

However, when enough soil has formed on the pebbles, another group of species mostly from thinner grassland habitats can occur. These include Autumn Hawkbit, *Scorzoneroides autumnalis*, Lesser Hawkbit, *Leontodon saxatilis*, and Thyme-leaved Sandwort, *Arenaria serpyllifolia*, in areas where proper soil has begun to form. This far up the shore the main maritime influences are very much reduced and the only coastal species that grow here are those with very broad ecological amplitudes. Some of these species are not really confined to the coast but grow there for other reasons. The large Perennial Sow-thistle, *Sonchus arvensis*, grows abundantly here and is a conspicuous feature of the shore as summer approaches. It can be a mature, tall plant with large dandelion-like flowers. It is widespread on roadsides and arable land, especially where manure and vegetable products have been dumped.

WILD CARROT

At the highest levels on the shingle ridge there is less
disturbance and a sandy soil begins to form. These areas are
shared by shingle specialists such as Sea Campion but the
presence of Wild Carrot indicates a developing soil.

TREE MALLOW

Numerous species can maintain a presence on disturbed ground on and near the coast. Some possibly native species have been brought into cultivation and subsequently escaped onto shingle ridges and resume a native lifestyle in almost 'natural' conditions.

A recent development that is affecting some of our shingle beaches is the gradual invasion by escaping garden species. Given that Biting Stonecrop can be so successful on the upper parts of shingle shores, on sand dunes and inland on buildings, far from the sea, it is not surprising that introduced succulents are now reversing the trend and gaining a toehold on dry, sunny sections of coastal shingle. The main culprit species is probably White Stonecrop, *Sedum album*, which has been observed on a number of rocky and shingle shores. Pellitory-of-the-wall, *Parietaria judaica*, a species well known to favour well-drained warm surfaces such as walls and coastal rocks, also occurs on the upper parts of shingle shores, though whether these are original natural habitats or areas to which it has spread from the built environment is not known. More challenging to explain is the occurrence of Fumitory species (*Fumaria capreolata*, *F. muralis* and others) on shingle shores. These are usually considered to be archaeophytes, but are often appear very successful on the upper, very natural parts of these shores.

Shingle shore species, communities and habitat can, therefore, be seen to relate in part to dune systems, both outer and inner, to rocky and sea-sprayed habitats and can also have a few species more or less confined to the shingle itself. They have a very distinctive physical presence and where they have formed – and the way in which they have formed – represents the outcome of many complex interactive geomorphological processes, which may be best recognised and interpreted by the use of good maps and aerial photographs. Luckily, there are many areas of shingle shore in Ireland that can be visited without permission from landowners. This greatly increases the pleasure and comfort that can be derived from these areas.

Rocky Shores

The coast of Ireland features a wide variety of rocky shores. These range from the steep wave-swept cliffs and peninsulas of the west coast to the lower and less precipitous headlands and promontories of the east. On all sides of the island the eroding sea has carved out huge exposures of bedrock. The subsequently created geomorphological features make a major contribution to the scenery and to the natural texture of the Irish environment. The cliffs of the west are so repeatedly pounded by huge ocean waves that plants rarely gain a roothold. It is usually only near the tops of these cliffs

CLIFFS

Sea cliffs in their majestic formations on the west coast are extremely challenging places for plants. Strong winds and severe poundings by the sea make living conditions impossible for most plants.

ROCK SAMPHIRE

Once it gains a roothold, Rock Samphire can cope with crashing waves, loose rocks, salt spray and other forms of environmental discomfort.

SEA-SPURREY

Sea-spurreys are prominent components of the vegetation of rocky sea cliffs. (See also right.)

that the most resilient of coastal plants can grow. On the south and east coasts conditions are less severe. Though still exposed to the waves and spray, the shore slopes less sharply to the sea, leaving an expanse of land where a very select group of plants can thrive. These, the plants of coastal rocks, live life in the spray zone.

By now, rocky coasts are one of the most undamaged habitats left in Ireland. Building opportunities are limited and cattle and even sheep are almost absent. Natural productivity is slight

here. There is very little soil and the little there is has formed in crevices between the bedrock. Soil formation is largely dependent on marine inputs in the form of decaying jetsam such as seaweeds and other organic matter cast up by the sea. This is supplemented by a constant supply of sand and pre-formed soil that trickles down from the upper sections of the shallow cliffs and then lodges in these natural cracks. Where the topography is suitable – gently sloping with plenty of niches where soil can form beyond the reach of the

SEA-SPURREY

The true spray-zone specialist is Rock Sea-spurrey, a plant with glandular hairs over most of its stems and an unwinged seed. Greater Sea-spurrey can be either hairless or have glandular hairs confined to the inflorescence and has winged seeds. Rock Spurrey usually occurs higher up the cliffs than Greater Sea-spurrey.

THRIFT

At well as inhabiting salt marshes Thrift enjoys great success in the spray zone, where it grows with various coastal lichens. Its sturdy root keeps it well anchored between the rocks.

highest waves – then rocky shore plants come into their own.

To survive here the appropriate plants must be both salt tolerant and built to withstand the impact of the strongest waves. Perennial species with deep rooting systems that can penetrate down into the crevices are at an advantage. The strongest waves may break off leaves, twigs and stems but perennial species with well-bedded roots can endure considerable punishment and put out new shoots later. Having fleshy leaves is an asset. Water stored in succulent leaves acts as a reserve and counteracts the drying effects of a salt-laden environment. At the tips of promontories, the rocks are exposed to spray coming from many directions, but in more sheltered areas it can usually come from only one direction. There are two plants here that are superbly adapted to this environment. Rock Samphire, *Crithmum maritimum*, a member of the Carrot family, is common around most of the coasts of Ireland, even growing with great success on piers and sea walls. It thins out on the colder coasts of the north of Ireland. In the past it was eaten as a vegetable. It has juicy leaves and produces heads of greenish-yellow flowers in summer and autumn. The similarly named Golden Samphire, *Inula crithmoides*, is a member of the Daisy family. It has bright yellow flowers like a ragwort and has dense, fleshy leaves. This is largely confined to the south and east coasts, extending from Kerry to Dublin. It is one of a group of southern plants that has made its way into Ireland spreading along the coast. The plants favour situations that are also bright, sunny and warm. Sea Lavender, *Limonium binervosum*, is another common species of the spray zone in the south of Ireland but rare in the north.

Another rare but conspicuous species where it occurs is Sea Wormwood, *Artemisia maritima*. There are a number of sea cliffs and exposed promontories on the east coast where it grows at the top of the spray zone and also, rarely, as a plant of upper parts of salt marshes. Threlkeld noted that 'The Country People make it into Sheaves and bring it in Carrs out of the adjacent counties of Meath and Louth to Dublin, of which our Ale-house keepers make their Purl.' Fortunately, the making of purl (an alcoholic drink made by infusing wormwood or other bitter herbs in ale or beer) fell out of favour just in time to save many colonies of this species. There are only two extant colonies of Sea Wormwood now known from Meath (Mornington) and Louth (Clogher Head), although some of the Dublin colonies have fared slightly better.

Another colourful member of this assemblage is Rock Spurrey, *Spergularia rupicola*. There are three species of Rock Spurrey around the Irish coast. This one does best in the spray zone, but the two other species can sometimes occur nearer the tide mark. Growing with Rock Spurrey in the spray zone can be found Thrift, *Armeria maritima*, which forms dense, leafy cushions. Its domed

SEA PLANTAIN

Sea Plantain can also grow some distance from the coast, growing as far from the sea as the shores of Lough Derg. It also occurs in association with unlikely congeners like Ling when growing in coastal heathland and on cliffs further inland.

growth form gives the whole plant an extra layer of protection from the waves. Its grip on land is reinforced by the extremely resilient roots that firmly anchor it in any suitable crevice.

Two common coastal Plantains also occur in this zone, Sea Plantain, *Plantago maritima*, and Buck's-horn Plantain, *Plantago coronopus*. These

SEA CAMPION

The dense flowering mats of Sea Campion have the appearance of a large smart alpine, especially when growing as tufts anchored in rock crevices on sea cliffs.

EXPOSED COASTAL HEATHLAND

ENGLISH STONECROP

Dense windswept mats of Ling are an unusual feature of rocky headlands on the west coast. Few other species can survive the hostile environment here.

English Stonecrop is well adapted to arid conditions. Where it grows on rock, its fleshy leaves soak up and retain rainwater before it disappears.

two species also have very strong rooting systems and produce dense leaf-rosettes that cling to the ground. In the severe winds on exposed coasts in the west of Ireland they can form a dense vegetation type known as Plantago-sward. Here the community includes a number of small annual species, Allseed, *Radiola linoides*, the more widespread Sea Pearlwort, *Sagina maritima*, and Sea Mouse-ear, *Cerastium diffusum*. Perennials here hunker down and make the best of things. Annuals live fast and die young.

In some places, individual rocks stand isolated from the main body of coastal bedrock, forming miniature islands, surrounded by seawater at high tide. The soils that have developed on their crests are usually very shallow and little influenced by the trickle-down soils from nearby cliffs that are usually washed away. Most of the soil that has developed on their upper parts has been formed from sea- or possibly wind-borne material. These areas are very exposed and have very few species. Deep-rooted plants have difficulty in sustaining themselves here.

The soils are so shallow that they can easily dry out in summer. Sea Mouse-ear is well geared to exploit this niche. It flowers early in spring and by early summer has died back, leaving only withered stems and viable seed in the shallow soil for the next generation. One of the many strains of Red Fescue, *Festuca rubra*, a grass widely used in the creation of lawns, is widespread throughout Ireland, both on the coast and inland. One of its many forms here has distinctly-coloured blue-green leaves. Red Fescue is often joined by another small wiry little grass, Sea Fern-grass, *Catapodium marinum*. These species occur around the upper parts of the spray zone and some can also grow on older walls near the sea. Here they find a man-made habitat that resembles in some ways their natural, more exposed home. Buck's-horn Plantain and Sea Fern-grass often grow in the more nutrient-rich areas at the base of the walls, while Sea Mouse-ear is commoner on the top.

Some of these species are not confined to salt-rich habitats. Interestingly, a few plants from this zone can occur inland. Thrift is common around the coast in a variety of saline habitats and then reappears on the tops of a number of our highest mountains in the north and west, where it looks like a very smart alpine. Similarly, Sea Plantain grows successfully in semi-natural grassland in shallow soils on lakeshores in Clare, Tipperary, Galway and Mayo.

Where the cliffs are more sheltered and shaded, another plant more usually associated with salt marshes occurs – Sea Aster, *Aster tripolium*. It is a member of the Daisy family and has flowers like a large daisy, but with the white ray-florets replaced by light blue ones. Slightly higher up the two stonecrops – English Stonecrop, *Sedum anglicum*, and Biting Stonecrop, *Sedum acre* – can handle the severe drought conditions along with a few other species that are not really spray zone species but occur here because they favour the shallow soils resting on the warm exposed bedrock.

Although these habitats are widespread all around the coast, the species composition changes from place to place. Species such as Rock Samphire and Sea Campion, *Silene uniflora*, are distributed more or less all around the coast, but others fare better in the south or north. Rock Samphire is a good example of a species that is common around the Atlantic coast of France and then in England and Wales. In contrast, some of the rocky shores in the north of Ireland have Lovage, *Ligusticum scoticum*. This is a northern species and is not known in Ireland south of Donegal, and Down, where it reputedly approaches its most southerly limit in Europe. It is joined by Rose-root, *Sedum rosea*, usually a plant of steep cliffs but which can descend almost to sea level in the north-west.

For many years spray zones were fairly secure habitats for the ecolocially-appropriate plants, safe apart from trampling by summertime visitors. However, in recent times the plant communities that grow here have come under threat from invasive garden species. The most troublesome of these is Hottentot-fig, *Carpobrotus edulis*. This was brought in by horticulturalists, but it has spread into habitats similar to those of its native home in South Africa. It is a large, heavy-leaved and very vigorously-growing species. In a few seasons it can engulf and destroy this very distinctive, colourful habitat that has formed and lasted for many years where nature intended it. The introduced species has created ecological havoc in the south of England and has already damaged the natural coastal vegetation of many areas in Dublin, especially on the Howth peninsula.

Canals

In a countryside to which access is increasingly curtailed, the canal system stands out as a remarkable feature of great interest to botanists, entomologists, ramblers and anyone who enjoys a safe quiet walk. The waters of the canals, unlike most of our rivers, are spared from large-scale sustained domestic, industrial or agricultural pollution. As a result, a number of water-loving plants can continue to live by canals long after they have been ousted from their natural areas. The network of canals was once far more extensive and many former canals have been abandoned or filled in. Those that survive perform a vital function for wildlife conservation.

CANALBANK

Slow-moving canal waters create an atmosphere of tranquillity where ramblers and naturalists can get close to nature. The banks have been colonised by tall emergent vegetation and the clear waters provide habitat for a number of true aquatic species.

YELLOW FLAG

A close relative of the garden Irises, Yellow Flag grows abundantly along the banks of canals. Its strong leaves can endure heavy grazing when it grows in damp pasture. On canal margins life is much less stressful.

The construction of the canal system altered the patterns of distribution of a large number of wetland species. Although Ireland has many lakes, there are very few in the south and south-east. Canals were built to move produce and people across Ireland at a time when the road system was poorly developed. The canals linked the flora of the lowland lakes with the river systems of the south-east, particularly the Barrow. The routes of canals such as the Grand and Royal can be envisaged as a series of separate artificial stepped channels rising gradually across the countryside. The water they contain is retained by a series of locks at each end of these steps. This water was acquired by connecting the canals into existing natural sources such as springs or small rivers. In some cases small canals (feeders) were dug to bring water from existing larger water sources.

Seeds and viable plant fragments began to spread from the central plain into the canal system lakes and the Shannon system. They were conveyed by the gradual movement of the water or dragged along to new areas by the canal boats. By 1904, the author of *Flora of the County Dublin*, Nathaniel Colgan, observed that the Royal Canal provided habitat for eight rare species (three flowering plants and five species of stonewort, which occurred nowhere else in Dublin). He was persuaded that all eight had made their way to Dublin from the Westmeath lakes or the Shannon. All have declined in recent years.

When first constructed, the sides of the canals were bare of vegetation. Over time, a number of aquatic species began to take hold on the sides of the canals as silt accumulated. At first a number of less vigorous but rapidly-colonising aquatic species became established. These were followed later by taller, more nutrient-demanding grasses, reeds and rushes. This succession resembles the manner in which smaller annual weeds on open ground are gradually ousted by larger, usually perennial species. These taller canal-side species are collectively classified as emergent vegetation, species that have their roots and lower stems in water, but whose upper stems, flowers and fruits are borne well above the water. They have similar growth characteristics but are not necessarily related. The free-floating species and those that have most of their leaves in water are considered to be true aquatics. Over time colonising vegetation threatened to impede the movement of the canal boats and was periodically cleared out. These clearings had the effect of re-stimulating the colonisation process, setting back the taller grasses but allowing the less vigorous aquatic species to flourish again. This pattern of clearing continued for many years until the canals fell into disuse. From then on, a dense floating mat of vegetation spread from the banks, sometimes extending to meet the vegetation growing from the opposite side. In this floating mat many other rare lakeside plants of the natural, floating scraw zone were able to take hold and flourish.

Drastic canal management by dragline excavators in recent years has resulted in the loss of much of this marginal habitat. However, some parts of the canal system have retained fragments of the less aggressive vegetation. There are surprise re-appearances by plants that have not been seen for many years. This sometimes happens when stretches of the canals have been temporarily dewatered when the banks are undergoing repairs. When the water is restored, some of these true aquatic species flourish, at least in the short term following disturbance. However, the heavier, more homogenous marginal vegetation gradually reasserts itself. These taller plants are not usually as affected by drastic fluctuations in water level. Being originally from reed-swamp and other lake-margin habitats, they came to the canal system with a built-in capacity to cope with the fluctuations that occur during routine canal maintenance.

On the other hand, many aquatic plants respond to changes in water level. In summertime, a number of low-growing plants of lakeshores flourish as water levels fall, especially toward the end of summer. They germinate, put on a spurt of growth and continue to flower and fruit well into the autumn on the bare exposed mud. Some seem to be stimulated into flowering by falling water levels. However, another group has the ability to grow in relatively deep water, seldom flowering and basically putting on (botanical) weight. When water levels are stabilised, the environmental stimulus that is provided by the sudden fall in water levels never happens. Needle Spike-rush, *Eleocharis acicularis*, flowers freely on lakeshores as water levels fall. In canals it remains in a vegetative state. Many other aquatic plants continue to grow vegetatively but seldom put their flowering heads up above water. They are, therefore, difficult to spot, as they often grow mixed with many other true aquatics in a kind of vegetable soup. Polarising sunglasses make it easier to see them but to examine them at close quarters it is usually necessary to haul them out, using a grab of some sort.

Once the vegetation is pulled out, it should be examined either over a plastic sheet or, better again, floated out in small quantities in a brightly-coloured plastic basin of water. There the plants can be rinsed out and allowed reassume their natural shapes, partly suspended and supported in the water. In this way a number of easily missed species may be found. This is the best way to find some of the bladderworts and the occasional water crowfoot. Fan-leaved Water-crowfoot, *Ranunculus circinatus*, for instance, occasionally flowers in canals. It is much more easily found by looking for its finely-divided leaves, which are arranged in a stiff plane. Unlike most other aquatics, whose leaves flop over when removed from the water, its leaves remain rigid. When they do flower, bladderworts are a spectacular sight. They have bright yellow flowers, borne on thin stems.

Because water movement is usually so slow, many of the plants that live in canals are more typical of lake margins than rivers. The canals usually flow through countryside that is rich in lime and can even bring lime-loving plants into areas that are otherwise acid. The vegetation of the canals to some extent resembles that of a long, narrow lowland lake. Visualise a cross-section across a canal. The emergent vegetation typically consists of a fringe of tall species such as Reed Sweet-grass, *Glyceria maxima*, Reed Canary-grass, *Phalaris arundinacea*, and Common Reed, *Phragmites australis*, nearest the bank, along with more colourful emergents such as Yellow Iris, *Iris pseudacorus*, and Meadowsweet, *Filipendula ulmaria*, Hemp-agrimony, *Eupatorium cannabinum*, Common Valerian, *Valeriana officinalis*, and Water-Plantain, *Alisma Plantago-aquatica*. Further out grow rooting plants with floating leaves, such as water lilies. In turn these are followed by rooted aquatics with leaves that remain submerged (although they may produce flowering stalks or spikes). Scattered through all this there are a few free-floating species such as duckweeds of various species (usually Common Duckweed and Ivy-leaved Duckweed). Yellow Iris is a very typical and tenacious component of the emergent fringe. Its flowers show it to be a close relative of the garden irises and it can sometimes be seen offered for sale in garden centres. It has a strong rooting system and, once established in suitable wet ground, can even withstand mowing and intensive grazing. For a species with this endurance, life on the margins of a canal offers few challenges. Another conspicuous component of the canal margins is Bulrush, *Typha latifolia*. It can invade the margins of pools and ponds and produces huge quantities of seeds that are equipped with little parachutes. The flowers are individually tiny but collectively form the large, sausage-shaped, brown structures that constitute the inflorescence. If these heads are properly dried, they are often included in flower arrangements. If they have not been properly preserved, they can go to seed, scattering thousands of seeds throughout the house.

The canals, in common with many other Irish habitats, have been invaded by exotic species. Shortly after they were first constructed, their waters were occupied by a plant that became

COMMON VALERIAN

Common Valerian has spread from wet marshy areas onto the canal margins, where it links up with many other species originally from nutrient-rich wetlands. With little in the way of grazing it can often form substantial clumps along with other emergent species such as Meadowsweet.

BULRUSH (GREAT REED-MACE)

Bulrush (sometimes called Great Reed-mace) is a tall and very successful colonist of open drains and ditches where it has spread from reed swamps and lake margins. On canal banks it can form spectacular emergent colonies, with its large, brown, sausage-like heads. In autumn these heads produce thousands of seeds. Flower arrangers often incorporate the heads into their designs. If picked at the right time and dried properly, they are an enduring feature in such arrangements. If they go to seed in the house they lose a good deal of their appeal.

known as Canadian Pondweed, *Elodea canadensis.* It is believed to have arrived sometime before 1836 and spread rapidly through the canal system. At various stages it threatened to choke the canals and had to be removed in great quantities, manually. In a short time it had spread from the Dublin canals to the Shannon system and beyond. It has now settled down and anyone unfamiliar with its history would take it to be a natural element of our Irish flora. A more recent invader, Water Fern, *Azolla filiculoides*, has been spreading lately. This is a native of tropical America and may have been brought into the country by aquarists. Its fronds often grow in large, reddish masses, covering the surfaces of canals, ponds and drains. Both these species can easily propagate from small broken-off fragments, a feature shared by many of our native aquatics. Some species that do not flower freely have another means of surviving or perennating. In autumn they produce vegetative structures known as turions. These look like dense, leafy buds, which fall to the bottom of the canal in winter as the parent plant disintegrates. In spring they resume growth.

Yellow water-lily, *Nuphar lutea*, must have claims to being the standard true aquatic canal plant. It has an unmistakable big yellow flower and large (30 cm) thick floating leaves, with a deep basal division. It also produces large, softer, submerged leaves with wavy margins. Sometimes these can be spotted in deeper waters in the absence of any flowers or floating leaves, as after the floating vegetation has been cut by the 'weed boats'. In late summer large fruits are produced, about the size of a small lemon, borne above the water initially but sinking later. A number of other species with a good proportion of their biomass invested in underwater leaves are similarly able to survive canal weed-control measures.

Botanists searching the canals should examine drains that sometimes run parallel to the canal. These are often rich in smaller emergent species and are sometimes cleaned out, allowing less vigorous plants of open water to succeed in the short term until the heavier emergent vegetation closes in again. In some areas these drains run through lime-rich marshland and have many interesting plants that are otherwise very rare in a locality.

Where canals were connected to the river systems, a degree of colonisation and recolonisation ensued between river and canal. Arrowhead, *Sagittaria sagittifolia*, is a typical canal plant in the east of Ireland and is also common in rivers linked to canals. It has a very distinctive above-water leaf, shaped like the blade of an arrow, and the flowering stems produce 3-petalled flowers, white with dark violet centres. It also produces long, narrow, submerged leaves completely different from the aerial ones. An even more attractive species is Flowering Rush, *Butomus umbellatus*. This is not a true rush and has a bright pink flowering head. The natural habitat of both species seems to be rivers and lakes and both are much commoner than is often realised. Like its close relative Arrowhead, Flowering Rush produces long narrow submerged leaves (in this case spirally-twisted), many of which fail to flower. When in blossom, it is unmistakable.

Horsetails are widespread along the canal system, especially in the fringe of marginal vegetation. These are not flowering plants but are related to the ferns, and reproduce not by seed but by spores. Water Horsetail, *Equisetum fluviatile*, which can get up to 80 cm tall, has an astonishingly hollow stem, almost like a drinking straw, and sometimes has rings (whorls) of branches arranged along it. It produces large blunt-topped cones about 15 mm long that produce the spores. A much more ecologically-interesting species is Variegated Horsetail, *Equisetum variegatum*. This is much rarer, usually encountered in fens and lime-rich marshes but has spread along the canal system from its original habitats. It also produces cones, but these are surmounted by a point, giving them the appearance of a tiny minaret. This species grows along the canals, usually higher up on the sloping bank, with its roots reaching down into wetter soil. The form that grows in the canals is consistently larger than the marsh form and is sometimes referred to as *Equisetum variegatum* var. *majus*. Other horsetails to keep watch for are Marsh Horsetail, *Equisetum palustre*, and Great Horsetail, *Equisetum telmateia*. Great Horsetail can be a metre or more high and has startlingly white stems. It is often found associated with natural mineral springs, often with other interesting wetland flora. Early in the year it produces massive cones almost 6 cm long on short pale stalks, which appear, produce spores and decay just as the non-fertile stems begin to appear above ground.

In this fringe of vegetation a plant that resembles a giant buttercup can sometimes be found. This is Greater Spearwort, *Ranunculus lingua*. It can be a metre tall and has flowers that are nearly 2 cm across. This, by now, is quite a rare species in Ireland but where allowed to grow properly is easily spotted.

Free-floating aquatics are easy to spot. The commonest species are Common Duckweed, *Lemna minor*, and Ivy-leaved Duckweed, *Lemna trisulca*. Common Duckweed produces thousands of tiny floating almost circular 'leaves' or fronds, each shaped like a miniature lily-pad. Ivy-leaved Duckweed is usually slightly submerged. It has more pointed slightly translucent leaves, which are

Duckweed

Various species of duckweed can completely cover the water surface of slower-moving stretches of canals and drains. Common Duckweed and Ivy-leaved Duckweed are the main canal species but other rarer ones occasionally occur. They are virtually free-floating aquatics and as such are liable to be washed away in faster-moving water.

splayed out with a main one joined on opposite sides of its base by two minor ones. There are two other duckweeds to look out for. One, Fat Duckweed, *Lemna gibba*, has greyish-green leaves that are swollen on the underside to the extent that the green parts are often tilted out of the water. The other, Greater Duckweed, *Spirodela polyrhiza*, turns up occasionally in abundance and can then virtually disappear from an area for some years. It has much larger leaves than the Common Duckweed, and has many roots descending from the leaves. In recent years another species, Least Duckweed, *Lemna minuta*, has begun to appear and seems to be increasing.

There is one other important true aquatic in the canals, Opposite-leaved Pondweed, *Groenlandia densa*. This has spread right into the centre of Dublin along the Grand Canal system and has also been found in the Royal Canal. It is not a particularly obvious plant, but is of interest as being one of a very small number of legally-protected species that live in or near the capital. Many of the better stretches of the canals are now much tidier than they were 40 years ago. However, there are still stretches that have managed to retain some of their more interesting flora. The continued survival of Opposite-leaved Pondweed in the waters of the Grand Canal indicates their enduring value as refugia for rare native species as well as commoner ones. Colgan commented in his *Flora of the County Dublin* that 'This species varies greatly in abundance according to the length of time the canal has been left undisturbed by cleansing or dredging. In some reaches of the canal near the city its dense masses almost monopolised the waterway in 1903, crowding out even the aggressive Canadian Water-weed (Elodea).' This seems about fair.

Hedgerows

The Hedged Landscape

Most of lowland farmed Ireland consists of tillage and pastureland enclosed by a network of hedges, which perform many functions. Hedges are clearly intended to separate cattle and other livestock from crops, but also to stop them from straying onto neighbouring property and roadsides. Enclosure makes a good deal of sense – cattle can be moved from one area of a farm to another when grass has been grazed down, when certain areas have become too wet or when the sward is beginning to cut up ('poaching'). In larger fields, grazing is nowadays often regulated by the use of electric fencing. Cattle are

HEDGEROWS

The varied character of Irish hedgerows is due in part to their past and present management history. Some of the oldest may have survived on ancient townland boundaries. Others were planted and let grow relatively freely. Some of the more modern heavily-trimmed creations would look more at home on a racecourse.

restricted to one section of a larger field, then moved on when they have eaten down the grass, giving the first strip a chance to put on new growth.

Episodes of woodland clearance of varying intensity have taken place since man began to farm the land in Ireland. However, major alterations in farming practice began, especially with the arrival of the Anglo-Normans. Large open fields were created and tillage increased.

Various attempts to enclose the land have taken place through the centuries. These efforts were usually linked to schemes to increase agricultural productivity and wealth. Bodies such as the (then) Dublin Society got behind these schemes and proposed lists of suitable species for planting. Some of the huge open fields of an earlier era were enclosed and hedged in the early nineteenth century. Indeed the encouragement of enclosure continued into the twentieth century.

The increase in agricultural productivity has greatly altered the character of the wild landscape. In many areas, species-rich grasslands have been transformed into species-poor green deserts of Rye grass and White Clover. As a result, hedgerows are now often the only areas where wildlife has any realistic prospect of survival. Today, there are thousands of kilometres of hedgerow throughout Ireland of varying value to wildlife, depending on the soils, terrain, agriculture and landscape history.

WHITE CLOVER

Increased agricultural productivity has entailed the conversion of species-rich semi-natural grassland to a very species-poor but nutritious sward. White Clover and various grasses have been widely sown. On good farmland the adjoining hedgerow bank is often the only area remaining where the local grassland species can survive.

HAWTHORN

The Hawthorn was widely adopted as a suitable species for hedging. It grows rapidly and produces many small sharp thorns, thus making an excellent stock-proof living fence. Also known as Maybush, its flowers appear after the leaves open and are a dominant colour feature, especially of more recently-planted hedges. See also overpage.

HAWTHORN

When growing alone Hawthorn assumes its true stature, that of a small tree with a distinct trunk. In the past, many isolated trees were said to be endowed with mystical properties.

watercourses or even streams. The presence of water enables a number of wetland species to spread and persist in otherwise dry areas. Fortunately, there are many other hedges with far more structural diversity and, therefore, a greater range of species. Some of these hedgerows retain elements of a woodland flora and may be survivors abstracted from the scrub woodland of earlier times.

The hedgerow, in its simplest form, consists of a simple row of a single planted species, usually Hawthorn, *Crataegus monogyna*. Hawthorn was chosen because it was quick growing and produced lots of robust prickly branches to form a usually impenetrable barrier that discouraged cattle from straying. Where these hedges have

The hedgerow is usually composed of two main elements – the hedge proper and the adjoining herbaceous strip. The hedge part is formed from trees, shrubs and woody climbers. It may be planted directly on the flat or more usually is set into the side of an earthen bank. This feature can often be seen when a hedge is set on a slope and a bank is cut, like a step, following the contour lines. Beneath this shrubby line grows a layer of non-woody herbaceous species. Planned hedgerows will often be arranged in straight lines, which sometimes relate to drains, modified

IVY BERRIES

The berries of Ivy provide an important source of food for birds in winter. The flowers from which they develop are less conspicuous greenish structures.

HAIRY BINDWEED

Many hedgerows have been invaded by various species of bindweed. The native species is Hedge Bindweed, *Calystegia sepium*, not because of its colour but because of its association with hedges (*sepium* = of hedges). The invaders have much bigger flowers. Large Bindweed, which usually has white flowers, is still spreading rapidly. Hairy Bindweed has pink flowers with white stripes and inflated bracts and is also spreading.

Blackthorn, which puts out its flowers before the leaves, was also widely used as a formidable hedgerow plant. These flowers will later produce sloe-berries. It can send suckers out into neglected pasture and may be enjoying something of a resurgence in some parts of the country.

been planted, they have, over a couple of centuries, acquired a few additional species such as Dog-rose, *Rosa canina* agg., various Brambles, *Rubus fruticosus* agg., Ivy, *Hedera helix*, and one of two other common species through natural colonisation from nearby sources. If cattle or sheep have access to the base of hedges of this type, then most herbaceous species have little prospect of

becoming established, let alone flowering and setting seed. Many of Ireland's hedges conform to this basic type.

Over 60 different species of tree, shrub and woody climber have been found growing in Irish hedgerows. Some of these are native species, others have been planted. Sometimes native species have been planted into hedges along with the foreign exotics. Some of these species have been around for so long that people presume them to be native. Beech, Sycamore, Horse Chestnut, many Elms and most conifers are all introduced. Some natives have subsequently seeded or otherwise spread into areas where they did not grow naturally. Sometimes trees or other species were planted for aesthetic or practical purposes. Domesticated apple trees were often grown and provided a useful supplement to the densely-cropping but usually much rarer native Crab Apple, *Malus sylvestris*. So-called 'Wild' Plums and Damsons were similarly useful. The fruits of species such as Bramble or Blackberry, Raspberry, *Rubus idaeus*, Blackthorn (Sloes), *Prunus spinosa*, and Elder, *Sambucus nigra*, also provided fruit that could be preserved as jams or drinks. In times of necessity or as opportunity dictated, fallen trees could be used for firewood.

Most of the original plantings derived from species that were locally available. The era of great landscaping brought in many ornamental tree species. More recently, other species have been brought into the country and some have become all too successful. One of the most conspicuous invasive hedge-forming species is a bushy shrub called Snowberry, *Symphoricarpos albus*. It spreads mainly by suckering shoots despite its very obvious white berries, and forms dense thickets where little else can grow. It is a native on the western side of North America. This is mainly a species of the roadside, where cattle cannot get at it. Many other species were also planted in recent times. There was a scheme to encourage roadside trees in Ireland in the 1950s and many roadside hedges have the benefit of attractive trees still growing in ecologically unusual situations. Bird Cherry, *Prunus avium*, with its large colourful pink flowers, may be one of these species. It is a true rare native species in some areas but can be found now growing often in otherwise undistinguished hedgerows. This is in essence the difference between the natural and the contrived. The natural patterns of species distribution, in hedges and elsewhere, have evolved over many years, and become the expression of how nature intends things to be. The alternative is called gardening.

SNOWBERRY

Snowberry has small pinkish flowers but produces huge showy fruits in autumn. In common with many garden plants it has spread well beyond its intended area by vigorous sucker growth. It came originally from North America.

The Hedge-forming Species

The present-day species composition of many hedges reflects many processes – ecological, historical and cultural. Despite this, the true natural patterns of occurrence of individual species can be detected. Once the local native species are identified, it is possible to work out why some species grow in particular habitats and why certain combinations of species occur in some areas but not in others.

Some areas are quite rich in species and this local richness is reflected in the diversity of the hedge-forming species available in the hinterland. To understand the reasons for some of this variation it may be useful to envisage two important ecological contrasts. The first, from base-rich to base-poor, will be familiar to most gardeners in relation to lime-loving and lime-hating species. The second is from wet to dry. Areas with lots of lime-rich and lime-poor soils and mixtures of wet and dry ground will have more species because of greater habitat diversity. The most species-rich hedges occur on the lime-rich soils of the Midlands. These have their own characteristic species, many of which rarely, if ever, make it into higher ground.

EUROPEAN GORSE

Known as Furze in the south, Whins in the
north and Gorse in the books, *Ulex europaeus*
is very important in hedge formation. In the
uplands it is often the main stock-proofing
shrub. With its dense and strong prickles it is
able to withstand wind as well as browsing by
livestock. On lower ground it is often used to
reinforce existing hedges, where it is planted
in a supplementary line close to the taller
hedge.

On higher ground where the soil is thinner, poorer and more acid, hedges do not grow as well as they do in the lowlands. Few hedge species can cope successfully in the cold wind. The shallow soils formed over bedrock are not deep enough to root in. However, in these areas, Gorse or Furze, *Ulex europaeus*, comes to the rescue. It has the capacity to grow on very poor shallow soils and because of its dense, prickly leaves it can function extremely well as a stock-proof barrier, especially in upland sheep country. In the past it had many other agricultural uses. Even in lowland areas, it was often planted in order to reinforce an existing hedge. The term 'Gorse' is not widely used in Ireland, being largely a book or urban name. In most of the south of Ireland, it is Furze and in the north, Whins. A related upland hedge-former is Broom, *Cytisus scoparius*. This species can often overtop lower-growing thinner hedges. Its individual flowers are similar to those of Furze, but it has no prickles, instead producing tall greenish twiggy shoots and masses of bright yellow flowers. In these areas it is joined by Rowan or Mountain Ash, *Sorbus aucuparia*, an acid-lover also able to tolerate a high degree of exposure. It is especially obvious in autumn when it produces great trusses of bright red berries. It has nothing to do with the Ash family, but is so-called because its leaves are like those of the familiar Ash, *Fraxinus excelsior*. It belongs to the Whitebeam family, many of which are planted in gardens and often included in suburban planting schemes. Another species that is well able to endure upland conditions is Eared Willow, *Salix aurita*. This is much lower-growing than most of the Irish willows and can often cope with poorer, wetter ground where most other species cannot manage. It is unmistakably a willow, but has distinctive ashy-grey much wrinkled leaves and small but prominent extra ear-shaped leaves (stipules) at the base of the ordinary ones.

MOUNTAIN ASH (ROWAN)

The bright red berries of Mountain Ash indicate that natural woodland species can still thrive, even in open conditions. Usually a plant of more acid upland conditions, it can also occur on roadside hedges where they adjoin boggy ground in the lowlands.

HAZEL (ABOVE AND BELOW)

The male catkins of Hazel produce clouds of pollen in spring. They appear long before the leaves. The female flowers are tiny structures, which will produce the large familiar nut in autumn. Hedges with Hazel often have many other native shrub species. See also p. 9.

Upland hedges also have isolated Holly bushes. It is often a woodland species but in Ireland can grow very successfully in hedgerows on lower ground. When it occurs on acid ground it can thrive in many different types of hedgerow. On lime-rich soils it is far less frequent and often only occurs in exceptionally species-rich hedges.

The midland hedges have many other attractive species. Some of the upland species can also grow in the lowlands, where they thrive on low-lying acid soils and peats. However, many lowland species cannot make it into the uplands.

One species that can grow in sheltered upland areas, but usually as a component in wooded ground, is Hazel, *Corylus avellana*. In the Midlands it comes into its own and can often be the main or dominant species in a hedgerow. In these situations, where the traditional planted species such as Hawthorn, *Crataegus monogyna*, are either missing or only present in small numbers, other species can be found. This may be because some of the hedges are actually survivors from an era before the clearings and major commercial plantings. In some instances it is possible to see the botanical similarities between present-day hedges and nearby woodland fragments. This is most obvious on some of the esker woodlands, where hazel woods seem to run on out into the hedges. Hazel-dominated hedges nearly always have other interesting species growing in and under them, and may be scrub relics. Hazel is notable in many ways. Its value as a coppice tree was appreciated by woodsmen for many years and when cut appropriately it can produce many stout pole-like stems from one stock. The flowers are unusual. It produces long dangling catkins in early spring, which makes it one of the first plants to flower in the year. The catkins are the male parts. Tap the stems and small clouds of pollen will puff out. The female flowers are small

GUELDER-ROSE (ABOVE) AND SPINDLE (ABOVE RIGHT)

On lime-rich soils, especially in the Midlands, a number of native tree and shrub species become more evident. Guelder-rose has large heads of showy white flowers from late spring onwards, which later produce large clusters of bright red berries. It is commoner on wetter ground. Spindle has far less conspicuous flowers but its bright pink fruits are unmistakable in autumn. It favours drier lime-rich soils.

structures, tucked away on the branches, concealed between reddish scales with the stigmas protruding to receive the wind-blown pollen (see p. 9). These tiny structures, if fertilised, will mature to produce the familiar hazel-nuts in autumn.

One of the most obvious flowering species is probably Guelder-rose, *Viburnum opulus*, which has large heads of white flowers. The outer larger ones are sterile. The smaller, fertile inner flowers produce lots of red fruits in autumn. Guelder-rose usually prefers slightly wetter ground. However, nearby it is often possible to find Spindle tree, *Euonymus europaeus*, on slightly drier ground. Spindle, in spring and early summer, is a very inconspicuous shrub or small tree. It has greenish stems and pale green petals. With the approach of autumn, the leaves turn reddish long before they fall and these flowers produce spectacular deep pink fruits that open to reveal a bright orange central structure. Both these species are commonest on lime-rich soils. In species-rich hedges they are sometimes joined by an unusual

ROSES

Various species of wild rose have come to live in hedges. Most favour lime-rich soils and a number of rare species have been found in Irish hedges. They are originally species of scrub and woodland-margins and therefore find the well-lit hedge a highly-suitable habitat. Their leaves and fruits in autumn are very distinctive, some being equipped with various glands that release smells of resin, turpentine or apples. The commonest species, Dog Rose, has no such interesting attributes.

whitebeam, with undivided leaves, usually very white on the underside. In Ireland we have a special one, Irish Whitebeam, *Sorbus hibernica*, which occurs wild nowhere else in the world. Rather like a number of its hedgerow associates, it is originally a woodland or scrub-woodland species, but appears occasionally but conspicuously on roadside hedges, especially in the central plain.

These lime-rich soils alternate with areas that are either waterlogged or adjoin drains running off raised bogs. In these places a number of native willows can be found, including Grey Willow, *Salix cinerea*, Eared Willow and Goat Willow, *Salix caprea*. It is possible to recognise these areas while travelling along a countryside road, by watching for where Spindle and Hazel give way through a transition zone of Guelder-rose and Grey Willow to acid-ground species such as Eared Willow and Birch, *Betula pubescens*. This can be very useful when searching for small and inconspicuous adjoining areas of present or former wetland such as fens, marshes and fragments of raised bog. These admixtures of different habitat types are the main reason why so many different species can be found close together in midland hedges.

The roses of hedges are not an easy group to deal with, because at first glance many appear very similar. This is a pity because there are many interesting species present in hedges, woodland margins and in adjoining scrub land. There are four main groupings of roses, all of which do very well in hedges. Most of the roses normally encountered belong to the so-called Dog-rose or *Rosa canina* group. In their simplest form, they have pink or white flowers, smooth fruits and leaves without hairs or bristles. This group is distributed throughout the island, but it is actually a hold-all category with a number of closely-related northern and southern species that have hybridised

extensively over the years. A more straightforward rose to recognise is Field-rose, *Rosa arvensis*. This is very common on roadsides, especially in the south and east but thins out rapidly as you go north. It clearly likes its sunshine and becomes increasingly confined to sheltered areas such as woodland margins in the north-west. It is usually the first rose to bloom in early summer and produces great sprays of cream-coloured flowers with noticeable yellow centres, and a distinct unified style. In autumn the fruits, which are more round than pear-shaped, have a distinct flat top and the fused style is more obvious.

The two remaining groups include species that are usually much rarer. The Downy roses have leaves that are generally covered with hairs and short glands. These glands extend onto the stalks of the fruits, the sepals and the fruits themselves and smell of resin. There are three species, Sherard's Downy-rose, *Rosa sherardii*, Soft Downy-rose, *Rosa mollis*, and Harsh Downy-rose, *Rosa tomentosa*. The most widespread species, *Rosa sherardii*, usually has large pear-shaped fruits that become very soft in autumn. The sepals are persistent and if you tug them off the top of the fruit will also detach. This species grows throughout Ireland, usually on slightly higher ground. A more spectacular species is *Rosa mollis*. This is mainly a northern species, with large round fruits and sepals that stand up straight on top of the fruits. It flowers and fruits earlier than the other species and can also grow well away from hedges on sand dunes and coastal heathland. *Rosa tomentosa* has shorter fruits on relatively longer stalks and grows mainly in the south.

The fourth group, the Sweetbriars, is very interesting. One of the wild species, Sweet-briar, *Rosa rubiginosa*, occurs naturally in limestone scrub country. It has sepals that stay erect on the fruits, and its leaves release a scent of apples, which

TRAVELLER'S JOY

Traveller's Joy is a close relative of the garden Clematis, though its flowers are not as showy as most. It is believed to be a native in the south of England but not so here. In recent years it seems to be getting commoner and is spreading to new ground by means of its feathered fruits, which become airborne towards the end of summer.

is produced from glands, tiny bumps, on the underside of the leaves, sepals and fruit stalks. Small-leaved Sweet-briar, *Rosa agrestis*, occurs in limestone scrub especially beside the large central plain lakes as at Lough Derg and Lough Ree, but is scattered around the Midlands. A third species, Small-flowered Sweet-briar, *Rosa micrantha*, is fairly common from Waterford to Kerry in sheltered ground, especially in Cork, and has recently been discovered in a few species-rich hedges elsewhere.

Plants that can climb up through the shrubs are at a great advantage in hedges. The two main climbers are Ivy, *Hedera helix*, and Honeysuckle or Woodbine, *Lonicera periclymenum*. They both produce large heads of flowers and later fruits. Ivy is unusual in that it flowers in autumn and even winter and its flowers are visited by wasps and winter-active flies. The flowers are not much to look at, consisting of five yellowish-green petals, 3–4 mm in length. Mature plants can climb 10 m or more on suitable trees. The fruits are blackish and globose and are an important food source for birds in winter. Ivy can grow in a wide variety of soils and is very tolerant of shade. This is usually not a problem in a hedge as it can always climb up into the light. Honeysuckle can be detected at a distance by the scent of its large fragrant flowers. The creamy petals turn a reddish-pink as they mature and are formed into a long tube about 5 cm in length, which spreads slightly open at the mouth. The flowers are visited by bumblebees and hawk-moths, whose long tongues enable them to reach down to the nectar at the base of the tube. It is also a species of sea cliffs and rocky places but the woodland-margin habitat provided by hedgerows is ideal for this species. Even when hedges are trimmed, it can grow back quickly. It occurs on a wide variety of soils. A number of garden honeysuckles occasionally spread into hedges and there is one interesting and long-established escape, especially in the north Midlands. This is Fly Honeysuckle, *Lonicera xylosteum*, which grows more as a free-standing shrub. The flowers are arranged in pairs and are about 1 cm long. Another climber that is becoming much commoner in Ireland in recent years is Traveller's Joy, *Clematis vitalba*. It is native in the south of England and known there as Old

Man's Beard. It is closely related to the Buttercups and true Anemones and of course to the garden species of Clematis, though they usually have much flashier flowers. When it gets established, especially on sunny, south-facing lime-rich slopes, it can take over great sections of landscape. It has become particularly common on exposures of glacial drift where these have been revealed by downwardly-cutting rivers.

There are a couple of low-growing woody species that are widespread throughout lowland Ireland in hedges. Tutsan, *Hypericum androsaemum*, belongs to the St John's-wort family. It has large yellow flowers and broad leaves and produces bright red berries in autumn. Despite its widespread distribution, there are usually only a few individual plants in any given area. However, it tends to be well recorded

TUTSAN

Tutsan is one of a group of small woody plants, barely qualifying as shrubs. It occurs in damp woodlands but has made the transition to shaded hedgebanks. Here it grows usually in small quantity but often in good company with other less common hedge-forming species.

because it can be easily spotted towards the end of the flowering season due to its colourful fruits. Although it is native, it can also be planted. It is also a woodland species and often occurs in slightly damp areas. Another species of wet swampy woodland margins is Woody Nightshade, *Solanum dulcamara*. This species belongs to the potato family and its flowers are shaped just like both potato and tomato flowers. The bright yellow anthers are pushed out to the front of the flower in the form of a cone and contrast vividly with the violet-purple petals. Woody Nightshade occurs naturally in the tall emergent vegetation of nutrient-rich lakeshore and riverside vegetation and on the upper parts of shingle shores. It can find an acceptable substitute habitat deep in hedgerows that have accompanying drains. In the south and

east of Ireland it is a fairly regular component of hedgerow vegetation. However, in the north and west it is often associated with old habitation and may in some areas have been introduced either as a medicinal plant or as an ornamental shrub. Threlkeld listed its many curative properties and gave four Gaelic names for it, including Slat Gorm, Dréimire Gorm, Mig buih and Mihagh Uisge, which testify to the colour of its flowers (*gorm* = blue, *buí* = yellow), the ascending habit (*dréimire* = a ladder) and the wetness of its habitat (*uisge* = *uisce* = water).

Where the ground is consistently water-logged farmers realised that conventional hedge-forming species could not grow and adopted a number of other wetland species instead. All that can be seen in some low-lying ground adjoining open drains are rows of planted non-native willows, such as White Willow, *Salix alba*, or the native Alder, *Alnus glutinosa*. Some of these grow to be fairly substantial trees and are often incorporated into hedges in slightly wetter areas also. However, it is these gappy and rudimentary drain-side lines of woody vegetation that stretch the definition of a hedge to the limit.

It is interesting to note that in Ireland there is little truth in the idea that the age of a hedge can be estimated simply by reference to the number of species it contains. The convenient equation developed in Britain of one species for every century of a hedge's existence does not hold up for Ireland. We do not have as many hedge-forming species and the number of species even within a county varies greatly with soil type and terrain. Areas with a mixture of base-rich and base-poor soils in sheltered lowland landscapes will have far more species present than in windswept mountainside areas with poor soils. At a local level, it is often possible to demonstrate that the hedges of townland boundaries, especially those on roadsides, have more and different species than the adjoining planted hedges. In general the boundary hedges have all the species of the nearby 'infill' hedges but also have many additional species not present in the newer hedges. There are abundant opportunities to test this in different parts of Ireland. However, in many areas the differences are not so obvious. This may be in part due to the fact that many of the more open parts of the countryside were maintained as open sheepwalk (unwooded parts of the countryside grazed by sheep) and where hedges occur, most are relatively recent in origin. In other areas, when hedges were being formed, locally-available species were employed rather than commercial stock from nurseries. The simplest way to test this idea is to compare hedges that adjoin each other at right angles, when one is a known townland boundary hedge and the other is not. Allowance should to be made for other ecological factors, such as the presence of a drain. This is always likely to bring in an extra woody species or two.

WILLOWS

Willows are often used to define property boundaries in areas too wet for conventional hedge species. In many instances they were deliberately pollarded to encourage denser growth. Many willows are pollarded incidentally while their hedges are being trimmed by mechanical cutters mounted on tractors. Their young new branches often sprout well in advance of the recovery of their neighbouring species.

BITTERSWEET (WOODY NIGHTSHADE)

Bittersweet had a number of native Gaelic names that reflected the colours of its flowers, its climbing habit and its association with water. It is usually found as a plant emerging from drains adjoining hedges, where its blue flowers with yellow centres are very obvious in summer.

LORDS-AND-LADIES

Lords-and-Ladies, or Cuckoo Pint, has a wealth of other vernacular names. It is a woodland plant that has spread successfully into hedgerows, especially those on lime-rich soils. The scientific name *Arum maculatum* indicates that the leaves should be spotted but most of the Irish plants are not marked.

Herbaceous Hedgerow Plants

Most of the herbaceous or non-woody species that grow in hedgerows are, like their woody counterparts, plants of the woodland margins. Many of these species require a certain amount of light and enjoy some protection from grazing from the twigs and thorns of the woody species that form the hedge. However, some of the woodland-margin species seem to do better in hedges, especially on lime-rich soils. Most hedgerows are best examined from the roadside but it is safer to view them in cul-de-sacs or in larger estates that have been converted to hotels or parklands. In these situations, particularly when grazing has been reduced, the herbaceous flora grows more luxuriantly and many of the plants achieve their true stature. It also becomes possible to get a clearer idea as to which species are more closely confined to the hedge since roadside verges, a little away from the line of the hedge, have their own rather different flora. In theoretically ungrazed situations the hedge proper is flanked by successive strips of low and lower shrubs, which in turn give way to robust herbaceous species and scramblers. In most instances this progression is severely interrupted either by grazing, tillage or by the roadside itself.

One of the most iconic species of the herb layer in a hedgerow is Lords-and-Ladies, Cuckoo-pint or Wild Arum, *Arum maculatum*. This plant has many different vernacular names in Britain, but not so here. It is common throughout Ireland, especially in hedges on lime-rich soils. However, its distribution at local level can be very patchy. This may to some degree be due to historical factors such as the presence of former woodland. Many

hedgerow species are natural inhabitants of woodland margins. They do not grow in deep shade, doing better nearer the dappled sunlight of the edges. The arrow-shaped leaves appear in spring and are shortly followed by a most unusual flowering structure, which resembles a small Altar-lily, better known in Ireland as Easter Lily, *Zantedeschia aethiopica*. The structure of the

GARLIC MUSTARD

In spring many hedgerows are fringed by the flowering stems of Garlic Mustard, whose leaves actually have a slight garlicky smell although it belongs to a completely different plant family.

inflorescence is very untypical of Irish species. From a distance a large (up to 25 cm) pale green sheathing structure known as a spathe arises. Protruding out of the centre of this is a dull purple structure known as a spadix. All the real flowers are concealed down within the spathe at the base of the spadix, very simple male flowers above and female flowers below. By early summer the spathe begins to wither away and the female flowers, by now fertilised, form distinctive clusters of poisonous scarlet fleshy berries. The plant is pollinated by small midges. Despite its specific name *maculatum* (spotted), most of the Irish plants are immaculate.

Another closely-related species with very distinctive white-veined leaves crops up occasionally. This is the Italian Lords-and-Ladies, *Arum italicum*, which is frequently cultivated in gardens and is often thrown out with garden waste. It can persist long after the associated horticultural rejectementa has decomposed.

Goose-grass, Cleavers and Sticky-back are all names applied to *Galium aparine*. This is a very well-known member of the many species that manage to more than hold their own in hedgerows. It is a scrambling plant and its leaves, stems and fruits are armed with little hooks that enable it to climb over other plants into the light. It is one of the first species to germinate in spring. The little globular fruits often get stuck in the fur of dogs. It has small creamy-white flowers and clusters of its leaves are arranged in a ring around the stem in groups of four. Growing in the same area is Ground-ivy, *Glechoma hederacea*, a fairly typical member of the Dead-nettle family. It has the square stem of so many members of this family and a characteristically-shared lower lip. In late spring it has little blue flowers and the leaves produce a scent that some people do not find pleasant.

Herb-Robert, *Geranium robertianum*, is remarkably successful in hedges. It is a true *Geranium*, as distinct from the indoor pot plants of that name that belong to the genus *Pelargonium*. Herb-Robert begins to flower at the end of April and can produce hundreds of separate reddish-pink blossoms through a flowering season that can go on to the end of September. There are various other species of *Geranium* in Ireland but this is by far the commonest, as it can also grow on roadsides, tumble-down walls and even on shingle-shores. The genus is collectively referred to as Crane's-bills because the pointed fruits with a swelling near the base containing the seeds are thought to look like the head and beak of a heron or crane.

Primrose, *Primula vulgaris*, is another species that does well in hedges, especially on the earthen bank within. Like Common Dog violet, *Viola riviniana*, it grows in clearings in woodlands and also on grassy slopes near the sea, often under Bracken. In some areas wild primroses have been fertilised by pollen brought from closely-related fertile garden hybrids, but it often hybridises with Cowslip, *Primula varies*. Dog Violet is the main species of hedge in Ireland. Confusingly, a much rarer species, *Viola canina*, is known as the Heath Violet. Dog Violet has big bright blue flowers. These are joined into a backwardly-projecting structure termed a spur. In this species the spur is white or pale blue and certainly much paler than the petals. These characteristics help to distinguish it from Wood Violet, *Viola reichenbachiana*, which is usually found in deciduous woodlands. Wood Violet has a much darker spur, the petals do not overlap and it is generally smaller-flowered.

Lesser Celandine, *Ficaria verna*, does very well in springtime in hedges. It is a member of the buttercup family but has far more petals than the other species. The flowers can form spectacular

PRIMROSE

Although typically a deciduous woodland plant,
Primrose is far commoner on hedged roadside banks.
Its attractiveness has resulted in many colonies being
almost exterminated by gardeners.

BUSH VETCH

In common with other vetch species, Bush Vetch has leaves equipped with tendrils that enable it to scramble up over other plants. It is remarkably successful in Irish hedges and on their associated roadside verges.

spreads of bright yellow colour from February onwards. The plants are very fast-growing, producing stems and leaves that are very soft and fleshy and die back once they have completed their cycle. By early summer there is often no above-ground trace of where the plants grew. Goldilocks, *Ranunculus auricomus*, is another woodland margin species. From a distance it looks like one of the commoner buttercups, particularly Meadow Buttercup, *Ranunculus acris*. However, it is often missing one or two or sometimes even more of its petals. Usually when Goldilocks is found in a hedge, other woodland species should be looked for. These include Barren Strawberry, *Potentilla sterilis*, Hedge woundwort, *Stachys sylvatica*, Wood Avens, *Geum urbanum*, Greater Stitchwort, *Stellaria holostea*, and Bush Vetch, *Vicia sepium*.

Because of their abundance throughout the countryside, hedges form an ideal habitat to study. They can be of interest to the expert and beginner, to botanists and landscape historians. The boundaries of many Irish townlands and land holdings are still physically defined by hedges. They are conspicuous features of the Irish landscape and we can often take them for granted. It is only when we visit other countries that we realise their cultural and natural significance.

GREATER STITCHWORT (ABOVE AND BELOW)

In early spring the flowers of Greater Stitchwort form great bands of white on roadside banks, looking like a giant Chickweed. It distribution is by no means even and in some areas it is only encountered in older hedges.

Natural Woodland

Lowland Ireland appears to be more wooded than it actually is. This visual deception is mainly caused by the large number of tall hedgerow trees that are spread across the countryside. The percentage of lowland Ireland occupied by native woodland is, in fact, extremely small. By now many lowland woodlands are mixtures of native species interplanted with foreign ones and even native Irish species may have been planted in some areas. The vegetation and flora of the woodland floor is often damaged through grazing, shading out and lack of structural diversity, and as a result has lost many of its most representative species. On more upland and less fertile ground the position is slightly different. Where land is unsuitable for ploughing, various forms of native woodland have fared better, although even this is often planted with unusual species. The ground flora usually gives a fairly good indication of the degree of naturalness of an individual woodland. Newly-planted woodland does not have the soil structure, associated biological processes, structural diversity or microclimate of a natural wood.

The huge swathes of conifers that have been planted on many parts of the landscape are essentially crops, converting moorland, bogland mountain wetlands and agriculturally-marginal grasslands into dark species-poor areas with a very reduced ground flora. In some areas plantings of this sort have failed, particularly on lowland bog margins. As a result, a semi-natural environment has developed, with some potential value to native plants. Indeed, some bog margins are now being colonised by Scots Pine, *Pinus sylvestris*, from seed spread from nearby planted parent trees. Although once a native Irish species, it died out as the climate changed. Its roots and stumps can often be seen preserved in peat bogs where newly-colonising saplings now grow.

Woodlands, and particularly tall oak woodlands, represent the end point in a vegetational succession in Ireland, which started with open ground dominated by short-lived annual species. These species were followed by longer-lived plants, grasses and various herbaceous species, then by various types of open and later closed scrub and smaller trees until at last the really big species came into their own. This succession can be seen where rough grassland is abandoned and various shrubby species begin to invade former pasture. In the long-term nothing overtops our native oaks, at least no native Irish species, although there are many ornamental single trees in the lowlands. Sadly most of our native woodlands have been cleared away, converted into timber for ships and buildings, pit props in coalmines and domestic furniture.

Woodlands can be classified into a number of major groupings but always with the caveat that there is some considerable overlap in their species composition. At an initial level of division there are woodlands dominated by tall native species such as oak. At the other extreme there are large areas of commercial forestry plantations usually dominated by introduced conifers. There are, however, large areas of introduced broad-leaved species in forests that might be mistaken for native woodlands. Broad-leaved usually deciduous species such as Beech, Sycamore, Horse Chestnut and many others are not native to Ireland, although all produce viable seed. We also have a number of rare native conifers such as Yew, *Taxus baccata*, and Common Juniper, *Juniperus communis*, which have survived in very special and select habitats. The clear-cut floristic differences between the introduced and the native are obscured by the recent tendency to plant deciduous trees from so-called native sources along the road frontages of conifer plantations.

A visit to an undamaged native woodland is a remarkable experience. The large boulders or exposed bedrock that are such a feature of these places are covered with mosses, liverworts and ferns. Trees of different sizes and species occupy different layers with seedlings, saplings and young trees mingling with older individuals. Where old trees have fallen, they are left to

YEW

Ireland has few native conifers. Yew is one. A rare native species, it is more usually encountered planted in churchyards.

WOODLAND FERNS

Many woodland ferns unfurl their fronds in early spring. The familiar 'Bishop's Crozier' shape is characteristic of many species.

be slowly assimilated back into the soil as a succession of insects and other invertebrates, fungi and bacteria break down their component parts over time. The continuity of generations of both long- and short-lived species is evident and there is an overall impression that the various topographical niches within the wood have been occupied by appropriate groups of species adapted to live just there. Some large species of ferns mature to form big shuttlecock-shaped clumps where grazing is absent. The main large fern species in limestone woodlands are Soft Shield-fern, *Polystichum setiferum*, and Male-fern, *Dryopteris filix-mas*. On earthen banks Hart's-tongue Fern, *Asplenium scolopendrium*, can become quite large. Although this and other ferns can spread into hedgerows, they grow larger and more luxuriantly in the comparative shelter of the forest. Woodlands in this condition are scarce nowadays. Because they are so often used for wintering cattle, they have lost a great deal of their ground flora, especially of species that might be flushing in early spring. However, there are various woodlands, often composed of introduced species, which may have been planted on the sites of former native woodlands. Long before the era of large-scale commercial plantings of exotic conifers, the economic importance of woodlands was appreciated. The retention of deciduous woodlands as part of the pleasure grounds of many large houses served to preserve many trees, forests and, fortunately, their associated ground flora. Woodcraft was a cultural art form and woods were managed by experienced woodsmen who would know which tree might be promoted to become a substantial element in a ship or large building, and which were destined to become broom handles or chair legs. Where an occasional tree was taken from a wood for a purpose, the indigenous flora was usually not damaged. However, when a wood or forest was clear-felled, light poured onto the former wood floor and many species accustomed to shade and cooler moister conditions dried out, shrivelled up and died.

Woods may have been planted if all the trees seem to be of the same age or if there are no typical woodland species present in the ground layer (even if there is an abundance of leaf litter on the ground), or if trees lack a good covering of mosses and liverworts. Woods showing little in the way of regeneration may have been heavily grazed, sometimes to the point where there are no young trees.

When properly developed, woodland plants can be seen to fall into three or four distinct layers. There are the canopy-forming trees whose branches and crowns meet and cast a dense shadow on the ground in the brightest summer. Beneath these there is usually a layer of younger trees and saplings working their way upwards to the light. These are joined by other woody species that seldom become really large – species like holly and hazel. Beneath these there are a number of young trees from seeds that have recently germinated. At ground level there is usually a layer of herbaceous vegetation lower down, and often with mosses and liverworts in the shaded areas. Where a clearing has occurred due to the removal or death of a large tree there is often a great spurt of recolonisation by seedlings, especially of Ash. These clearings then become gradually occupied by a dome of regenerating saplings, with the tallest and longest established in the middle of the opening, tapering off to the smallest towards the shaded margins.

develops best on rocky ground or esker ridges which, despite being free-draining, are unsuitable for agriculture. The main native trees now standing on limestone are Ash, *Fraxinus excelsior*, and Hazel, *Corylus avellana*. As woodlands were cleared or at least partially converted to pasture, Hazel increased dramatically and still forms a powerful presence in woodland. It springs to life early in the year, putting out its catkins from January on, long before the larger trees close off

LEAF LITTER

On the woodland floor the process of recycling continues through the year. Fallen leaves gradually decompose, often where a network of ivy stems and mosses covers the ground.

Woodland on Limestone Soils

The typical oak of lime-rich soils is Pedunculate Oak, *Quercus robur*. Well-developed native oak woodland on limestone is now rare in Ireland. It

the light supply to the lower layers. It often forms a low canopy with Ash, whose leaves emerge from their black buds quite late in spring. As a result, the ground flora of Ash-dominated woodland will receive more light than that which grows under different species-canopies. Furthermore, Ash leaves are divided into separate sections and although the

WOOD SPEEDWELL

The pale lilac-blue flowers of Wood Speedwell contrast with those of the far commoner Germander Speedwell, which has a much stronger blue colour.

RAMSONS

Ramsons or Wild Garlic can totally dominate the floor of many woodlands. It is a genuine native species and can persist in hedgerows after the previously adjoining woodland has been cleared.

THREE-CORNERED GARLIC

Three-cornered Garlic, a garden species, is set to become a major pest on some of our roadsides and woodland edges.

leaf outline is large there are many gaps that let light through even in high summer. Wych Elm, *Ulmus glabra*, with its huge, rough asymmetrical leaves, also grows in deciduous woodlands but many trees may have been planted. Ash, on the other hand, has no trouble regenerating in woodland on deeper soils. Although willows are usually considered to be typical of wetlands, there is one species, Goat Willow, *Salix caprea*, which is often found in relatively dry woodlands. For a willow, it has very broad leaves, which are densely-felted on the underside.

Other woodland trees also flower early in spring. One of the most attractive is Crab Apple, *Malus sylvestris*. This is the species whose small brownish globose fruits are produced in abundance

in early autumn and collected for making apple jelly. It is a true native species, although often encountered in situations where it may also have been planted. It resembles the various cultivated apples. Key points of difference are in the leaves, which are long-stalked and almost circular in Crab Apple, and especially in the fruit stalks and calyx, which are hairless or almost so. Most garden apples have shorter leaf-stalks, leaf-blades are longer than broad and the fruit stalks and calyx are much hairier.

There is one tree species that is endemic to Ireland – Irish Whitebeam, *Sorbus hibernica*. This is closely related to many of the other whitebeams of Western Europe and is widespread throughout the central plain. It is most often seen as a small

(LEFT TO RIGHT): WOODRUFF, SANICLE AND ENCHANTER'S NIGHTSHADE

Woodruff and Wood Sanicle are typical species of deciduous woodland and can tolerate quite low light conditions where few other species can cope. Enchanter's Nightshade can also cope with dark woodland conditions and sometimes forms large stands, especially where leaf litter accumulates.

hedgerow tree but it is also present in woodlands if these have formed on shallow soils where limestone lies close to the surface. Although it is conspicuous in open ground, especially as a young tree, it is often difficult to see in mature woodland as its leaves are up in the darker canopy along with other species. It is often found more easily in woodland in early autumn when its leaves and bright red fruits fall to the ground.

Most of the herbaceous species that live on the woodland floor must begin to grow fairly early in the year or else they will be shaded out completely. Thus although they are usually found in woodlands and hedges they are seldom found elsewhere. They will not grow well in strong sunlight. One of the first species to flower is Wood Violet, *Viola*

reichenbachiana. This resembles the commoner Dog Violet, *Viola riviniana*, which also occurs in woods, though usually in brighter areas. Wood Violet differs from its commoner relation in having a smaller flower, petals more spaced out (not overlapping to the same degree) and the projection at the back of the flower (the spur) is darker than the flowers. The leaves are usually a brighter green and they form in a cluster, branching out from the stem some distance from the ground where leaf litter would have accumulated over the winter. Wood Violet can flower from March on and it is usually a good indicator of older (though not necessarily 'ancient') woodland. When Ivy has formed a thin network of stems on the ground, it can trap the leaf litter and prevent it from blowing

WOOD ANEMONE

Wood Anemone forms great drifts in many woodlands, its white flowers contrasting strongly with their dark green foliage in springtime. Many woodland plants flower early in the year before the woodland canopy closes in. Where Wood Anemone occurs many other uncommon woodland species may also be expected.

away. There are a number of species which, together with Wood Violet, are usually found on lime-rich woodland soils. These include Wood Speedwell, *Veronica montana*, Goldilocks, *Ranunculus auricomus*, Ramsons, *Allium ursinum*, Bluebell, *Hyacinthoides non-scripta*, Woodruff, *Asperula odorata*, Wood Sanicle, *Sanicula europaea*, Wood Anemone, *Anemone nemorosa*, Enchanter's Nightshade, *Circaea lutetiana*, Bugle, *Ajuga reptans*, Pignut, *Conopodium majus*, Early-purple Orchid, *Orchis mascula*, and Broad-leaved Helleborine, *Epipactis latifolia*. Some of these can manage in dry woodlands where few native species form the canopy. Wood Sanicle seems to be able to survive in relatively non-natural woods, as can Wood Speedwell and Enchanter's Nightshade. Most of the others demand slightly better quality woodland conditions.

Wood Anemone is one of the most spectacular woodland species. It appears in spring and forms great stands of white or whitish-pink flowers and is a relation not only of the garden anemones but also of garden plants such as the various species of Clematis and Pulsatilla. One other member of the Buttercup family is widespread on woodland margins. This is Goldilocks. It has the same petal colour as our familiar buttercups but from a distance can be seen to have large clusters of

BUGLE

Bugle is found in woodlands, especially where the ground is slightly damp. Garden cultivars with copper-coloured leaves are grown in shaded gardens.

EARLY-PURPLE ORCHID

In woodland clearings and trackways Early-purple Orchid adds a splash of exotic colour to the woods in spring. Becoming a rare plant now in the east of Ireland, it still flourishes in the west, growing abundantly on open lime-rich grassland.

BROAD-LEAVED HELLEBORINE

Though not often noticed, the flowers of Broad-leaved Helleborine are spectacular constructions. The individual flowers, typically orchid-shaped though small, are similar to its much larger-flowered relatives. Broad-leaved Helleborine has been lost from many of its sites in the east of Ireland but persists in some and puts in an occasional re-appearance when conditions are favourable.

WOOD ANEMONE AND LESSER CELANDINE

Wood Anemone and Lesser Celandine often occur in combination on the fringes of deciduous woodland, even spreading onto roadside verges.

divided leaf-like structures in the upper parts of the stem, giving the whole plant a bushier appearance. Closer examination often reveals that it lacks one, two or more of the five petals it should have. These have not fallen off. The flowers open with the petals already missing. The other commoner member of the Buttercup family in woodlands is Lesser Celandine, *Ficaria verna*. It has many more petals and is a much more low-growing species, which flowers not only in woods but is common on roadside verges and hedgerows.

VIOLETS (ABOVE) AND BARREN STRAWBERRY (ABOVE RIGHT)

Violets and Barren Strawberry are among the first species to flower in springtime while there is plenty of light reaching the floor of the woodland. They both grow up through the leaf litter, weeks before other species get started.

Ground Ivy is unrelated to the climbing plant of walls, but belongs to the family that includes the Mints, Dead-nettles and Bugle. It can form dense stands on woodland clearings and has successfully colonised roadside verges and hedgerows.

The other great plant of woodlands is Bluebell, *Hyacinthoides non-scripta*. This can cover huge areas of woodland and is by no means restricted to lime-rich woodland. Another species, Spanish Bluebell, *Hyacinthoides hispanica*, a garden plant, has often escaped or been plentiful in woods. Hybrids between the two species are now widespread. In many areas the native species grows out under

Bracken, *Pteridium aquilinum*, along with Pignut, Common Dog Violet, Primrose, *Primula vulgaris*, Barren Strawberry, *Potentilla sterilis*, and Ground Ivy, *Glechoma hederacea*. Although all these plants can occur in woodlands and woodland margins it seems that they are also able to grow quite well away from conventional woodland where they are sheltered by the Bracken that forms a sort of woodland substitute. Some may even be surviving elements of an earlier scrub woodland flora that has been cleared back and is now gradually reverting.

A number of other woodland-margin species are widespread and in Ireland are often encountered in hedgerows. Primrose, Lords-and-Ladies, *Arum maculatum*, Ground Ivy, Wild Strawberry, *Fragaria vesca*, and Barren Strawberry, Herb-Robert, *Geranium robertianum*, Germander Speedwell, *Veronica chamaedrys*, Wood Avens, *Geum urbanum*, and Bush Vetch, *Vicia sepium*, are usually found in brighter areas, near trackways or in clearings, and in roadside verges.

If the woodland is near a river, the stems of a big rough evergreen horsetail, Rough Horsetail, *Equisetum hyemale*, are often evident in large stands.

A number of rare species occur where there is a substantial build-up of leaf litter. Some of these live in clearings or beside woodland tracks as they prefer dappled light. The legally-protected Hairy St John's-wort, *Hypericum hirsutum*, though a rare species in Ireland, is very conspicuous in deciduous woodlands along the Liffey Valley in Dublin, as are Yellow Weasel-snout, *Lamiastrum galeobdolon*, and the beautiful grass Wood Melick, *Melica uniflora*. Rarer species include Toothwort, *Lathraea squamaria*, and Ivy Broomrape, *Orobanche hederae*. Bird's-nest Orchid, *Neottia nidus-avis*, and Yellow Bird's-nest, *Hypopitys monotropa*, derive their nourishment through saprophytic or parasitic involvements with other species in the woodland.

LORDS-AND-LADIES

The bright scarlet fruits of Lords-and-Ladies are spectacular elements of the woodland floor in autumn, persisting long after the unusual flower has long since disappeared. See p. 176.

All four of these species are unusual in that they lack chlorophyll and do not produce conventional leaves.

The distribution of accumulation areas for leaf litter is often of importance to woodland plants. Leaf litter gradually moves to the bottom of the slope. But where there are large boulders, sudden dips and other obstructions, fallen leaves accumulate and other species can grow. In areas where water occasionally rests, the flora can be further modified and enriched.

In common with most mature ecological habitats, there is a natural sequence of gradual colonisation, which leads over to time to the establishment of canopy-forming woodlands. In the case of woodlands on limestone soils, rich with exposed rocks and boulders, semi-natural scrub woodland develops, a process stimulated by a reduction in grazing levels. For some time many species of grassland flowering plants find shelter close to the burgeoning scrub cover. This habitat is particularly characteristic of lakeshores, notably in the central plain, especially in areas where lake levels were lowered by twentieth-century drainage schemes. As a result, new lime-rich soils previously under water were exposed and colonised not only by herbaceous species but also by scrub, which includes a number of nationally rare shrubs. Two species of rose spread out from pre-existing wood margins here, Sweet-briar, *Rosa rubiginosa*, and Small-leaved Sweet-briar, *Rosa agrestis*.

Woodland on Acid Soils

Native woodlands of a sort have survived on many acid soil areas, particularly in areas where usually fairly thin soils have formed on steeply-sloping terrain, often with huge boulders or protruding bedrock evident. Although the soil in these areas is free draining, little agriculture is possible here as the soil is so poor. As a result, a number of grazing-sensitive species of plant are particularly well represented in these areas. The oak woodlands of Killarney and elsewhere are very well known for their state of naturalness. However, in many areas, woodlands were severely exploited for the production of charcoal to be used in smelting and were felled in great numbers. Other woods were cut down and grew again, and small parts of some

WOODLAND RECYCLING

Decomposition and recycling continue through the year. Fungi are major contributors to these processes, especially in autumn.

SESSILE OAK (ABOVE) AND HOLLY (ABOVE RIGHT)

As the leaf canopy closes, the supply of light to the woodland floor is drastically reduced.
Few species can cope with this. Holly is one of the more successful species in this situation.

may never have been exploited. In some of these areas, irrespective of their history, the flora often takes on an almost jungle-like appearance. Many of the trees are densely clothed with mosses, ferns and large, trailing lichens. As well as having Birch and Mountain Ash, these woodlands also contain Yew and Strawberry-tree, *Arbutus unedo*. Planted Yew trees are a feature of many churchyards and this species has often been used as 'Palm' on Palm Sunday. Strawberry-tree was also taken into cultivation and there are many fine specimen trees to be seen in larger gardens of a certain era. Grazing by deer can be a problem. One of the biogeographically-intriguing species here is Irish Spurge, *Euphorbia hyberna*, which occurs in great abundance on many of the sheltered woodlands of Kerry (but also in Cork, Waterford and elsewhere), even spreading onto sheltered roadsides, hedgerows and damp lightly-grazed grasslands. This is one of the species that do so well in the south-west and which are either very rare or absent in Britain, as in the case of the Strawberry-tree. The former distribution of trees is enshrined in place names that often indicate the species in question. The

preponderance of the element -dair, anglicised and contained within place names such as Derry, testifies to the former abundance of oaks. Many other trees gain entry in the place names registers. Willows, in Latin *Salix*, make their way into place names with endings such as –saileach or saileog, such as Cloonsellan (a meadow with willows) in both Longford and Roscommon or Lough Sillan in Cavan, or Kilsallaghan in Dublin.

The dominant tree at the end of the ecological succession here is Sessile Oak, *Quercus petraea*. However, other smaller trees such as Holly and Mountain Ash are well able to colonise or hold their ground in adverse conditions. They grow very well where the woodland canopy is poorly developed. These and other species can often be seen nowadays on open slopes on higher ground when rough land is abandoned. Typically these species and a variety of brambles may be seen in open rocky ground growing up through a great sea of encroaching Bracken. In more sheltered areas these trees can form small forests and copses, often following the course of rivers and streams where there is more nourishment and shelter. Here they

FOXGLOVE

Foxglove thrives on many acid soils and occurs on woodland margins, tracksides, rocky exposures and sheltered areas on heathy ground. It is also grown in gardens and sometimes escapes but usually does not persist – at least not on lime-rich soils.

are often joined by mature stands of Hazel, *Corylus avellana*.

The ground flora is dominated by a number of species many of which also occur in open acid-ground conditions such as heathland, moorland and bogland. Because these are open ground species, they grow best under openings in the canopy where individual trees have fallen and let light onto the woodland floor. They also occur prominently along trackways through the forests as well as on their margins. Most of these are slow-growing species, a necessity here because there is so little in the way of nutrient. Bilberry, *Vaccinium myrtillus*, is particularly successful here, producing green to reddish tubular flowers in late spring on strong twiggy shoots and black edible berries later in the year. It grows well on the drier spots in the wood, where it is joined by Foxglove, *Digitalis purpurea*, Ling, *Calluna vulgaris*, Wood Sage, *Teucrium scorodonia*, and Common Cow-wheat, *Melampyrum pratense*. Foxglove is a wonderful plant for revealing the presence of dry acid soils. When it is encountered, many of its regular botanical associates will also turn up nearby. Wood Sage, an unusual-looking plant with pale greenish flowers, a distinct square stem and leaves that appear wrinkled on the upper surface, is usually not far away on trackside banks. These in turn are joined by the yellow-flowered Tormentil, *Potentilla erecta*, and large clumps of the Wood-rush, *Luzula sylvatica*, further into the wood. Two species of St John's-wort also grow here. Slender St John's-wort, *Hypericum pulchrum*, is indeed a striking upright plant, with opposite leaves and yellow petals that are reddish when opening. The sepals and the edges of the petals are densely clothed with small black glands. This usually grows on the trackside banks, with its close relative Trailing St John's-wort, *Hypericum humifusum*, crawling over bare gravelly ground.

A number of these species can also hold their own in conifer plantations, where there is sufficient light, by

COMMON COW-WHEAT

Common Cow-wheat is a colourful component of the native woodland floor on acid soils and can also be found on formerly wooded rocky ground, even when thinly planted with conifers.

WOOD-RUSHES

Wood-rushes grow with great success in shaded situations on acid soils, often becoming the dominant vegetation.

197

WOOD-SORREL (ABOVE AND LEFT)

Wood-sorrel is one of the first flowers to bloom in woodland. Although it can grow on various soils, it is at its best on acid ground. On lime-rich soils it often occurs on mosses growing on fallen tree-trunks some distance from the ground. Its solitary flowers are usually veined with delicate mauve. Many other members of the genus *Oxalis* have been brought into cultivation and several have escaped. Wood-sorrel is a genuine native species in Ireland.

tracksides, and where mountain streams cut down through the newly-planted stands of commercial forestry. If the trees have been planted sufficiently far back from the banks, a reduced woodland flora can be found containing species with more specialised requirements. Heath Milkwort, *Polygala serpyllifolia*, will turn up in these gaps along with Wood-sorrel, *Oxalis acetosella*. Welsh Poppy, *Meconopsis cambrica*, with bright yellow flowers, occurs in many Irish woodlands, either as a rare native or as a garden escape. It is not always easy to decide which. Another rare native species, Columbine, *Aquilegia vulgaris*, has similarly had

its natural range obscured by the proliferation of garden escapes.

One species that is particularly characteristic of these acid oak woodlands is Hard Fern, *Blechnum spicant*. This is an interesting species because it produces two types of frond. Through most of the year it sustains a substantial tuft of long pinnate fronds, which spread outwards. It also produces another set of fronds, narrower than the others, which are held stiffly erect. The lobes of these fronds (pinnae) are narrower and fertile, covered by dark brown soris which contain the spores. These spores are minute and are wafted on the

Some woodland ferns do much better on acid soils and some can even cope with the low-light conditions that prevail in densely-populated conifer plantations.

wind in their thousands, some eventually to form new plants. There are other large ferns in these oak woods. The acid-ground counterpart of the more ubiquitous Male-fern is Golden-scented Male-fern, *Dryopteris affinis*. This is a fine fern, also with the typical shuttlecock-growth form. It may be recognised from a distance because the stalks of the individual fronds are covered with a dense clothing of golden-brown scales. These scales are particularly evident in late spring when the fronds are unfurling and contrast strikingly with the bright green pinnules. Two other acid-ground ferns are Broad Buckler-fern, *Dryopteris dilatata*, and Hay-scented Bucker-fern, *Dryopteris aemula*. The latter looks like a smaller and softer version of Broad Buckler-fern with paler green fronds and pinnules that are often turned up at the tip. In the east of Ireland this species is usually found in sheltered humid woodlands, especially near streams and waterfalls. However, in the mistier west it turns up on roadside bedrock exposures and in shaded hedge banks as well as in woodland.

Wet Woodland

Wet woodlands develop where soil is waterlogged for long periods of time. They form in all sorts of land where drainage is impeded, but especially in the flood plains of rivers, and the edges of bogs and lake margins. Depending on the nature of the soil, the ground flora can take on a base-rich, neutral or base-poor character. Many wet woodlands have formed on the edges of bogs and the flora is, therefore, acid. Where the fall of land is gentle these woods can form extensive bands of vegetation with the upper limits of flooding tracked by the presence of Grey Willow, *Salix cinerea*. They do not develop well in situations where grazing is intensive. Wet woodlands are difficult and dangerous to walk through. In well-developed examples there are numerous trees and fallen logs alternating with wet pools and muddy areas. There is a great feeling of the primeval about these areas, an impression interrupted occasionally by the presence of barbed-wire fences and drainage ditches. The main tree-forming species over most of lowland Ireland are Alder, *Alnus glutinosa*, and Willow, *Salix cinerea* ssp. *oleifolia*, usually with Downy Birch, *Betula pubescens*. These are medium-sized species and each grows up to battle it out in the canopy. Archaeological evidence indicates that the Alders that once grew in Ireland were far larger than those that grow today. Beneath the canopy and usually nearer the brighter edges of the wood grow Guelder-rose, *Viburnum opulus*, Mountain Ash, *Sorbus aucuparia*, and Buckthorn, *Rhamnus cathartica*. This type of woodland is also very common on the former edges of drained raised bogs, especially where the peats give way to mineral soils. Here Downy Birch comes into its own,

especially in the absence of grazing. It can become established very rapidly and can form substantial copses in less than 10 years. Hedge Bindweed, *Calystegia sepium*, and Woody Nightshade, *Solanum dulcamara*, climb up through this marginal vegetation. If the woodland is open enough Yellow Flag, *Iris pseudacorus*, Meadowsweet, *Filipendula ulmaria*, Hemp-agrimony, *Eupatorium cannabinum*, and Common Valerian, *Valeriana officinalis*, can flourish. These are not really woodland species but rather are typical of bog margin wetlands. They are sheltered by the woodland and also by the general reduction in levels of grazing, which is discouraged due to the extreme wetness of the land. Some of these wet woodlands, especially the more peaty ones, have Royal Fern, *Osmunda regalis*, and more often, Broad Buckler-fern. It is often possible to judge the extent of winter flooding on these wet woodlands by examining the height of the mud caked onto the trunks of the trees or by watching out for tufts of loose grasses, leaves and other debris caught in their lower branches. This flooding can be quite some distance from the summer levels of the nearby lakes, depending on local topography. The extent of woodland-floor flooding is sometimes indicated by the presence of open patches devoid of vegetation or colonised by the runners of invasive grasses such as Creeping Bent, *Agrostis stolonifera*. If the water stays at a low level for the entire summer and early autumn, then other species can stake a claim. Where these woods form on the margins of lakes, the seeds of some of the lakeshore species are washed into the woodland and can grow, at least in the more open sections.

GREAT HORSETAIL

The young stems of Great Horsetail are typically associated with wet seepage areas both in and outside woods. As the year progresses their stems will become taller and almost white between the much darker nodes.

WATER AVENS

Water Avens is typical of wet soils in sheltered woodland and also on shaded stream sides in upland areas. It was one of the first plants to be recorded in Ireland, from woodland at Castletown in Celbridge, Co. Kildare, where it still lives.

Wet woodlands also formed on lime-rich soils on slopes where there is usually a spring supplying water. This water trickles down over initially more open conditions and in time the area becomes colonised by various willows, Birch and a number of wetland herbaceous species. The most spectacular of these is Great Horsetail, *Equisetum telmateia*, recognisable by its size (up to 1 m) and its almost white stems. These grow with another species characteristic of spring sources, Marsh Hawk's-beard, *Crepis paludosa*. This looks like lots of other yellow composites but has a very distinct leaf and a dull brown pappus. Both these species and others that grow with them, such as Ragged Robin, *Lychnis flos-cuculi*, and Water Avens, *Geum rivale*, are also found in open, flushed, ungrazed ground. If grazing is prevented, this type of woodland can form very quickly. It is often possible to find the dying stems of Furze, green at the top, growing up through this woodland. These shrubs were present on the drier areas of these wetlands but were not able to grow upwards towards the light as the willows and other species took hold.

There is a natural progression in the formation of wet woodlands. Areas that are permanently submerged are not likely to become colonised by non-aquatic species. Germination will usually take place when water levels have fallen. Prolonged flooding inhibits the establishment of many species and if water levels stay high through the year a flora develops that is more typical of wetland than woodland. Some plants have the capacity to form long-lived tussocks, which grow along with the rising waters and gradually over the years form substantial 'trunks'. Chief among these is Greater Tussock-sedge, *Carex paniculata*, which can tolerate extended periods of inundation and form a 'trunk' nearly half a metre high crowned with a spray of strong, narrow, green leaves, resembling a young tree fern. It is a species of more open sedge-swamp and gradually contributes to the build-up or colonisation of intermittently-flooding land. Other species can then follow. Various grasses such as Reed Canary-grass, *Phalaris arundinacea*, are also well adapted for life in areas with fluctuating water levels.

The riparian trees of many Irish rivers are of non-native species. Some of these may have been planted originally to prevent erosion of the riverbanks by the movement of the waters. However, many have subsequently spread either by seed or viable twigs to new ground. This is often noticeable where a river has been straightened. Most of the water is carried down the newly-planned line of the river but the by-passed sections, resembling ox-bows, still retain some water. These areas are often colonised by various native and non-native willows and by Alder. The main non-native species are Crack-willow, *Salix fragilis*, and White Willow, *Salix alba*, but other species such as Almond Willow, *Salix triandra*, and Purple Willow, *Salix purpurea*, also occur. Where there is a good covering of willow and Alder, tall herbaceous species thrive and form a dense undergrowth, enjoying the nutrient-rich waters of the river, which has deposited a rich layer of alluvium, leaf-litter, branches and even trunks of trees.

Threats

The major threat to native woodland is felling. Sadly, most of the damage has already occurred. Grazing, especially in winter, is also very injurious, especially when cattle feeders are installed in small woodlands.

An ongoing threat to surviving woodlands has been the spread of non-native species, particularly those with broad evergreen leaves. The main culprit here is Rhododendron, *Rhododendron*

DECAYING BIRCH

Leaves, twigs, even the branches and trunks are all eventually recycled by insects, woodlice, millipedes and, most obviously, by fungi.

ponticum. It was, like so many other species, introduced by gardeners. Most Rhododendron species are lovers of acid soils, and they have become particularly invasive in woodlands on such soils. Because the leaves are evergreen, daylight rarely reaches the forest floor, particularly at that crucial phase in spring before the leaves of the tree-canopy flush. Therefore little regeneration of woodland trees and herbs can take place.

RED CAMPION

Red Campion can form substantial stands in woodland clearings in early summer. Though quite common in the northern parts of Ireland, it becomes much rarer in the south.

Rivers

W hen individual drops of rainwater fall to earth, they evaporate rapidly if they land on warm, dry surfaces or are released back into the atmosphere through leaves if taken up by the roots of plants. However, most precipitation finds its way back to the sea, either quickly by escaping directly into the network of drains, streams and rivers or more slowly as its winds its way underground.

Rivers usually have many contributary sources. They generally form on higher ground as networks of fine seepage lines, dripping out of the covering of moorland vegetation to

RIVERS

Near the source, most rivers are too severe an environment for broad-leaved water plants. The constant shearing by the water's movement would shred their leaves. Despite this, a few species can manage here, though usually growing in the shelter of larger boulders.

form tiny rills, trickles and streamlets. These can run dry in summer. After extended periods of heavy rain they can explode from that same boggy moorland, shooting out dramatically at the point where the sodden peat lies directly on the underlying bedrock. Where this happens near roads fringed by high peaty banks the effect can be spectacular as a soup of peat, sand and gravel is literally projected out onto the road by the water. This force, whether converging dramatically on one point or relentlessly trickling through the soil and vegetation cover, gradually erodes both organic and inorganic material and moves it to lower ground.

In the higher reaches, streams are, in relative terms, fast moving, where the steeply-shelving topography speeds their course. They can form torrents that cut down into the substrate and carve out gullies from the mountain peats, sandy gravels and bedrock. The shearing and abrasive effect of these fast-moving streamlets makes it virtually impossible for many plants to grow in these areas. Sand, silt and other potential food material cannot settle. This is compounded by slow rates of growth in these areas because of low nutrient availability. Very few true aquatic plants can grow here and those that can have very narrow leaves and swaying stems that give and move with the current. Broad-leaved species such as water lilies would be cut to shreds in this environment. The true aquatic plants that do survive are usually species that also live in acid-water lakes and can cope with low levels of nutrients. One of the few that can grow here is Alternate Water-milfoil, *Myriophyllum alterniflorum*. Water-milfoils can lose many of their leaves without permanent damage but remain anchored to the substrate and grow on again. In rivers, even this species is usually found growing on the lee side of more substantial boulders where some silt and gravels accumulate.

Where the streams have changed course, small ox-bow features survive along the original line and here other true aquatics can grow in conditions where abrasion is less significant. Eroded silts and gravel are deposited here in quieter backwaters where small quantities of nutrient accumulate. A few species can take advantage of this. Floating Club-rush, *Eleogiton fluitans*, is one, with long narrow leaves and flowering stems that rise above the water in summer. Another, with similar-looking leaves, is Bulbous Rush, *Juncus bulbosus*. Both of these can cope with fluctuating water levels and flower successfully in the semi-terrestrial conditions that develop in summer. In the margins of these upland areas of sheltered still water two members of the Buttercup family grow. Lesser Spearwort, *Ranunculus flammula*, is fairly widespread and looks like many of the more familiar yellow-flower species but differs in having long, narrow tapering leaves and can grow also in many lowland situations both in shallow water and on permanently wet ground. The other species, Round-leaved Crowfoot, *Ranunculus omiophyllus*, is much more restricted in its distribution. It has white petals and obvious floating leaves divided into three segments. With a leaf shape like this it would be under pressure in the fast-moving waters but often occurs in pools and drains adjoining the streams. It is mainly found in hillier areas from the Dublin Mountains around the higher stretches of the south-east to Cork and Kerry. It is not known from the north or west of the country. Despite living in colder upland areas, it is usually one of the first species to flower here and can be seen in blossom as early as May. Other species from the mountain bog pools can occasionally grow here also, but there are often more interesting species to be found on the margins of the streams and the adjoining rocks.

Most of the interesting plants in these areas belong to the non-flowering groups, especially the liverworts and mosses. True aquatic mosses grow here and are especially suited to life in this habitat. One of the main species in these upland waters is the Alpine Water-moss, *Fontinalis squamosa*, which clings to rocks in fast-flowing streams in contrast to its close and commoner relative, Greater Water-moss, *Fontinalis antipyretica*, in lower-level, richer waters. The down-cutting gullies formed in these eroding situations provide a sufficiently humid environment for many mosses and liverworts and higher plants that are unable to grow out on the exposed moorland. Of the flowering plants, a number of saxifrages make it onto these rocks, especially on their more protected sides. Chief of these is Starry Saxifrage, *Saxifraga stellaris*, which forms mats on rocks but also grows in seepages in the adjoining moorlands. Water here is rich in oxygen, poor in nutrients and usually unpolluted. The true aquatic flora, though poor in species, is very natural and relatively unaffected, at least directly, by intensive agriculture and other human influences. Though restricted, the range of species is interesting ecologically and can be seen to alter as the stream moves to lower ground. Several species from upland habitats have closely-related counterparts in the very ecologically-different lowlands.

The distinction between higher and lower ground is not simply one of altitude. Many other factors combine to change the physical and chemical properties of the water in its transit from upper ground. Climate

WATER-CROWFOOTS (ABOVE AND BELOW)

Water-crowfoots are close relations of the buttercups. Their white flowers, held above the water in early summer, emerge from floating mats of stems and leaves that can rise and fall as river levels fluctuate. Some species have both floating and divided leaves. Many former colonies of the large riverine species have died out due to water pollution.

YELLOW WATER-LILY

Yellow Water-lily occupies the quieter
backwaters of lowland rivers. It produces
the familiar lily-pad leaves on the water's
surface and also has larger softer
submerged leaves. Plants with this design
are not built for speeding waters.

and weather are different, as is the soil through which the river passes as it changes from the base-poor moorlands to the richer, more mature soils of the lower ground.

There are many interesting plants to be seen growing in the waters and on the riverside margins, partly due to the surrounding terrain. Rivers coming off the moorland can often enter into large open plains where their courses change. The sands, gravels and peats from these higher areas are washed down into these valleys (many of which have been altered by glacial action), and have been spread across their floors. Large open areas characterise their margins and rivers meander across the more level ground. These areas are often covered with layers of sandy material and the rivers cut deeply into some places, undercutting the banks at one point and depositing the eroded material downstream. By-passed stretches of river are evident in these level areas and here some wetland aquatic species grow, usually species more typical of wet grasslands.

One of the true aquatics of this region of most rivers is the Stream Water-crowfoot, *Ranunculus penicillatus*. In late spring this is a marvellously obvious species, covering stretches of the river with its large white flowers held above the water in their thousands. It produces long (2–3 m) underwater stems as well as tassels of submerged deeply-divided leaves and floating lobed leaves. This species is still very successful in relatively unpolluted upland waters but many of its former sites in the lowlands have been lost. There are two other large-flowered water-crowfoots in Ireland (Pond Water-crowfoot, *Ranunculus peltatus,* and Common Water-crowfoot, *R. aquatalis*) in slow-moving rivers, pools and lakes. There are two rarer species. Brackish Water-crowfoot, *R. baudottii,* usually lives in slightly salty drains near the sea and

the very rare River Water-crowfoot, *R. fluitans*, in north-east Ireland. These are not easy species to distinguish morphologically. Their success or lack of it can provide an indication of water quality. In the lowlands, agricultural and domestic pollution has greatly increased the amount of nutrients in the water, resulting in the loss of many colonies of these interesting species.

Like water-crowfoots, pondweeds belonging mainly to the genus *Potamogeton* have species that are characteristic of different parts of the river course and the different species reflect the nutrient burden and pollution levels endured by the river. Some Pondweed species have both floating and submerged leaves and others have underwater leaves only. In the moorlands, Bog Pondweed, *Potamogeton polygonifolius*, can grow in still sections of the upland streams where there is no shearing factor. At lower levels Broad-leaved Pondweed, *Potamogeton natans*, is the most obvious and widespread species in a variety of water types, and on clear, clean lime-rich waters Shining Pondweed, *Potamogeton lucens*, is often evident. This is one of our most distinctive pondweeds, its semi-transparent submerged leaves revealing an amazing network of veins that are seldom so evident in other species apart from Perfoliate Pondweed, *Potamogeton perfoliatus*. This species can tolerate slightly higher levels of eutrophication than many of its relatives.

In lower and usually more eutrophic and polluted waters Curled Pondweed, *Potamogeton crispus*, and Fennel Pondweed, *Potamogeton pectinatus*, are usually the most resilient species, growing in waters where few other species can survive. Neither produces floating leaves. The former has wavy leaves about four times as long as wide. The latter species produces huge long strands of underwater stems bearing dense clusters of long, narrow leaves. From a distance it could be confused with some of the water-crowfoots but these are usually much rarer in polluted waters.

There are two other species of water-milfoil native to Ireland, Whorled Water-milfoil, *Myriophyllum verticillatum*, and Spiked Water-milfoil, *Myriophyllum spicatum*. Both species produce large mats of submerged vegetation, their leaves being deeply divided into many linear segments arranged like a feather (pinnate). Both also produce spikes of flowers that emerge from the water. Whorled Water-milfoil is confined largely to clean lime-rich waters but Spiked Water-milfoil has increased in eutrophic waters in recent years, tracking the elevating levels of nutrients in our rivers. Recently another species has appeared in Ireland, which may become invasive, Parrot's-feather, *Myriophyllum aquaticum*. This has been brought into the country by aquarists and water gardeners and has either been thrown out or has accidentally escaped into ponds and slow-moving rivers elsewhere.

There is one species of Water-crowfoot that can occur in base-rich though not necessarily polluted waters, Thread-leaved Water-crowfoot, *Ranunculus tricophyllus*. It has small white petals and it does not usually produce floating leaves although it has lots of submerged ones. This species is very successful in small drains feeding into larger rivers. A second species with even smaller flowers and undivided leaves often grows in similar eutrophic conditions. This is Ivy-leaved Crowfoot, *Ranunculus hederaceus*. It is a bare-mud and inundation specialist growing especially where drains feed into smaller rivers where back-flooding sometimes occurs.

Some truly colourful emergent species (as well as some uncolourful ones) grow on the margins of lowland rivers. These are not true aquatics – their lower parts are firmly anchored in the shallower waters at the margins of our larger rivers, but the flowering stems and leaves are carried well above the water. By far the most attractive of these is Flowering Rush, *Butomus umbellatus*. This is unmistakable when in flower with its huge head of pink flowers but is often not so obvious when flowering stems are not produced. Like many aquatic species, it also produces underwater leaves, in this case long and spirally-twisted, but many plants do not flower consistently. Indeed, it often fails to produce good fruit and there is some discussion as to whether it is native in all its sites in Ireland. Another colourful emergent is Arrowhead, *Sagittaria sagittifolia*, which is common especially in the south-east. It has also invaded the canal system, particularly the Barrow Navigation, the Boyne and the Shannon, where various lengths of these rivers have been by-passed by stretches of canal. Yellow Water-lily, *Nuphar lutea*, is highly successful in rivers once the water is not too deep.

Many other tall plants fringe our rivers. Most of these are grasses, many equipped with the ability to grow taller and taller. Some of these also grow in lakes and sometimes form huge stands where water speeds are not too high. Submerged accumulations of water-borne shingle have formed in rivers where obstructions such as bridges reduce the through-flow. Being composed of non-silty matter such as pebbles and even small boulders, they provide a resistant substrate where some emergent species can become established and remain. Common Club-rush, *Schoenoplectus lacustris*, often grows here. Similarly some pondweeds can gain anchorage on these submerged shoals. Nearer shore the main big emergent grasses are Common Reed, *Phragmites australis*, Reed Canary-grass, *Phalaris arundinacea*, and Reed Sweet-grass, *Glyceria maxima*. Reed Sweet-grass is an

BROOKLIME

Brooklime (one of the Speedwell family) is a common
species of wet muddy ditches and can re-assert its
presence when drains are cleared to improve water flow,
often forming substantial clumps on the edges of the
water course.

WATER FORGET-ME-NOT

Forget-me-nots (*Myosotis*) grow in both wet and dry situations. Our wetland species have the hairs on their calyx lying flat while the dry-ground species have spreading hairs.

interesting species because it can form a floating mat of vegetation, where the rhizomes are intertwined densely.

There are three species of Figwort native to Ireland and all grow on and very near riverbanks. They are usually about a metre tall and have numerous brownish-purple flowers with paler green areas. Common Figwort, *Scrophularia nodosa*, is by far the most widespread, and can extend onto roadsides and wet waste ground in cities. The stems of all three species are strongly four-angled and, except for Common Figwort, have obvious extra projections (wings) along the edges. Water Figwort, *Scrophularia auriculata*, is patchier in its distribution. It occurs commonly in some river systems but is rare in others. The rarest of the three is Green Figwort, *Scrophularia umbrosa*. It is locally common on the Liffey in Dublin and Kildare and in a few other parts of the country. In its Dublin and Kildare sites it can often grow to over 2 m and stands out from the other species by flowering in late summer and having bright green foliage. The figworts have five stamens but only four of them are functional. The fifth is a modified organ (a staminode) attached to and projecting slightly upwards from the inner part of the corolla tube. It is differently shaped in all three species. It is almost the same colour as the tube and tricky to spot but can be most easily seen by slipping a thumbnail between it and the corolla tube.

The difference between a deep drain and a small stream is not always clear. Many drains were cut close to the line of existing natural streams, especially where raised bogs were being drained. They usually run in relatively straight lines and the original course taken by the river is often nowadays obscured. Having served their purpose, these deep drains are sometimes abandoned for extended periods of time. When they are not cleared out, a range of more-or-less emergent species comes to occupy their silty and marly beds. Taller species growing here include Bulrush (Great Reed-mace), *Typha latifolia*, and two species of bur-reed, Branched Bur-reed, *Sparganium erectum*, and more rarely the rather similar Unbranched Bur-reed, *Sparganium emersum*. These deep cuts are often difficult to examine safely and a long stick is advised for testing the depth of the mud.

Occasionally these drains are cleared out and the flow of water again becomes evident. The muddy fringes of the drains are then colonised by a variety of common species including Fool's Water-cress, *Apium nodiflorum*, Brooklime, *Veronica beccabunga*, Blue Water-speedwell, *V. anagallis-aquatica*, and Water Forget-me-not, *Myosotis scorpioides*. Rarer species such as Trifid Bur-marigold, *Bidens tripartita*, Nodding Bur-marigold, *Bidens cernua*, and a Whorl-grass, *Catabrosa aquatica*, also thrive in the short-term on the muddy fringes until they are closed out as the next round of taller emergent species gets underway.

As many home owners can ruefully testify, flood plains tend to flood. Extended periods of rainfall result in the inundation of great areas of low-lying countryside. This has been going on for thousands of years. Silt, sand and other organic materials, translocated from their point of origin to low-lying land, are deposited often some distance from the main watercourse and will remain there until another larger flood. These flooding episodes bring large volumes of nutrient-rich silt into areas and can often alter the character of the vegetation at a local level. The emergent vegetation of river margins in the past often extended far from the present-day banks of the river and it is often possible to ascertain the potential range of flooding

JAPANESE KNOTWEED

The banks of many Irish rivers have been invaded by the notorious Japanese Knotweed, another uninvited colonist, not so much a garden escape – more an eject.

by reference to these satellite colonies of taller vegetation.

In recent years the banks of many rivers have been invaded by a number of well-known species. The most obvious of these is Indian Balsam, *Impatiens glandulifera*, which can form immense stands often up to 3 m high, with huge pink flowers. The species was brought into Ireland as a garden ornamental (originally from the Himalayas), but spread very quickly along Ireland's waterways. Despite its size, it is an annual and can grow speedily. Little can grow on the mud beneath its rapidly-expanding foliage. After flowering, the fruits contort and snap open, casting the seeds some distance from the parent plant. The fruits will do this even before being fully ripe if held in the hand for a few seconds.

The other major invasive species of riversides is Giant Hogweed, *Heracleum mantegazzianum*. Originally from south-west Asia, this species has spread along many watercourses. Its stems and leaves release a chemical that causes serious skin irritations, particularly in strong sunlight. It continues to colonise new ground despite attempts to eradicate it in some areas. Another notorious invader of riversides, as well as urban waste ground, railway sidings and abandoned gardens, is Japanese Knotweed, *Fallopia japonica* (*Reynoutria japonica*). This species is now exceedingly difficult to eradicate.

All these species have a track record of engulfing the native flora and are poised to do further damage. Rivers provide an ideal means of transport to new locations for their seeds and viable roots. It only takes one seed or one fragment of living root to start a new colony and wipe out another stretch of our diminishing natural heritage.

Lakes

Ireland has a variety of water bodies ranging from the spectacularly large Lough Neagh, which borders five counties in the north, to tiny ponds and pools. Depending on how and where they formed, they can have many different physical and chemical characteristics resulting in very different floras.

The upland corrie lakes formed by glacial action usually have exceedingly nutrient-poor waters. Most of the Irish uplands are of 'acid' rocks, and any water that has accumulated in these great excavations has run off from the surrounding uplands. The prevailing low levels of nutrient in the hinterland show up in the slow rates of plant and animal growth in these waters. These areas are still relatively cold and winter snow lingers here, especially on north-facing slopes. Very few aquatic plant species can grow in these mountain lakes.

The rocks associated with these lakeshore upland areas are often spectacularly covered with mosses and liverworts, especially those species with essentially northern or western distributions. Cooler and more shaded conditions make it easier for these plants to survive in these areas and many are much commoner on acid rocks such as granite.

One specialist plant of this habitat is Quillwort, *Isoetes lacustris*. This is fairly widespread in this type of lake, especially in the west, and also in other acid-water lakes with rocky floors. It also occurs in clear mountain lakes on high ground in the east of Ireland in the Wicklow Mountains and also in the Mournes. There is a second Irish species, Spring Quillwort, *Isoetes echinospora*, much rarer and confined to the Atlantic side of Ireland. Both species grow permanently submerged in the cold clear water of these upland lakes and are usually found washed up on lakeshores. They are close relatives of the ferns and produce spores. Spring Quillwort has long narrow stiff leaves (hence the name). In cross-section these leaves will be seen to have four chambers running their length.

There are many lakes that have formed in depressions within the western blanket bogs. These are also usually very nutrient poor but often include a number of interesting species. The most obvious of these is White Water-lily, *Nymphaea alba*. This species has often been planted in the lowlands of Ireland where it can clearly survive but its favourite

LAKESIDE EMERGENT VEGETATION

Lakeshores have a distinct band of tall emergent vegetation comprising
species that can cope with fluctuating water levels. Meadowsweet,
Great Willowherb, Reed Canary-grass and, in deeper water, Common
Club-rush are typical inhabitants of this environment.

natural home is in clear nutrient-poor water and it is a conspicuous feature of the blanket bog lakes from Cork to Donegal. Strangely it is almost unknown in the south-east. Where it does occur, as in the Wicklow lakes, it grows with another acid-water specialist, Water Lobelia, *Lobelia dortmanna*. This species usually grows in shallow water, forming a dense mat of short, stubby leaves on the gravels between the larger rocks on lakeshores. In summer it puts up above the water tall racemes of pale lilac flowers.

Alternate Water-milfoil, *Myriophyllum alterniflorum*, and Floating Bur-reed, *Sparganium angustifolium*, can also cope with these starved conditions. The Water-milfoil is a submerged plant putting its flowering heads over the water only occasionally but this bur-reed can be spotted from a distance by its exceedingly long, narrow and floating leaves (up to 1 m) in these usually upland waters. Both species can occur in slightly more nutrient-rich conditions but their lowland relatives are seldom found in these upland waters.

A number of very narrow-leaved plants forming floating mats bobbing just below the surface can also be spotted in these areas. The commonest is usually the floating version of Bulbous Rush, *Juncus bulbosus*, but the rarer Floating Club-rush, *Eleogiton fluitans*, grows in a similar way. Both species can also grow and flower on exposed mud when water levels fall but can equally produce flowering heads, which arise from the mat of semi-submerged vegetation that could otherwise be easily overlooked. Some of these can also grow in bog pools and drains. A far more colourful species, Lesser Bladderwort, *Utricularia minor*, whose flowering stems bear a few pale yellow blossoms, also arises from a mat of submerged vegetation. It occurs naturally in base-poor pools, including bog holes and drains

WHITE WATER-LILY

White Water-lily is widespread in lakes and pools, especially in the north and west.

FLUCTUATING WATER LEVELS

The shallow margins of some lakes may dry out completely in summer, leaving only bare mud.
For some species this is a challenge and for others, with different life strategies, an opportunity.

associated with peat cuttings. In all these species the entire mat of leafy vegetation can rise and fall with the water levels and provides a floating platform from which the flowering stems rise.

Slender Naiad, *Najas flexilis*, is also an acid-water species. For many years it was thought to be exceedingly rare in Ireland, usually found washed up in the drift-line of small lakes. Recent sub-aqua investigations have shown it to be somewhat commoner. It is one of the small group of species that occurs in Ireland and Scotland and just about in England, but is widespread in North America.

However, there is a far more obvious North American species unknown in mainland Europe that occurs in many bog pools in Atlantic Ireland (and western Scotland), and is especially conspicuous in the Connemara area. This is Pipewort, *Eriocaulon aquaticum*, which produces tall, leafless stems arising from a matted perennial underwater rosette. These stems are surmounted with a little knob of densely-packed flowers.

In many upland areas reservoirs have been constructed by damming up the exit points of rivers in great natural valleys. These artificial lakes are of interest because they often present a bare lakeshore composed of silvery sand, especially in the draw-down zone – the area between the upper and lower water levels. In times of drought the water levels in these reservoirs fall and areas that are usually submerged are exposed to the air. Large tracts of muddy open ground are left uncovered and if drought persists many short-lived plants of natural muddy lakeshores can appear, at least for a season. These include Red Goosefoot, *Chenopodium rubrum*, Marsh Cudweed, *Gnaphalium uliginosum*, Water-pepper, *Persicaria hydropiper*, and its relative Small Water-pepper, *Persicaria minor*, as well as other usually annual species normally associated with wet muddy ground on poor soils. One of the most enduring species is Amphibious Bistort, *Persicaria amphibia*. This is an unusual species in that it can live both on land and in water. In lakes and ponds it produces large floating leaves and dense heads of pink flowers, but flowers less successfully on drier ground. Where the draw-down zone is narrower, a limited lakeshore flora develops, usually dominated by perennial species

AMPHIBIOUS BISTORT

Amphibious Bistort, a relative of many garden weeds, can have both dry ground and aquatic lifestyles. It is often abundant in the draw-down zone of lakes and reservoirs.

FLOODED WOODLAND

Where water levels have fallen in the past, trees and other emergent vegetation can become established on the exposed muds. When water levels rise again these areas give the impression of islands, sometimes with the trees emerging directly from the water.

more typical of marshy ground. However, most reservoirs have areas where submerged soils lie nearer the usual water surface and these are often worth checking out whenever levels fall. True aquatics are often surprisingly uncommon in these reservoirs and grow best in small sheltered coves.

One species that is very typical of the draw-down zone is Shoreweed, *Littorella uniflora*. This usually grows on the flooded margins of natural lakeshores and it normally comes into flower when water levels fall in summer. It is a relative of the Ribwort Plantain, *Plantago lanceolata,* of garden lawns. On the shores of natural lakes it comes suddenly into flower soon after the winter flooding subsides, in company with many other species that tolerate periodic inundation. On reservoir shores it can form dense mats of thick, almost cylindrical leaves, which are spongy when viewed in cross-section and lack partitioning. When in flower it is unmistakable, producing long stamens almost 2 cm in length, with the anther bobbing in the wind at the end of each. Another species with similar growth habits is Needle Spike-rush, *Eleocharis acicularis.* It too is a species of natural lakeshores and flowers rapidly once the waters recede. It is now beginning to appear in the draw-down zone of Irish reservoirs.

Many Irish lakes have been partly drained and their new lower levels regulated by weirs and small dams, resulting in the loss of the shoreline zone's structural diversity and characteristic mixture of ephemeral species. Consequently, perennial species can spread into the areas that would previously have been inundated. This is clearly beneficial for these usually taller and long-lived species but profoundly bad for the smaller and/or short-lived species of the innundated zone. Casual grazing can be beneficial here where cattle hoofs open up the sward and create small areas of open ground.

One most unusual landscape type – and hence habitat – largely characteristic of Ireland is the turlough. Turloughs are ephemeral lakes found mainly in the limestone areas of Clare and Galway. They receive their water from fissures and holes in the underlying substrate. In this way water can rapidly flood these areas and similarly be lost from them. The vegetation of these areas is to a large extent determined by levels of inundation and the differing abilities of various species to cope with the drastically-altering water regime. The levels of many shallow lakes can also fluctuate. Depending on the fall of the land and the local soils, this can result in large exposures of muddy or marly ground. On a small scale this provides habitat for the suite of these ephemeral lakeshore species. In landscapes where there is a large number of small lakes with different drainage characteristics, this can result in the retention of higher levels of biodiversity. Even if one lake and shore have a 'bad' year, there are others in the vicinity from which seed may spread or be transported by birds or even by water if the lakes are linked by rivers or streams. Many of the plants from these shores have seeds that can remain viable for many years and can germinate when the right sequence of environmental conditions recur.

Other plants may not be so lucky. One such is Irish Fleabane, *Inula salicina*, a perennial and one of our rarest native plants. It is of great interest as one of those species that grows in Ireland but not in Britain. It was known from a number of spots on the northern end of Lough Derg on the Shannon, where it grew in joints in the exposed limestone bedrock near the average waterline. Its decline has been attributed to eutrophication of the waters but

LESSER POND-SEDGE

Tussock-forming sedges can maintain themselves in areas where water levels fluctuate. Once established, they grow upwards. Collectively, species with this growth habit contribute to the gradual infilling of ponds and lakes.

also to the stabilisation of the lake levels following the construction of the Shannon hydro-electric dam. It looks like a small Elecampane, *Inula helenium*. Another species, from more or less the same area, mainly in the Shannon basin by Lough Derg and upriver by Lough Ree, is Water Germander, *Teucrium scordium*. This species is now rare in Britain but occurs in great quantity in the band where lakewater laps over pebbly, partly-vegetated ground. It is a robust little plant with pinkish-mauve flowers and wavy-edged leaves. It spreads by stolons, which may be a useful strategy if its ability to flower and set fruit is impaired by sudden summertime flooding. It seems to have coped better with the lake-level changes, helped by a low-growing habit that keeps a good deal of the plant living beyond and below the browse of cattle.

Lakes, especially those on the more fertile ground, which in Ireland usually means on limestone, can accumulate large quantities of silt washed in from upstream sources. Where this silt is not scoured out by the movement of water it settles and becomes colonised by the taller emergent plants of riversides. Many of these plants, such as Common Club-rush, *Schoenoplectus lacustris*, grow well in lake margins and rivers and can form huge stands spreading out into the lakes where the water is shallower. Where there are plenty of nutrients in the water a number of fairly widespread species appear. Yellow Water-lily, *Nuphar lutea*, is one of the most obvious and is much more at home in the calmer water of lakes than in faster-flowing rivers. In these shallow nutrient-rich waters other species that are favoured by these conditions also thrive. However, in recent years a number of alien species have also found these areas very suitable and their numbers have exploded. Curly Waterweed, *Lagarosiphon major*, an aquarist's plant, is one such species.

On the water surface tiny green discs of Common Duckweed, *Lemna minor*, are usually fairly common in sheltered areas. They can completely cover the surface of the water, especially where it is fairly nutrient-rich. A new species, even smaller Least Duckweed, *Lemna minuta*, has recently arrived in Ireland. Its initial discovery sites indicated that it was an introduction but it has since spread into other more natural habitats. There are three other native duckweeds. Fat Duckweed, *Lemna gibba*, does very well in nutrient-rich waters, and often forms an almost complete covering of the water's surface. Its fronds swell up on the underside, making the green discs tilt at an angle. A larger species, Greater Duckweed, *Spirodella polyrhiza*, has, as its specific name suggests, many roots. Both of these species can fluctuate very much in number. A pond covered in either for one year may have only a few plants the following year. All these species have circular fronds. A fifth species, Ivy-leaved Duckweed, *Lemna trisulca*, has narrow pointed fronds, often linked together, and usually occurs slightly below the surface of the water. Water Fern, *Azolla filiculoides*, was widely cultivated for garden ponds, where it covered the surface with a thick, chunky layer of clustered small green, floating leaves that become redder in autumn. It has been turning up in nutrient-rich lakewaters and canals recently.

Most of the lakeshores have large bands of tall emergent species, typically the large grasses such as Common Reed, *Phragmites australis*, Reed Canary-grass, *Phalaris arundinacea*, and sometimes Reed Sweet-grass, *Glyceria maxima*, as well as Bulrush, *Typha latifolia*, and Yellow Loosestrife, *Lysimachia vulgaris*. These usually take hold where there is abundant silting. However, in areas where silt does not accumulate,

YELLOW LOOSESTRIFE

Yellow Loosestrife is one of several tall and colourful species that grow on the margins of lakes and flooding rivers, where they stand above the altering water levels.

COMMON REED

Common Reed can cope with deeper water than most of the emergent species.

another group of species appears. These are mainly shorter species that are able to cope with fluctuating water levels once their roots and lower stems are kept wet. The most obvious of these is Water Horsetail, *Equisetum fluviatile*. This horsetail has a most unusual structure in that its stems are virtually hollow, almost like a straw. When it grows in shallow water it usually produces simple unbranched stems, which are usually about 60 cm tall. These stems have cones at the tips that produce spores rather than seeds and in this respect it is a relative of the ferns. On more transitional ground, such as swampy woodland, it can get much taller and produces numerous rings of long branches and begins to look like most other horsetails.

Another semi-emergent species of the shallower waters is Mare's-tail, *Hippuris vulgaris*. It has rings of leaves around its stems superficially resembling the whorls of horsetail branches. However, Mare's-tail is a proper flowering plant, although the flowers are not very obvious. They are formed at the base of the flat, narrow leaves and are usually only visible as anthers, there being virtually no proper petals produced. The flowers, such as they are, are borne on stems that emerge above the water's surface. Mare's-tail also produces large soft, floppy leaves on long, thick submerged stems. Another species with very different above and below-water leaves is Arrowhead, *Sagittaria sagittifolia*. The arrow-shaped leaves are unmistakable, as are the white flowers, but the underwater leaves are completely different, long strap-shaped structures. This species is usually found throughout the canal system and can still be encountered in lakes in the Midlands.

One of the more attractive plants of these shallow waters is Frogbit, *Hydrocharis morsus-ranae*. This is more often recognised by its leaf, which resembles a small greenish-brown lily-pad. This is a free-floating plant but the leaves are often seen settled on peaty mud when water levels fall in summer. It is still found in many of the lakes of the Midlands and north Midlands. It has white petals also grouped in threes, an arrangement characteristic of a number of other attractive flowering plants growing in the emergent zone. These all have three lilac-mauve petals with a small white eye. The most frequent of these is Water-plantain, *Alisma plantago-aquatica*. It has tall flowering stems that branch and branch again to form large inflorescences with hundreds of separate flowers. A closely-related species, Narrow-leaved Water-plantain, *Alisma lanceolatum*, grows in similar situations. Lesser-Water-plantain, *Baldellia ranunculoides*, is a less assertive species, lower growing and often with its leaves floating or held slightly above water. It is largely confined to shallow waters on the edge of lakes and pools and can also occur in recently-cut drains through fens and other lime-rich habitats. A fluctuating water level does not usually trouble species with these growth forms until it falls to the point where farm animals can graze down to them. When this happens, taller plants can be trampled or eaten. The edges of many winter-ponding areas throughout the country are by now grazed to the point where no waterside emergents survive.

Water plants are particularly vulnerable to the effects of eutrophication. Bad as these effects are in river systems, they can be even worse in smaller lakes. In warm weather the water levels fall, nutrient levels increase and algal growth proliferates. In recent years, the mix of plant species is gradually changing in many lakes. Species of clean water are challenged by those that thrive on nutrients. The vagaries of seasonal effects such as sunlight, leaf fall, turbidity and levels of run-off

COMMON REED

Dead stems of Common Reed washed up by winter flooding will be deposited and eventually recycled on the drift line of lakes and rivers.

Pondweed and Water Plantain

Two contrasting growth forms – the long-stalked floating leaves of true aquatics such as Pondweeds rise and fall with water levels while the emergent species like Water Plantain just grow and grow, keeping their leaves and future flowering stems well out of the water.

Bladderworts

Bladderworts are at their best in shallow water. They often flower in high summer just as water levels begin to fall.

all contribute to these enforced changes in the composition of the flora.

A number of rare native species have come under pressure from the usual sources – drainage, infilling of pools and a general increase in eutrophication. Coupled with this is the general standardisation of environmental conditions. For years, I had been fishing submerged leafy fragments of a bladderwort out of a peaty reservoir in Co. Kildare. One dry and sunny year, water levels fell and there were hundreds of plants of the species in flower, the submerged leaves having settled in the mud, the flowering stems standing upright and colourful. I have been back to the same site on many occasions. The submerged stems and leaves are still there but I have not seen it flower since.

Fens

I reland is well supplied with water and soils rich in lime. Rainwater may leave an area rapidly, in streams. In other cases the transit of water is much slower and exerts far more influence on the flora of the countryside. Instead of flowing over the ground, even intermittently, it percolates slowly through peats, raw gravels and soils. The rate is influenced by many factors, including the slope of the land, the depth of the soil and its capacity to retain water. Soil that is very large-grained (literally with more pores) sheds water much faster than soil with more fine-grained material. Similarly, deeper mature soils with higher levels of humus will retain moisture better than thin, dry, shallow soils.

Where water is released gradually it passes through the soil until it reaches bedrock. As it does, it is influenced by local soil chemistry. Base-poor water emerging from moorland areas may wind up in streams and runnels but a good deal of it will continue to pass through the soil. Where the land levels off, these underground waters will slow and form damp patches. If there is a dip in the land, small pools may form. In the course of moving from point of fall through soil to free movement in stream or river, water may stall many times, and pick up different soil chemicals at different stages of its passage. It may even form small pools, which may be transitory or semi-permanent. These flushed areas, where water, minute particles of silt and soil chemicals have moved slowly through the covering of earth and peat, will develop different qualities at different points in the landscape. The character of the plant species living at these different stages will reflect the nature of the soil beneath. Water will usually start off in a base-poor state but will become more base-rich as it moves onto lower levels. It also picks up nutrients. Usually on more upland ground, even in upland grassy pasture, the subterranean routes taken by moving water are indicated by the distribution of various species of rush. Sometimes the line of rushes is well-defined and seems to wind downhill as would a small stream, conforming to the slopes of the land. In other areas large dense stands of rushes indicate areas where the underground flow of water was arrested, having reached a level area or a band of

(LEFT TO RIGHT): OPPOSITE-LEAVED GOLDEN SAXIFRAGE, GREAT HORSETAIL AND YELLOW PIMPERNEL

Where springs issue from the ground, wet muddy conditions often ensue. On slightly shaded ground this becomes an ideal habitat for species such as Opposite-leaved Golden Saxifrage, Great Horsetail and Yellow Pimpernel, all of which grow on the margins of wet scrub and woodland.

impervious and often silty material. These areas are often churned up by cattle.

The most interesting botanical ground often occurs where water passes through these contrasting transitional zones – the area where the glacial drift thins out and gives way to moorland or on lower ground the interface between the more substantial esker ridges and adjoining raised bogs. These intermediate zones, though widespread, are seldom large in extent and are not easily found. They are often very narrow and their width can fluctuate from year to year depending on rainfall. Drainage operations on lower ground, often some distance away, can draw down the ambient water table by a few centimetres and wipe out rare species, especially smaller ones. Similarly, small

local drains can intercept the natural percolating water flow and re-route it into larger drains, water troughs and drinking ponds. These areas are often, therefore, at their best in late spring and early summer, just as they come into flower before being eaten or crushed.

Most of these percolation features are most easily observed in upland areas where natural vegetation survives better. It is a very different matter on lower ground. Here the soils are deeper and have been largely converted to pasture and tillage. An extensive system of land drains mops up most of the water that falls locally. Where these soils are exposed naturally, their lime-rich character becomes more evident. Over time some of the lime-rich material has been washed down into the lower horizons of the soil. Different layers of soil are sometimes revealed. This is most easily seen on the sides of recently-constructed motorways: mature soil with lots of roots and decayed plant material on top, bedrock at the bottom and soils with water oozing out in between. The sides of large rivers in the lowlands provide a natural example of these exposed layers. Where rivers have cut down through the glacial till, they create slopes. Depending on the local topography, which is in turn related to the disposition of bedrock and nature of glacial deposits, these slopes may be steep or gentle. Many of the steeper ones, unfit for farming, are left largely alone and have retained or reverted to scrub woodland. Water is often released onto these slopes and trickles down through the exposed and often lime-rich soils. Where enough light reaches the ground, these wooded wet areas often have Great Horsetail, *Equisetum telmateia*, Marsh Hawk's-beard, *Crepis paludosa*, Opposite-leaved Golden Saxifrage, *Chrysosplenium oppositifolium*, Ragged Robin, *Lychnis flos-cuculi*, and Yellow Pimpernel, *Lysimachia nemorum* – all of which present a very natural aspect. On bare muddy ground in these situations it is often possible to see detached flakes of calcium carbonate on the mud or forming nearby on the sides of rocks, fallen tree trunks and even on undecayed leaf litter, looking like limescale deposits from electric kettles.

However, where these features have developed in open sunnier ground, the flora is often spectacular. These flushed areas, especially when used only for light summer grazing, are characterised by a number of wetlands species that are often very rare in the hinterland. Even where light grazing has occurred, the flora is still of interest. In fact, in some instances some species are confined to open muddy areas where the ground has been poached. In these situations the mud is often a paler shade of brown, indicating the higher levels of lime in the soil.

RAGGED ROBIN (ABOVE AND BELOW)

The heavily-incised showy petals of Ragged Robin usually indicate the presence of other even more interesting but less obvious species.

One of the most recognisable species here is Common Butterwort, *Pinguicula vulgaris*. This has large rosettes of bright yellowish-green leaves clinging in a star shape to the bare muddy ground. It produces very unusually-shaped dark violet flowers, solitary at the end of flowering stalks about 10 cm high. The leaves feel oily to the touch and are equipped to trap small flies and other insects, which are ultimately assimilated into the plant's tissues as a form of supplementary nutrition. Flies trapped on the surface of the oily leaves are gradually dissolved over time and their dried-out legs, wings and body parts are visible on the leaves long after the more nutritious parts have been absorbed. Another plant very characteristic of this type of ground is Grass of Parnassus, *Parnassia palustris*. This is also a very conspicuous species in late summer, with a large single flower atop a flowering stalk 15 cm or more tall and a disproportionately small leaf at the base of the stem. It is difficult to spot in early summer. No such difficulty attaches to another member of this group of species, Bog Pimpernel, *Anagallis tenella*. It is a low-growing plant, with most of its growing stems crawling over bare mud and thin vegetation. It comes into flower in early summer, often forming great masses of pale pink flowers. It is especially common in areas where the ground water seems to issue from the soil. There are other species that are associated with these areas, such as Knotted Pearlwort, *Sagina nodosa*, Brookweed, *Samolus valerandi*, Few-flowered Spike-rush, *Eleocharis quinqueflora*, Lesser Clubmoss, *Selaginella selaginoides*, Marsh Lousewort, *Pedicularis palustris*, Fragrant Orchid, *Gymnadenia conopsea*, Marsh Helleborine, *Epipactis palustris*, and Variegated Horsetail, *Equisetum variegatum*.

This list of species is similar to that of dune slacks, and in many ways the two habitats are similar, both requiring lime-rich but low-nutrient conditions. Water that has travelled for a long distance above and below ground may have acquired many additional nutrients along the way. When this happens, even if the structural attributes of the slope seem favourable, the flora will be more typical of river valley flood plains and be less interesting. On the other hand, waters that have originated nearer the point of exit from the ground may have high levels of calcium carbonate but may carry fewer nutrients and, therefore, support this more unusual combination of plant species.

COMMON BUTTERWORT

Common Butterwort, a species of true fens and lime-rich wetlands, has basal rosettes of leaves covered with an oily substance. Small flies are trapped on its leaves and are gradually absorbed by the plant.

GRASS OF PARNASSUS

Grass of Parnassus is typical of lime-rich wetlands and was once widespread. It has become much rarer in recent times following the gradual lowering of the water table and the subsequent loss of wetland habitats.

COLT'S-FOOT

Colt's-foot frequently colonises bare areas on slopes where water pressure has caused soil to slump outwards. It has also colonised many types of dry, sandy wasteground.

Percolating water, charged with calcium carbonate, can often be seen dripping off the face of low cliffs by the sea. This happens typically where the burden of boulder clay or even blown sea-sand rests on exposed bedrock a little above the high tide mark. There is usually a fairly clear distinction between the two materials. Ground water that has been moving slowly through the lower parts of the soil meets bedrock, is unable to travel down any further and, therefore, follows the fall of the bedrock itself. Eventually the water emerges into the open air when it meets the coast and drips down the face of the cliff. White-staining deposits on the rocks and even on some of the plants indicate the course taken by these lime-rich waters. A few species can grow in this almost soil-less environment. One of the most consistent is Brookweed and there is often a smaller species, Slender Club-rush, *Isolepis cernua*, growing out of cracks in the rocks. Brookweed, which grows in fens and other lime-rich ground inland and not just at the sea, is able to cope with conditions that are clearly far too salty for many non-coastal species. Furthermore it is rooted in very shallow soils trapped in the jointing of the exposed bedrock, even in situations where it must be lapped by the higher tides.

Where these percolating waters continue to flush through the boulder clay and over the coastal rocks, they modify the trapped salt marsh vegetation that sometimes forms a little lower down the shore. They can even influence the salt marsh vegetation that sometimes lies between the point of emergence of the freshwater and the upper levels of the salty tides. In these areas the saline influences are reduced, allowing a number of rarer species to occur. A good example is Strawberry Clover, *Trifolium fragiferum*, which often grows where freshwater passes through shallow soils near the coast. Percolating and emerging ground waters

are also found where other coastal species such as Parsley Water-dropwort, *Oenanthe lachenalii*, and Wild Celery, *Apium graveolens*, are found. These species are usually present at the upper levels on salt marshes and are seldom inundated for any great length of time by the sea. The supply of freshwater further reduces the saline influence in these areas and allows these and other species to grow well in these rather specialised areas.

On the coast the effects of ground water are often very obvious. After extended periods of rain a large volume of water builds up in the soil, usually escaping via drains, streams and rivers. However, where water builds up behind the earthen cliffs resting on bedrock, they become so saturated that they collapse outward onto the shore, taking with them soil, loose boulders and vegetation from higher up the cliff. These slumping features are especially common where the bedrock is near the level of the shore, where the base of the earthen cliffs is undercut by wave action. These areas of loose collapsed soil will vegetate gradually but most, being of unconsolidated material, are swept away. However, where these slumpages have survived, a flora develops that is reminiscent of some inland flushed and fen situations. Common Butterwort, Lesser Clubmoss and Black Bog-rush, *Schoenus nigricans*, can all occur where ground water has continued to flow and wave action has not washed these features away. Counterparts of this phenomenon can sometimes be identified inland, in very steep river valleys, where fallen material is eventually washed away by the river. In both of these situations Great Horsetail often indicates the line where the waters originally emerged, joined by Hemp-agrimony, *Eupatorium cannabinum*, and Colt's-foot, *Tussilago farfara*.

In inland situations where there is an abundance of calcium carbonate in the soil, it is

TORMENTIL

Tormentil is a species with a wide ecological amplitude, being able to grow in a variety of habitats ranging from heathlands to lime-rich damp soils.

sometimes transported, concentrated and deposited along a series of small but related emergence points. Often these areas are covered up by taller vegetation, especially in the absence of grazing, and characterised by slightly harder terrain, which feels crunchy underfoot. On examination, the ground will be seen to be composed of creamy-white material, crispy rough and brittle to the touch, where lime has either been deposited directly onto solid material such as pebbles, or has been assimilated by certain mosses and charophytes. These areas usually indicate that a spring head or seepage line is present nearby.

Many of the species mentioned above are also encountered in midland fens. True fens are formed on peat, not the acid rainfall-dependent peats of the raised bogs, but the ground-water peats that preceded their formation in large depressions in the lowland landscape. Many fenny lakeshores also support these species, especially in lime-rich areas. Here, even if there is a little more nutrient available than usual, the heavier grasses are restrained by lingering flood waters of previous winters so the surrounding vegetation is usually thinner. It, therefore, includes more species than grow on the deeper, better drained, often grazed soils higher up on the lakeshore. Where ground waters percolate down from higher ground through grassland onto these lakeshores many extra species can be found, especially when the water table is high and there is a continuity of water supply through the summer months. The flora of the wetter areas above lakeshores again depends on the characteristics of the flush. Gently percolating waters moving across lime-rich soils contribute to greater species diversity. One of the most obvious fen plants is Meadow Thistle, *Cirsium dissectum*. This is an unusual-looking thistle because it generally has a single almost leafless tall stem clothed with whitish hairs. The leaves, almost all basal, are not as prickly as the dry-ground thistles and have a dense pile of white felt on the underside. This often grows with Black Bog-rush, which forms large tufts rising above the surface of the fen. Fen Bedstraw, *Galium uliginosum*, is usually common in more open ground but is also able to scramble up over other vegetation, despite its delicate growth. Eyebrights are not robust plants and Scottish Eyebright, *Euphrasia scottica*, is one of the most delicate. It grows up from the area between the tussocks of the larger species with the appearance of a plant struggling to get up to the light. These larger tussocks comprise a microhabitat in their own right. Sometimes these can be quite tall and their upper layers are so far distant from the lime-rich ground water that they provide habitat for some of the species more normally found in raised bogs such as Cross-leaved heath, *Erica tetralix*, and even Ling, *Calluna vulgaris*, as well as a number of less ecologically-pigeonholed species such as Tormentil, *Potentilla erecta*.

In areas where a mixture of fen peat and wet mineral soils abut onto each other, a number of usually taller species grow. Blunt-flowered Rush, *Juncus subnodulosus*, and Black Bog-rush are usually fairly prominent. In some of the larger fens there are systems of upwelling springs usually indicated by the presence of bare patches of muddy ground where a number of species such as Few-flowered Spike-rush, Bog Pimpernel and Broad-leaved Cotton-grass, *Eriophorum latifolium*, occur. This last species resembles the much commoner Bog Cotton, *E. angustifolium*, but has much wider and paler green leaves and conspicuous blackish scales in the inflorescence. The rare Intermediate Bladder-wort, *Utricularia intermedia*, often occurs on these open muddy areas, its tiny leaves spread out on the mud and other stems with tiny bladders for trapping minute invertebrates submerged in the watery mud. It flowers very rarely in Ireland. Where these upwelling springs have not been damaged, low mounds of lime-rich material builds up, vegetated by a number of rare or ecologically-significant mosses. From a distance these mounds look like accumulations of mosses formed in a dome. However, the core of the dome is usually quite solid, being composed almost entirely of calcium carbonate re-deposited either directly or through plant growth processes. This solid material is referred to as tufa and is a very important indicator of the continued or former presence of very rare ground-water conditions.

Many inland areas are not rich in calcium carbonate but are flushed by ground water, bringing about a fairly obvious enhancement of the local flora. A number of species are fairly tolerant of a wide range of flushed conditions. They are quite common in base-rich areas but can also occur in more base-poor environments. Widespread species include Water Mint, *Mentha aquatica*, Lesser Spearwort, *Ranunculus flammula*, and Marsh-bedstraw, *Galium palustre*. Fen-type vegetation also occurs around the edges of raised bogs where the ground water, which is usually rich in lime,

GREAT WILLOWHERB

Great Willowherb is one of the species that can grow within taller fen vegetation. It often forms extensive stands, competing successfully with more robust-looking species.

comes into contact with peats of various sorts. This results in a very mixed pattern of vegetation with base-rich and base-poor, dry and wet influences, operating at close quarters. Where pools and drains have been dug the pattern becomes even more complicated.

One of the most spectacular plants of taller fen communities is Saw Sedge, *Cladium mariscus.* This is a very large plant with long leaves with sharply serrated edges that can cut the skin of humans. It can form huge stands where little else can grow, with the exception of Great Willowherb, *Epilobium hirsutum,* and the even taller Common Reed, *Phragmites australis.*

When left to their own devices, fens may gradually develop into a particular type of scrub woodland. Drainage and grazing have usually prevented it from happening. Fragments of this type of vegetation are to be found around many lakes and on bog margins where agriculture is not feasible. As well as the usual swamp woodland species here, Alder Buckthorn, *Frangula alnus,* Common Buckthorn, *Rhamnus catharticus,* Guelder-rose, *Viburnum opulus,* and Bog Myrtle, *Myrica gale,* occur. Alder Buckthorn is usually found in these situations as isolated small trees although it can occur commonly on much drier ground elsewhere. Common Buckthorn and Guelder-rose are often found in wet woodland and even in hedgerows where roads and causeways pass through former wetland areas. Bog Myrtle is an interesting and more widespread species. Its leaves and buds release an aromatic fragrance. It is a low shrub and grows typically on the edges of former raised bogs where they interfaced with mineral soils. Many other interesting species will also be encountered with it and many small-scale ecological puzzles will be presented. There are many examples of species with contrasting habitat

BOG MYRTLE

Bog Myrtle is a low-growing shrub that has aromatic leaves, which give off their scent if rubbed. It grows on the edges of bog and fens, often forming small natural shrubberies where grazing is absent.

allegiances growing closely together. The two louseworts Marsh Lousewort, usually in fens, and Lousewort, *Pedicularis sylvatica*, usually on more acid soils, can be found within a few metres of each other, and other species familiar from the dune slacks such as Marsh Pennywort, *Hydrocotyle vulgaris*, and Devil's-bit Scabious, *Succisa pratensis*, grow commonly with species from much more acid soils. Ground water rich in lime still continues to flow into the depressions in which the fens and bogs originally formed. The interaction with the various types of peat, wet or dry, exposed or 'reclaimed', has created a number of fragmented habitats that still contain many botanical surprises.

Heath

Heathland vegetation is typically dominated by low-growing shrubs. It forms on shallow non-productive soils, usually over acid bedrock. It can occur on relatively flat free-draining ground or on dry scree slopes. Many of the heathland soils that have developed *in situ* are peaty and low in nutrients. Although they have usually formed in areas of high rainfall, the water normally runs off quickly. Growth rates are very slow here and many of the dwarf shrubs, though small, can live longer than some tree species. Ling, *Calluna vulgaris*, when allowed to mature, can reach 20–30 years old. The low levels of agricultural productivity of these soils have meant that they have not been heavily grazed. However, various price-support mechanisms rendered some of these areas economically viable though not ecologically sustainable. As a result, some grazed heaths have now become species-poor grassland.

IRISH HEATHLANDS

Irish heathlands are of great interest because they have a number of heather species that are rare or unknown in Britain.

IRISH HEATH AND GORSE

Irish Heath forms large tall stands and flowers early in the year on rocky ground in the west, often at the same time as Furze (Gorse).

LING (LEFT) WTH BELL HEATHER

The reddish-purple flowers of Bell Heather contrast with the paler blossoms of Ling. Both are typical species of dry heathland and form a dense cover of vegetation, which occasionally goes on fire to restart the colonisation process. Bell Heather is the species that most characterises dry heathland in Ireland. It forms dense carpets of purple flowers in summer and early autumn, often growing and flowering with Western Gorse.

Heathland is usually a very dry habitat, especially in summer, and as a result fires often break out. The leaves of Ling and other species do not break down readily and there is, therefore, an abundance of inflammable material lying on the ground beneath the dwarf shrubs. The main species that characterise Irish dwarf heathland are Western Gorse, *Ulex gallii*, and Bell Heather, *Erica cinerea*, with Ling. Western Gorse is a widespread species in Ireland. It seldom gets as tall as (European) Gorse, *Ulex europaeus*, and flowers mainly in autumn,

unlike European Gorse, which begins to flower very early in the year. Furze can often occur on deeper pockets of soil in heathland areas and it is sometimes difficult to distinguish a large well-grown Western Gorse from a young or stunted Furze. The shallow, dry soils tend to inhibit taller trees and although birch seedlings can get established they are usually killed off again by burning, at least in the driest areas. Even when rain falls, the water is retained in the upper layers of the peaty soils and when the sun shines this evaporates quickly. Most of the species have adaptations that enable them to cope with extended periods of drought. The most obvious strategy is to produce narrow leaves, which reduce water loss. This feature is shared by all the major heathers and is taken to an extreme in the case of the two Gorse species where the leaves are modified to sharp spines.

All of these species have a high woody content and can burn very easily once a fire has started. In high summer they can burn so vigorously that nearby housing is occasionally threatened. Planned burning to stimulate new growth is still a feature of heathland management. Following a burning incident, large areas of heathland may be left entirely devoid of vegetation for several months. This can be seen in the vegetation for many years afterwards. There is often a distinct boundary between a large stand of mature Ling, flowering well but with its stems and branches spreading out or falling back to the ground, and the contrasting adjoining stands of younger plants, also flowering only 10–20 cm high with branches held erect. The species associated with these different burning episodes give us an insight into the way in which the vegetation recovers after fire. However, even in the autumn after a burn, some plants begin to germinate and by spring a number of fast-growing annuals have already started to grow. As is usual in open unvegetated areas, the annuals come in first. Sheep's Sorrel, *Rumex acetosella*, and Heath Groundsel, *Senecio sylvaticus*, appear fairly rapidly. The Heath Groundsel looks quite like the garden groundsel but is covered with a dense clothing of sticky hairs and glands, which release a resinous scent. The plant can be spotted even from a distance because sand, grit and feathered seeds are trapped by the sticky glands. Sheep's Sorrel colonises rapidly and can even mature in the same year as the burn took place. Seedlings of Ling, which germinates rapidly on open peat but much less successfully under dense cover, will also be found. In spring unusual seedlings with three-lobed leaves like a shamrock may be seen on the otherwise bare peat. These are likely to be the very young leaves of Western Gorse or even European Gorse, utterly different from the prickly spiny leaves that either species will produce later in life.

Annual plants can get through their life cycle fairly quickly, often in a few months, and are not troubled later by excessive drought. Long-lived perennials like English Stonecrop, *Sedum anglicum*, have a succulent strategy. This species lives on the bare rocks scattered through the heathland with its roots insinuated in tiny cracks. It soaks up whatever rain falls and stores it in the leaves like so many species from arid parts. The soil on these rocks is even more shallow, often only present where blown grit, sand and even ash has accumulated. A few species find their base here, especially where some of the local soil rides up onto the side of the rocks. A good example is Heath Bedstraw, *Galium saxatile*, a relation of the Goose-grass of our hedgerows, but much smaller. This, along with Tormentil, *Potentilla erecta*, Heath Speedwell, *Veronica officinalis*, and Heath Milkwort, *Polygala serpyllifolia*, will spread out from these isolated rocks. These small rocks, protruding through the peat, get very warm in summer and support a group of small short-lived grasses. Two of these, Early Hair-grass, *Aira praecox*, and Silver Hair-grass, *Aira caryophyllea*, are annuals and are particularly abundant here and are often joined by a much taller perennial species, Wavy Hair-grass, *Deschampsia flexuosa*. All three have very fine leaves and shallow rooting systems, can cope with very arid conditions and manage to exist in circumstances where many other plants cannot survive.

GOLDEN-ROD

Golden-rod grows best on open sloping ground beside trackways running through heathland, especially near the coast. However, it can occur commonly on shallower soils and on rocks on open woodland.

One of the most successful rare species in these burnt-ground situations is Climbing Corydalis, *Ceratocapnos claviculata*. Though not a widespread species, Climbing Corydalis can often be found where scrubby heathland reverting to scrub has been burned. An annual, it germinates early in the year, and its stems climb up over the burnt-back stems of scrub and produce small creamy-yellow flowers in spring.

In the west of Ireland one other amazing species appears often abundantly on heathland. This is St Dabeoc's heath, *Daboecia cantabrica*. It is very common throughout large sections of Galway and Mayo on rough heathland. It has large bell-shaped flowers and is one of the small group of plants that occur in the west of Ireland, but not in Britain, and also appears in the Iberian Peninsula.

Despite its fairly uniform cover of dry-ground vegetation, wet areas occur within heathland. Sometimes there are with natural depressions in the bedrock, sometimes in areas that have been quarried, and there are always watercourses, above or below ground. In summer some of these watercourses appear entirely dry but can be recognised by the presence of deep-rooting rushes or even by the way in which the leaves of some of the softer grasses have been washed and flattened by flash flooding. In winter some of these watercourses can become small streams and the existing vegetation often shows signs of having been swept by water running over rock. Loose peat can be washed by rain and also by wind and deposited some distance from its point of origin. One or two species track this, one of the more obvious being Lousewort, *Pedicularis sylvatica*, which sometimes seems to be growing on bare peat, in contrast to its more usual wetter moorland habitats. Some of this material will accumulate in depressions in the otherwise shallow-soil landscape

BOG ASPHODEL

Bog Asphodel indicates areas of wet heathland and
moorland. However, it is often at its best on boggy ground.

Burnet rose (above) and Spring Squill (below)

Coastal heathlands are often characterised by the presence of Burnet Rose. In more open grassy situations, Spring Squill is a colourful springtime feature of many promontories where shallow soils predominate.

and form deeper peaty soils with intermittent supplies of rainwater. Because they are formed in depressions, these soils are likely to stay in place longer and retain their water more effectively.

Topography determines where water will flow, where nutrients will travel and where more mature soils will begin to form. The wetter areas are less likely to be burned and even if they are, they recover quickly. In these situations the dry heathland loses its character and can become more like other habitat types. In some areas Bracken, *Pteridium aquilinum*, takes over and overtops the heathland vegetation, shading it out. On slopes and even on old broken-down dry-stone walls, Bilberry, *Vaccinium myrtillus*, grows well along with Hard Fern, *Blechnum spicant*, and here trees such as Birch and Mountain Ash thrive. There is one species of willow often found here. Eared Willow, *Salix aurita*, is usually a low-growing tree, 2–3 m high with ash-grey small wrinkled leaves. Many of these species can also be encountered on the margins of lowland raised bogs and also in sheltered areas in moorland. Where water accumulates, pools and shallow muddy areas introduce additional structural diversity into heathland. Various wetland margin species of base-poor ground appear such as Marsh Speedwell, *Veronica scutellata*, and Marsh Violet, *Viola palustris*. The presence of Round-leaved Sundew, *Drosera rotundifolia*, Bog Asphodel, *Narthecium ossifragum*, and various species of Sphagnum moss recall the species that occur around the edges of bog pools in raised bogs.

At much higher elevations, well above the (former) tree line, combinations of wind and high rainfall greatly restrict the number of plants that can grow. Soils are exceptionally thin and the sloping ground is usually quite free-draining. The soil, such as it is, is mixed with shallowly-bedded fragments of bedrock. In many cases the erosion of the former covering of peat has now exposed solid bedrock. There is little here to retain rainwater. In these wind-swept areas, Fir clubmoss,

KIDNEY VETCH

Kidney Vetch usually occurs as a yellow-flowered plant but in some coastal areas it has cream-coloured petals.

Huperzia selago, and Alpine clubmoss, *Diapasiastrum alpinum*, are often striking components of the vegetation. In the east of Ireland these are limited to higher ground but in the north-west they can come close to sea level. Indeed, Fir clubmoss is a component of certain types of raised bog vegetation in parts of the Midlands. On the mountain tops they grow with a number of very low-growing, narrow-leaved grasses that can withstand the constant exposure. They are joined by an extremely tough rush, Heath Rush, *Juncus squarrosus*, which has a dense leaf-mat and produces strong wiry flowering stems that can endure the strongest winds. In very natural upland habitats Bearberry, *Arcostaphylos uva-ursi*, clings to the ground. In crevices in exposed

bedrock, Dwarf Willow, *Salix herbacea*, manages to survive.

It comes as some surprise, therefore, that the same Heath Rush and a grass from the uplands, Mat-grass, *Nardus stricta*, are present in a number of lowland grassy situations. This has come about where long-established free-draining grassland has been both leached and heavily grazed for many years, such as the Curragh grasslands in Co. Kildare. Both of these species are locally common on this low-lying ground but grow within sight of the Wicklow Mountains, where they are abundant on higher ground.

Sometimes a heath-like vegetation forms over limestone bedrock. This occurs particularly in the west of Ireland where heavy rainfall has leached out much of the available calcium carbonate from the soil, which is often thin enough in the first place. This results in unusual combinations of lime-loving and lime-intolerant species growing in close proximity. Though ecologically perplexing, these areas are very interesting since they contain large numbers of species in quite small areas. As well as Ling and Bell Heather, these areas also support other low-growing woody species such as Burnet Rose, *Rosa spinossisima*, and, more rarely, Bearberry and also Crowberry, *Empetrum nigrum.*

Sometimes the covering of glacial drift that envelopes much of lowland Ireland thins out. In many parts of the east coast the acid rocks are covered by some of this material and results in a soil that contains a mixture of peaty and mineral material. The very colourful Spring Squill, *Scilla verna*, comes into flower here from April, looking like a miniature version of its close relative Bluebell. It grows with plants often found in coastal grassland, such as Kidney Vetch, *Anthyllis vulneraria.* It is abundant on many of the heathy semi-natural grasslands on headlands along the coast. Even after it has gone out of flower its dark fruits can be found lying about on the grass as the stems and leaves die back.

Pathways cut through the heathland create steep trackside banks and here a number of herbaceous species such as Golden-rod, *Solidago virgaurea*, Sheep's-bit, *Jasione montana*, and Slender St John's-wort, *Hypericum pulchrum*, grow well. These exposed banks are constantly eroding and seldom become heavily vegetated. Therefore these and other outwardly non-competitive species can maintain themselves in more open conditions where they are less likely to

be engulfed by larger plants. Rarer species of this open, often stony habitat include the annuals Small Cudweed, *Filago minima*, and Common Cudweed, *Filago vulgaris.* Both of these require open ground conditions. Rarer still are Heath Cudweed, *Gnaphalium sylvaticum*, and Sand Spurrey, *Spergularia rubra.* Their most natural habitat is open areas in heathland and there are old records for many of these from stone quarries and walls, where they occur in the thin skin of moss that forms on the top of low dry-stone walls. They are sometimes found on open gravelly ground beside forestry tracks, where they seem to have spread from natural populations nearby. They may also have been spread in soil on the wheels of heavy forestry machinery moving from one area to another. Many of these species flourish for a few years as long as the habitat is open, but gradually they are shaded out by encroaching, more robust vegetation.

In recent years surviving heathlands have come under constant threat from invasion by Rhododendron, *Rhododendron ponticum*, especially in the areas where water lingers. The cessation of burning, accidental or otherwise, in some areas has led to a gradual reversion to scrub or light woodland. When burning occurs, Rosebay Willowherb, *Chamerion angustifolium*, invades rapidly, initially in slightly damper areas. It can totally engulf and shade the sides of many of the watercourses that wind their way through the heathland. Overgrazing has damaged many heathland areas and converted much of the marginal ground to grassland, resulting in the decline of many ecologically-restricted species and their replacement by much commoner ones.

SHEEP'S BIT

Sheep's-bit is widespread on shallow acid soils growing on rocks and open tracksides through heathland. It can even grow on leached dunes and is often found on walls. It avoids limestone soils.

RHODODENDRON

Rhododendrons first invaded our native woodlands and are now beginning to spread into other habitats such as blanket bogs and heathland. Very little can grow in the shade cast by their dense leathery leaves.

Bogs

Bogs develop in areas where water-logging has greatly curtailed the rates at which plant material such as leaves, twigs and stems decay. As a result, there is a gradual build-up of dead and slowly-decaying vegetable matter. The easiest way to observe this is to examine a recently-exposed turf bank from one of the 'raised bogs' of the Midlands. At the top there is a layer of living material, including mosses, heathers, some sedges and grasses. Directly beneath, a layer of very spongy turf is formed, loose and crumbling, composed mostly of dead Sphagnum moss and roots. Further down the profile, the material is denser and even from a distance will be seen to contain preserved

BLANKET BOG

The peaty deposits of upland Ireland have been exploited for peat, though not to the same extent as those of the midland bogs.

fragments of tree bark and twigs embedded in the older peat. Various layers with different colours and textures can be discerned. These layers correspond to different phases of colonisation by different types of vegetation and are in effect a vertical cross-section of the bog's history.

Living bogs are usually characterised by the abundance of Sphagnum mosses that grow actively and abundantly on the surface. These mosses are extraordinary plants and are able to absorb water many times their own weight. There are many Sphagnum species, some of which are characteristic of different types of bog. The individual species with their respective ecological requirements contribute hugely to the manner in which different bogs have formed.

A handful of this peaty material, taken from the face of the bog and teased out in a bowl of water, will reveal many other plant and animal remains such as seeds, leaves, stems of plants and sometimes even the preserved wing-cases of beetles. Fruits, especially of sedges and pondweeds, are particularly useful as they often have characteristic features that preserve well and can be compared with more recently-grown specimens for identification purposes. The occurrence of these preserved fragments and their position in the environmental timeline gives an indication of the relative stages at which different environmental conditions prevailed.

The material is best examined when it is taken fresh from the face of the bog. Material that has dried, such as sods of turf, is difficult to re-hydrate although the twigs and roots are very visible. Examination of the material with a hand lens will even reveal the presence of mosses, often with the leaves still intact. With a microscope it is possible to see the cells in the leaves, remarkably preserved. Bog historians are also able to extract and examine

the pollen of plants, which is often preserved in abundance within the peat where it fell thousands of years ago. Researches of this sort have made it possible to trace the way in which the vegetation at a site has changed over time and helps us understand the current growth processes in a bog.

The lowest layers contain remains of plants associated with lime-rich and nutrient-rich conditions. Over time these plants gave way to species more typical of neutral ground water. Eventually acid-ground species came to the fore as the growing bog gradually lost contact with ground water sources and became more dependent on rainfall.

In certain instances, especially towards the margins of the bogs, drainage ditches are several metres deep. It is then sometimes possible to see the white marly material that underlies many bogs. It is like putty when taken from a freshly-exposed surface and contains the visible shells of water snail species that lived in the lime-rich waters of the site thousands of years earlier.

In the past many raised bogs would have had a wet area, usually towards their centre. Here the influence of the underlying base-rich waters had not been completely lost. These features have almost all disappeared by now as a result of drainage operations, leading to the subsidence of the bogs themselves. When a bog is very wet, the water imparts a degree of buoyancy to the dead and living vegetation. This is why living bogs have a bouncy water-bed feeling. When the water is drained off, the bog surface is lowered, becomes hard, dry and increasingly dominated by Ling, *Calluna vulgaris,* which can cope with the dryness.

The peats that are thus preserved, their energy locked up for thousands of years, have been used in Ireland and elsewhere as fuel, harvested and stacked manually as 'turf' sods for generations.

BOG ROSEMARY

Bog Rosemary is an early-flowering member of the Heather family. It is particularly associated with raised bogs, where it is visited by spring-flying butterflies and other insects.

More recently, industrial-scale peat extraction has produced milled peat, used as fuel in power stations, for the production of peat briquettes or sold in bags as 'peat moss' for horticulture.

There are usually considered to be three different broad types of bog in Ireland. Raised bogs are most widespread in the Midlands. Mountain (upland) blanket bog is mainly in areas of impeded drainage on higher ground and lowland blanket bog occurs mainly in the west but usually at lower altitudes.

Raised Bogs

Raised bogs are the main type of bog over most of lowland Ireland. Most of these bogs have been heavily exploited for fuel and other purposes and many have lost most of their natural vegetation. They formed initially in lake basins, which gradually became vegetated and eventually filled in with mixtures of silt, plant and animal remains. The ground water would originally have been rich in minerals but over time the vegetation altered. A succession of wetland plants with progressively less dependence on the lime-rich ground waters would have developed on a site. Over time these plants were replaced by others even less dependent to the point where eventually the species living currently on the bog receive virtually all their water from the rain. The vegetation of the bog continues to grow and gradually builds up to form a dome of peat crowned with a living layer of bog plants. There is very little nutrient input and little in the way of recycling of fallen leaves and dead plants. Many bogs are now not actively growing and many wetland species have disappeared locally.

A walk across an undamaged raised bog can be a fascinating exercise. The soft, wet ground is covered with shallow pools often filled with Sphagnum mosses. It is easy to forget that there is usually no solid bedrock or soil here and that the entire feature – with the exception of the living layer – is made almost entirely from the accumulated remains of dead vegetation. Usually the bog has been cut along the margin and, therefore, it is necessary to find a safe way around the steep exposed faces that often have deep and dangerous waterlogged areas to the front. Once up on the growing surface, it becomes possible to envisage the extent to which the bog has grown vertically by looking back at the starting point. A glance in the opposite direction may indicate that there is another rise and a walk of several hundred metres before the highest point of the bog dome is reached. Towards the top of the dome, evidence of former pools may be seen and in some areas there may still be sufficient open water to maintain an aquatic flora. More often all that now remains is a series of dried-out depressions.

Bog vegetation was occasionally set afire to kill off the old Ling and stimulate new growth. If the bog has remained unburnt for some years, both the ground and even some of the living bushes will be covered with various species of lichen, particularly of the genus *Cladonia*. These include the familiar Pixie-cup lichens with bright red tips but there are many other species. Once burning has taken place, many of these lichens are destroyed. Similarly, various mounds of Sphagnum mosses, which constitute a specialised habitat for a small number of liverworts and some rare invertebrates, are wiped out and take many years to recover.

Drainage ditches now cut through most of the main raised bogs but bogs take a long time to die fully. There is an order in which the species die off, shallow pool-dwellers first, followed by other deeper-rooted wetland species. The areas nearest the cuts still retain some water and, therefore, hold on to some of the more interesting wetland plants.

Away from the drains, the dry surfaces of many raised bogs are nowadays dominated by Ling. Here and there in the surviving bog pools and drain-edges some of the more enduring bog plants can survive a little longer. Cross-leaved Heath, *Erica tetralix*, usually the most conspicuous other species, has pink bell-shaped flowers and narrow leaves covered with tiny hairs. Another member of the heather family is Bog Rosemary, *Andromeda polifolia*. It flowers relatively early in the year, before the other heathers have begun to bloom. Round-leaved Sundew, *Drosera rotundifolia*, is usually still to be found commonly, but in many of the dried-out bogs in eastern Ireland even this common species can be hard to find away from the drains. In most of the wetter areas Bog Asphodel, *Narthecium ossifragum*, is still to be found, joined by White Beak-sedge, *Rhynchospora alba*, and 'Bog Cotton' or Common Cottongrass, *Eriophorum angustifolium*. Another related species of Bog Cotton, Hare's-tail Cottongrass, *Eriophorum vaginatum*, often occurs out on the bog surface on drier terrain. It forms

ROUND-LEAVED SUNDEW

Living raised bogs support an abundance of Sphagnum mosses, usually accompanied by Round-leaved Sundew.

BOG ASPHODEL

In wetter parts of the bog, by drains and abandoned bog pools, Bog Asphodel maintains a presence, long after many of the rarer species have been lost.

Bog Cotton, officially Common Cottongrass, can form dense stands, often where the bog has been cut away.

dense tufts with hundreds of leaves arranged like long pins in a pincushion, with the familiar tuft of cotton formed into a single unit at the top of the flowering stem. Bog Cotton has a similar but larger and more diffuse white tuft, composed of three or more distinct clusters. In less damaged bogs and especially further west the bog flora is often richer. The Great Sundew, *Drosera anglica*, and Cranberry, *Vaccinium oxycoccus*, are commoner and Brown Beak-sedge, *Rhynchospora fusca*, is more frequent in some of the wetter bogs.

The faces of many of the smaller bogs are being exploited by bucket-diggers that excavate the peat and form it into cylindrical shapes, and cut these into sod-shapes as they lie on the ground. In this way even quite small bogs are losing their flora with only the most ubiquitous and tolerant species persisting. Where they were originally cut by hand and where each turf cutter worked his own bank, the ground was often organised in distinct rectangular sections, which re-flooded after abandonment. The waters are gradually recolonised by a few aquatic species, especially Lesser Bladderwort, *Utricularia minor*, Bogbean, *Menyanthes trifoliata*, Marsh Cinquefoil, *Potentilla palustris*, and an acid-ground pondweed, Bog Pondweed, *Potamogeton polygonifolius*.

BOGBEAN

Bogbean can colonise the wet pools left behind after turf-cutting has been abandoned and in time will contribute to their infilling.

HARE'S-TAIL COTTONGRASS

Hare's-tail Cottongrass forms distinct tussocks on bogland. It has a single terminal spikelet contrasting with that of Common Cottongrass, which has two or more spikelets and is hence generally larger.

MARSH CINQUEFOIL

The spent flowers of Marsh Cinquefoil present a sinister appearance in autumn as the seeds ripen. It colonises bog pools and also occurs beside runnels through living bogs.

The edges of many dried-out raised bogs have by now been invaded by Birch, usually Downy Birch, *Betula pubescens*, and Bracken, *Pteridium aquilinum*. However, in some of the deeper, shadier and now almost dry drainage cuts a number of acid-ground ferns can be found. As well as relatively common species such as Hard Fern, *Blechnum spicant*, and Broad Buckler-fern, *Dryopteris dilatata*, large stands of a rarer species, Narrow Buckler-fern, *Dryopteris carthusiana*, can grow well. Bilberry, *Vaccinium myrtillus*, grows successfully on the sides of these drains and as an understory shrub in the birch woods.

One of the more bizarre non-native species to have become established in Irish bogs is a North American species of Pitcher Plant, *Sarracinea purpurea*. This species and a few others were planted on Irish bogs many years ago. Most colonies died out but some have endured and, more seriously, have now been discovered in areas where they were almost certainly not planted. The usual other invasive species such as Rosebay Willowherb, *Chamerion angustifolium*, and more recently Rhododendrons are now also encroaching on the margins of bogs.

In some areas the raised bog has either grown out or slumped out over the adjoining mineral soils. This makes for an unusual mixture of habitats, which are often more species-rich than the adjoining bogland. If there is sufficient water available and if grazing levels are low, then a sort of heathery grassland often appears with species from a wide range of habitats, including fen and marsh growing close to typical raised bog species.

By now many of the largest bogs have been totally worked out by mechanical cutting to the point where the lowest parts of the exploitable peat meet the underlying marly subsoil. From a distance these spots can be identified by their paler colour.

BRACKEN

The unfolding fronds of Bracken indicate the approach of spring. On the dried-out edges of bogs Bracken has now taken hold, creating a form of shelter for species that would otherwise not be able to grow in these areas.

In some areas a sort of semi-natural recolonisation, comprising a very eclectic combination of species, is taking place, dictated to some extent by the species that survive in the hinterland. In the short-term, some nearby drains are colonised with unusual combinations of wetland plant species, lime-haters and lovers alike, bringing a little variety to an otherwise 'brown desert'.

Upland blanket bog develops on the slopes and plateaus of mountains where the better mineral soils of the lowlands and valleys thin out. These upland bogs are covered with various types of wet peatland and many Sphagnum mosses. Some of this peatland has been cut – usually by hand on a small scale – resulting in the formation of bog holes, deep drains leading nowhere and even small isolated ponds. Large-scale peat extraction is almost impossible here. Where rainfall is very high and the underlying bedrock is gently concave, long-since filled-in lakes occur. These may be peaty in character but with dense coverings of scraw-like vegetation or accumulations of deep peat.

These boggy moorland areas are often bleak and treeless, maintained in this condition by extensive sheep grazing and burning, interacting with colder and harsher, wetter environmental conditions. A botanist could spend a great deal of effort and not discover many plants of interest. Having found all the main species, the best approach is to search for variations in the habitat. A quick glance at the Ordnance Survey Discovery Map of the area will show small trickles of water. Where they are bridged or culverted there is often access to the more interesting areas of boggy moorland upstream. Even when there is no water evident on the map, sudden bends on the road with corresponding variations in the contour lines usually indicate potential areas of different habitat.

The vegetation of these areas includes many species from the raised bog such as Round-leaved Sundew, Ling and Cross-leaved Heath. However, Purple Moor-grass, *Molinia cerulea*, is much commoner here than on raised bogs. One of the more obvious relatively large plants is Green-ribbed Sedge, *Carex binervis*, whose flowering stems can often be a metre high. There is one species of orchid that occurs in moorland and seldom elsewhere. This is Lesser Twayblade, *Neottia cordata*, which comes into flower in late spring. It usually lives on mossy ground under Ling, is only about 5 cm tall, has pale greenish-brown features and is, therefore, often overlooked. Higher ground may have Crowberry, *Empetrum nigrum*, and Bilberry, *Vaccinium myrtillus*.

Before the mountain areas had become covered with mossy and boggy vegetation, rainwater would have run off rapidly, gathering in the dips of the bedrock. Rain continues to fall but nowadays it must make its way through the covering of vegetation, peat and fragmented sand and gravel covering the bedrock. The main areas of interest are usually where there are evident watercourses working through the bogs. These can normally be spotted by the presence of rushes and other vegetation clearly following a meandering course determined by the contours of the underlying bedrock. These water movements are like very slow-moving streams nudging their way through the peat and indeed often join other similar flows eventually to form small streams. This ongoing movement of water leads to a translocation of nutrients, which then become concentrated along the sides of the watercourse. Where these watercourses intersect with open hard surfaces such as forest trails or when they run alongside moorland tracks, they make contact with deeper mineral soils and here the vegetation becomes very different. Many species recorded from moorland habitats are in fact often associated with these flushed areas. Species such as Marsh St John's-wort, *Hypericum elodes*, Pale Butterwort, *Pinguicula lusitanica*, the legally-protected Bog Orchid, *Hammarbya paludosa*, Marsh Violet, *Viola palustris*, and Lemon-scented Fern, *Oreopteris limbosperma*, will appear along these mossy trickles and minor drains. This is especially evident when the water moving off the moorlands begins to make contact with glacial drift on the lower slopes. In areas with more soil, other species, several of which would appear in fens and even on Midland lake-margins, may appear. These include Black Bog-rush, *Schoenus nigricans*, Lesser Clubmoss, *Selaginella selaginoides*, Round-leaved Crowfoot, *Ranunculus omiophyllus*, and Lesser Skullcap, *Scutellaria minor*. However, the mix of species depends very much on local soil conditions and many other interacting environmental factors.

LESSER BLADDERWORT

In acid-water bog pools Lesser Bladderwort flowers. The submerged leaves are equipped with tiny bladders that trap minute water invertebrates, thus supplementing their diet in nutritionally-challenged conditions.

Lowland Western Blanket Bogs

Lowland blanket bogs constitute a very special element of the Irish landscape. They cover great low-lying areas of the west of Ireland and are particularly well developed in areas where annual rainfall levels are not only high but distributed throughout the year. While this has a depressing effect on sun-loving plants and animals, a number of plants do particularly well here. Chief among these are the bryophytes – the mosses and liverworts, the latter being the most spectacular feature of many of the western bogs, especially near open pools and flushes.

As in other bog types, there is a build-up of bog mosses and other vegetation due to slow rates of decay on waterlogged soil. In common with mountain blanket bog, they have formed on acid mineral surfaces rather than in substantial water bodies. The flora contains several species that are common to many peat and wet heath formations. They share a number of species with those of wet heathy habitats such as Lousewort, *Pedicularis sylvatica*, Heath Milkwort, *Polygala serpyllifolia*, and Tormentil, *Potentilla erecta*. Even slightly higher ground will have dry heath and heathery vegetation intermingling with species from much wetter ground. These plants are common to various types and states of blanket bog, reflecting the broad tolerances of a number of species that can all grow in these very nutrient-poor conditions.

LOUSEWORT

Lousewort occurs commonly on the bogs and moorlands and in these areas is often one of the few flowering plants that actually produces something that looks like a proper flower.

A number of rarer plants should be watched out for here, especially the rarer sundews, Oblong-leaved Sundew, *Drosera intermedia*, on more open, wet, peaty ground and Great Sundew, *Drosera anglica*, in wetter areas, along with both Bog-sedge, *Carex limosa*.

Local flushing occurs and adds an extra ecological dimension as well as extra species. A case in point is Black Bog-rush. Though usually a species of lime-rich fens, lakeshores and coastal flushes, this species occurs widely with blanket bog systems in the west and has stimulated much debate as to the factors that govern its distribution.

SUNDEWS (ABOVE AND RIGHT)

All three Irish species of Sundew occur in various types of bogland. They have leaves densely covered with sticky glands that trap insects. The bigger species can catch quite large insects – even damselflies.

It also occurs on flushed areas in upland mountain bogs along with Pale Butterwort and other species that signal increased nutrients. Blanket bogs are usually much shallower than their raised bog counterparts. Where they have formed on gently sloping ground they are in closer contact with underlying bedrock, as is the water that percolates through them. Where dips in the bedrock occur, deeper peat forms. Where these dips are deep enough, pools or even small lakes form. The area between the open water and the surrounding bog is often less heavily vegetated and here bladderworts can also be found along with other less competitive species. Depending on the pattern of glacial deposits, the nature of the bedrock, the character of water supply (intermittent, flowing, percolating) and of land use of the area, many interesting variations in the flora can occur. By watching for slight changes in the landscape, noting where the water flows and gathers above or below ground and by spotting changes in the colours of the vegetation, extra species will be found and new insights gleaned from the landscape.

MARSH ST JOHN'S-WORT

Marsh St John's-wort fares best where water running off mountain slopes gathers in flatter areas. Its densely-hairy perennial leaves make it recognisable long after the petals have fallen.

Dry Grasslands

Grass grows well in Ireland. Rainfall levels are relatively high and are distributed through the year. Temperatures are relatively uniform with little in the way of extreme cold or heat. The growing season for grass runs for about nine months of the year, a reality that can be confirmed by any lawn enthusiast. Deep, mature, well-developed lime-rich soils especially in the lowlands are particularly suitable for grassland production. On good grazing land the water table is at an appropriate level, growth continues, land is not poached by cattle nor does it dry out in summer. All of these factors are good for grazing. Where there is a surplus, grass can be dried as hay or preserved as silage to be eaten by overwintering cattle. Grass for silage can be cut more than once a year. To stimulate growth, extra fertiliser is applied. To increase agricultural productivity further certain strains of particular species, especially Rye Grass, *Lolium perenne*, and White Clover, *Trifolium repens*, are grown. These species are selected because they produce large quantities of nutrient-rich herbage. A few of the most resilient low-growing natural grassland species can survive here. Taller native species and those with more specialised ecological requirements have no chance.

From a distance the lush green covering may suggest a habitat of environmental richness but nothing could be further from the truth. It was not always like this. Survey data accumulated on the distribution of plants show a historical landscape with many more grassland species present than occur nowadays in the same areas. By the end of the nineteenth century many of the pastoral areas had already lost many grassland species.

This dearth of species must have been due in no small part to the extent of tillage in the years preceding these botanical surveys. The notorious potato famines indicate the dependence of a huge population, largely tenant farmers, on a single species of food plant. The distribution of lazy beds (broad potato ridges), whose remains are still visible on higher ground and poorer soil, testifies to the extent of tillage in areas where today only sheep graze. However, even well before the major famine, the percentage of land in tillage even in the eighteenth century was comparatively high. When the potato crops failed and failed again, the social structures of the countryside also changed. The number of very small farms decreased as the patterns of agriculture altered in the face of a declining population. Gradually former tenants became landowners. Pasture increased, a phenomenon that continued for many more years, but the nature of the soil had been altered. The amount of long-established permanent grassland, maintained in that state by light grazing since the removal of the woodlands, must have been very small in some areas. Land that had been tilled, ploughed, harrowed and possibly even weeded did not acquire native grassland species simply because a crop of grass seed had been sown. Recent trends in grassland husbandry have been even more inimical to the survival of the grassland flora. Fertilisers boost the growth of agricultural strains of nutritious grasses and clovers, out-competing many of the smaller and less aggressive grassland species. Cattle are much heavier and with additional food supplements become even heavier. They eat more and cause more compaction of the soil through their constant trampling.

Given these factors, it is not surprising that good quality natural species-rich grassland is such a rarity now. Indeed, most of our best areas of natural grassland are by now really confined to areas of agriculturally-marginal ground on steep slopes, on various types of rocky ground inland or near the coast, or on the margins of wetlands and river valleys. In their different ways these habitats sustain the remnants of the natural flora, a flora whose species tell us a great deal about the underlying soil conditions. It is not always easy to spot these areas of biodiversity interest from low-lying vantage points. However, from higher ground or with the aid of aerial photographs it is possible to identify some. Whether with the naked eye or with binoculars, the simplest guide is the changing colour of the vegetation. Ignore the rich green areas and watch for slightly sloping ground with a paler yellowish-green covering of grasses and more colourful flowering plants. These areas are often more free-draining and because they are sloped, at least on the south-facing side, the sun's rays will warm up the soil more effectively than it does the level ground nearby. Slightly reddish-brown vegetation may indicate the presence of Purple Moor-grass, *Molinia cerulea*, and with it an assemblage of species that prefers wetter conditions.

There are a number of areas where fragments of the original grassland flora survive. Small old churches were often built on rising ground, especially in the Midlands. The adjoining churchyards, especially those with associated graveyards, were often developed long before the advent of fertilisers and herbicides. They have often been cared for in a way that allows natural grassland flora to survive. The grass is cut, the clippings are taken away and the flowers appear year after year. The grasslands in these churchyards often feel springy when walked on due to the large amount of grassland mosses that have also survived. Sometimes the surrounding stonework and tombstones, which indicate local stone, also carry coverings of lichens, the dates on the tombstones indicating when they became established.

The Midlands of Ireland are traversed by winding ridges of gravels known as eskers. The word esker crops up in place names in many parts of Ireland. The main dry route through ancient Ireland from east to west was via the Eiscir Riada, which ran as a sequence of ridges through the bogs and swamps of the central plain. These gravel ridges formed under the ice sheets, where they were deposited by glacial melt-water. They are composed of loose material, sand, gravel, pebbles and larger pieces of rock that have been smoothed around the edges, rather like stones on a sea shore but not to the same extent. These esker ridges can be quite steep and because of their sandy composition can become very dry in summer. They have often been cut into for sand and gravel. Where this has happened it is usually possible to examine the exposed earth profile. At the upper parts of these features the covering of proper mature soil is usually very thin, often less than 30 cm, below which there is little living material, rather a dense mound of relatively inert sand, gravel and boulders. There is little humic material here to retain water. Rainwater runs off quickly and deep-rooted, nutrient-demanding species are at a disadvantage. Less robust species with lower nutrient demands thrive, once the grassland has not been heavily fertilised and grazed. Moraines, terminal or lateral, and other glacial depositional features have covered much of the lowlands with rich free-draining soils. Another important depositional glacial feature in grassland areas is the drumlin. The term is incorporated into many place names especially in the north of Ireland, but drumlin landscapes are also a major landscape in parts of the west and south-west. They consist of low hills, usually with a long gradual slope on one side and a much shorter and steeper one on the other. These areas are usually heavily grazed, are not rich enough in lime or sufficiently free-draining to support a typical Midlands lime-loving flora and tend to become heathy in the drier areas.

GENTIANS (ABOVE RIGHT) AND LADY'S-MANTLE (RIGHT)

Dry grassland is becoming much rarer and, as a result, many of our most colourful species are disappearing at a local level from many areas. The formerly widespread Field Gentian and Autumn Gentian are in decline and the various species of Lady's-mantle are similarly suffering.

COWSLIP

Cowslip was once widespread in lime-rich pastures and still occurs
on roadside verges and on shallow soils over limestone.

(LEFT TO RIGHT): BLACK MEDICK, DOVE'S-FOOT CRANE'S-BILL AND MEADOW VETCHLING

Dry, well-drained, lime-rich sandy soils support a diverse flora of generally common species such as Black Medick, Dove's-foot Crane's-bill and Meadow Vetchling. These species prefer sunny situations and all have spread onto roadside verges and other dry-ground situations such as abandoned sandpits and even urban waste ground.

Grassland species did well in the Midlands, not only on the true well-defined eskers, but also on many other free-draining sunny soils, which would have had similar properties as far as the plants were concerned. Cowslips, *Primula veris*, Pyramidal Orchid, *Anacamptis pyramidalis*, Green-winged Orchid, *Anacamptis morio*, Centaury, *Centaurium erythraea*, Autumn Gentian, *Gentianella amarella*, and various species of Lady's-mantle, *Alchemilla*, turn up in the less-damaged areas. One of the rarest of Irish violets, Hairy Violet, *Viola hirta*, occurred and still does in some of these sites as well as in a number of sand dune grasslands in the east of Ireland. Many of these are often to be found close to stands of Furze where grazing pressure is less. Some of these species also grew, and still do, on thin, shallow grassland formed over isolated limestone outcrops. It is sometimes difficult to decide whether the habitat is thin, shallow grassland over bedrock or protruding bedrock with pockets of soil covering the depressions. In both cases the rock is near the surface and the soil is shallow, warm and free-draining. A number of common species grow here, including Black Medick, *Medicago lupulina*, Dove's-foot Crane's-bill, *Geranium molle*, and Meadow Vetchling, *Lathyrus pratensis*. Autumn Ladies-tresses, *Spiranthes spiralis*, is also one of the rare orchid species that turns up on limestone-rich outcrops as well as sand dunes.

Undamaged pastures still survive, showing where some of these plants once grew. There are botanical clues in the landscape, mostly low-growing species that can survive grazing.

LADY'S BEDSTRAW (ABOVE) AND MARJORAM (BELOW)

Both Lady's Bedstraw and Marjoram are typical of very well-drained sunny soils. They and many other similar species are extremely sensitive to heavy grazing and are now more often encountered, therefore, on roadside verges, where they cling on.

Tormentil, *Potentilla erecta*, Bulbous Buttercup, *Ranunculus bulbosus*, Lesser Hawkbit, *Leontodon saxatilis*, Spring-sedge, *Carex caryophyllea*, Field Wood-rush, *Luzula campestris*, and indeed Cowslip all have a lot of their biomass concentrated close to the ground and can persist in lime-rich pastures once the grassland is not ploughed up. Three widespread grasses should be watched out for, Crested Dog's-tail, *Cynosuros cristatus*, Downy Oat-grass, *Avenula pubescens*, and Yellow Oat-grass, *Trisetum flavescens*, which looks like a miniature version of the former grass. Another very distinct species is Quaking-grass, *Briza media*. Until recently, some larger tracts of grass have been maintained as unimproved lawns, seldom if ever fertilised, especially around large institutional buildings. Because of this it is sometimes possible to find some of these species even in built-up areas, where sheep and cattle have not grazed for many years.

Another group of herbaceous species of these free-draining lime-rich soils is far more sensitive to grazing, mainly because they are taller and so get eaten. These usually occur where land has been fenced off near the steeper edges of sandpits. In heavily-grazed terrain there is often a gap of about a metre where some of these species find a sort of refuge, although most can manage almost as well on some of the ungrazed roadside verges nearby. From a distance the blue flowers of Knapweed, *Centaurea nigra*, and Field Scabious, *Knautia arvensis*, and the yellow petals of Lady's Bedstraw, *Galium verum*, and Bird's-foot Trefoil, *Lotus corniculatus*, are evident and where these can occur other species also cling on. Ox-eye Daisy, *Leucanthemum vulgare*, Rough Hawkbit, *Leontodon hispidus*, Marjoram, *Origanum vulgare*, Wild Carrot, *Daucus carota*, Carline Thistle, *Carlina vulgaris*, Salad Burnet, *Sanguisorba minor*, Kidney Vetch, *Anthyllis vulneraria*, Yellow-wort, *Blackstonia perfoliata*, various Eyebrights and occasionally Greater Knapweed, *Centaurea scabiosa*, occur in very thin grassland and also on more open ground within the sandpits. One of the most enduring species in the face of heavy sheep grazing, despite its upright stature, is Burnet Saxifrage, *Pimpinella saxifraga*.

Many of these species also occur on railway sidings and embankments where the track has cut through gravel ridges. These features are in a sense similar to motorway cuttings, although they have by now usually been colonised by heavier perennial grasses and even scrub, which reduces the number of colourful herbs. These railway sidings often provide a selection of sites in different stages of recolonisation. Sometimes the vegetation has been sprayed with poisons or burnt and the colonisation process, at least by annuals, is to some extent then reactivated.

Open ground in gravel ridges is a very special habitat. Where sandpits have been dug and abandoned there is a limited time-window before they become colonised. If left alone, a natural succession of species ensues, annuals preceding perennials, herbaceous perennials preceding scrub. This sequence can take many years and directions, a process extended by the low nutrient levels of the remaining gravels, which at least fails to encourage the most nutrient-demanding species. In addition, within the gravel quarries various exposed sandy faces become recolonised at different rates. Little piles of worked sand will acquire their own dry-

OX-EYE DAISY

Ox-eye Daisy flourishes where lime-rich grassland has been cleared and a species-depleted type of vegetation struggles to recover the lost ground. It also occurs in quantity on various other nutrient-poor soils.

Where dry lime-rich grassland is allowed to grow properly it presents an amazing array of colourful species – Marjoram, Common Knapweed, Wild Carrot, Yellow-rattle and many more.

ground species. Flat compacted areas nearer the water table will flood intermittently and support a short-lived and transitory land flora in the interim. These areas where the water table fluctuates above or below the floor of the sandpit are usually recognised in dry weather by a combination of Silverweed, *Potentilla anserina*, with its long runners spreading over the bottom of the pit, and various dried-up mosses looking long dead but reviving in the next shower.

In many areas this was the natural ecological progression and it was possible to visit some of these abandoned sandpits over time and study the process of recolonisation. The open, crumbling faces of these excavations are often hotter and drier in summer. These habitats are quite rare in the landscape and are inhabited by a number of our rare dry-ground annuals, which require dry, lime-rich, loose, open sandy ground – a combination of factors no longer common in the Irish landscape. Two legally-protected species, Red Hemp-nettle, *Galeopsis angustifolia*, and Basil Thyme, *Clinopodium acinos*, are nowadays largely confined to this type of habitat. In the past some of these species were also found in cornfields, but that was before selective herbicides and high-production agriculture. These are species that occur fairly early on in the colonisation sequence. Bee Orchid, *Ophrys apifera*, Mountain Everlasting, *Antennaria dioica*, Mouse-eared hawkweed, *Pilosella officinarum*, and Thyme, *Thymus polytrichus*, appear, especially where there are large quantities of pebbles in the ground or where the sands have been lightly leached. The heavy perennial vegetation takes time to get established on these nutrient-poor soils and that gives these in open ground space and time. In the interim, Creeping Cinquefoil, *Potentilla reptans*, like its relative Silverweed, extends its runners far over the open

KIDNEY VETCH

Unusual colour variations of Kidney Vetch occur especially near the coast. On some coastal headlands the cream-coloured form is predominant instead of the more usual yellow forms.

EYEBRIGHT (ABOVE) AND GREATER KNAPWEED (ABOVE RIGHT)

When left unploughed and unfertilised, lime-rich grassland contains many surprises. A number of different species of Eyebright live in these conditions. Where grazing levels are low, Greater Knapweed forms large, almost herbaceous-border standard clumps.

ground, sets new plants, and to some extent consolidates the loose sand over which it spreads.

Many of these species also occur in sand dune systems and here find sufficient points of environmental similarity. Some also turn up on roadside verges where the road has been cut through gravel ridges. Others, especially those with no close association with the coast, may have occurred on natural sandy exposures, such as in steep river cuttings through glacial drift, and made their way subsequently into gravel-pit country. As the colonisation sequence continues, rare shrubs

such as Sweet-briar, *Rosa rubiginosa*, appear where grazing has been excluded.

Many of these sandpits do not last long and in many instances the transition from open sandy annual communities to closed scrub is never completed. At one stage gravel would have been drawn by the cartload from a gravel pit as occasion demanded. This meant that there was a degree of ongoing disturbance that allowed many annual communities to continue. Plants could mature, flower and set enough seed to allow the next generation to succeed. Modern extraction methods

Mountain Everlasting

Mountain Everlasting is frequent on shallow soils over limestone rocks and can also grow on screes and leached sand dunes.

Wild Thyme

Wild Thyme is common in older leached dunes. If sniffed, its leaves do indeed smell of thyme. It also grows on shallow soils over various rock types in inland situations.

with mechanised diggers and large gravel trucks mean that gravel ridges in pasture can be identified, excavated fully, levelled off and restored to a form of thin grassland in less than a decade. The rates of gravel extraction and landscape 'restoration' are so rapid that most of the rarer species are not able to become established even if they do occur in the vicinity.

Many of the smaller gravel pits are maintained in a semi-open state and used as feeding areas for cattle. This results in major inputs of cow dung into nutrient-poor systems, promoting the growth of large coarse vegetation such as nettles and docks and the steady killing off of the annual communities. A further indignity is heaped on some of these areas by their use as landfill. In these situations, not only are the rarer species engulfed with various types of dry filling and domestic waste but also with the unwanted contents of various gardens, including the usual crop of subjects ejected because of their invasive tendencies. They carry on invading in these rare habitats resulting in the occurrence of bizarre combinations of species, native and invader, in some of these sites.

Where lime-rich grassland sits atop low sea cliffs a thin band of usually ungrazed vegetation survives. This is generally quite distinct from coastal grassland and lacks most of the salt-tolerant species usually only encountered by the coast. The normal indicative species are present, Field

AGRICULTURAL GRASSLAND

Most agricultural grassland is unsuitable for lime-rich grassland species. A few species such as Ribwort Plantain and various sorrels can cope up to a point but there is usually little here to interest the field botanist.

Scabious, Knapweed and Bird's-foot Trefoil, but this is often a good place for Pale Flax, *Linum bienne*. Wild Flax was once a widely-recorded species in thin grassland in the east and south-east and still occurs in such situations rarely. However, it also turns up on the coast in ungrazed and dry and lime-rich situations. It is the wrong shape to last long in modern pastureland.

Another very rare habitat occurs near the sea and contains a number of our rarest native clovers. This is a sort of thin grassland that has formed over very shallow soils, often less than 1 cm in depth. It can be found where very thinly-vegetated soils, sometimes with a lime-rich component, grade into heathy grassland. The extreme shallowness of the soil and its low productivity have rendered it unsuitable for normal grazing. Rabbits are the main herbivores. The main danger to these rare communities is from encroaching Brambles, *Rubus fruticosus* agg., Furze, *Ulex europaeus*, and Bracken, *Pteridium aquilinum*. Even though these species cannot root and spread in the exceedingly shallow soils, they can become established in deeper pockets of soil nearby. Brambles are particularly invasive and a single bush can throw out rooting stems a metre or two in all directions in one season, engulfing other smaller species in a few years.

These very rare habitats have usually developed on sunny, well-drained situations. They are, therefore, usually encountered close to the sea, although the rare species they support are not in themselves necessarily salt-loving. The main species here are a group of clovers, Bird's-foot, *Ornithopus perpusillus*, Rough Clover, *Trifolium scabrum*, Knotted Clover, *T. striatum*, Clustered Clover, *T. glomeratum*, Bird's-foot Trefoil, *Lotus corniculatus*, and Hairy Bird's-foot Trefoil, *Lotus subbiflorus*. Despite their rarity these species have held on better than many other species of more agriculturally-suitable ground. As a group they are more or less limited to rocky often peninsular ground from Cork to Down, although Knotted Clover gets around as far as Kerry on limestone rocks near the sea. Even if these rare clovers are not present, other uncommon species sometimes occur, most of which are winter annuals and best looked for between April and June. After seeding they shrivel up and become very hard to find.

The best grasslands survive, therefore, in agriculturally-marginal situations. Infertile soils are not sufficiently exploitable to be economically viable. This is most evident on higher ground and on free-draining base-poor ground in the lowlands. On higher ground in Ireland most upland grassland is acid, due to the character and nature of the underlying bedrock. Not only is the soil shallower and less productive it is also dry, at least on the steeper slopes – ideal ground for sheep. Botanical indicators of acid soils and grassland are by now more easily found on roadside verges and tumble-down dry-stone walls where the sheep cannot get. Sheep's Bit, *Jasione montana*, Sheep's Sorrel, *Rumex acetosella*, Foxglove, *Digitalis purpurea*, Slender St John's-wort, *Hypericum pulchrum*, and Wood Sage, *Teucrium scorodonia*, are mostly tall-growing species and so would have difficulty surviving in sheep country. Where the soil gets even thinner in the pasture, Ling, *Calluna vulgaris*, begins to appear. This is usually the most grazing-tolerant of the taller woody dwarf shrubs and can tough it out much longer than most herbaceous perennials.

In a small area on the borders of Dublin, Wicklow and Kildare, one of our most interesting species was once plentiful. This is the Mountain Pansy, *Viola lutea*. Its typical ground was on very thin grassland soils over shales, at the upper limits of the glacial drift. Here the soils were leached, becoming slightly acid and lightly grazed. It even grew among Ling and Western Gorse, *Ulex gallii*. It resembles a very large-flowered form of the

MILKWORTS

Where the lime-rich soils give way to more acid ground the species-mix changes, Common Milkwort yielding to Heath Milkwort on the more heathery ground.

pansy that occurs commonly in sand dunes. It can still be found in these areas but usually occurs now on dry-stone walls partly covered with heathy vegetation. The populations have declined seriously in recent years. There are curious pockets of large-flowered pansies in some of the sandhills in Clare that may also be this species. Two other native violets from the acid grassland to heathland transition zone have similarly declined. Heath Dog-violet, *Viola canina*, and the much rarer Pale Dog-violet, *Viola lactea*, like Mountain Pansy, are ascending herbaceous perennials of open ground and are, therefore, very sensitive to sheep grazing. Heath Dog-violet is still present in sand dunes, especially in ungrazed leached systems. These and many other species with growth forms that render them susceptible to grazing are again caught in an environmental pincers: too much grazing and they are eaten; too little grazing and the open, mixed heathy-grassy ground conditions they require are lost to encroaching Bracken, Brambles and resurgent Gorse.

On slightly higher ground the effects of the drift are greatly reduced and most of the grassland presents a heathy character. Many plants of heathland begin to appear, including Heath Rush, *Juncus squarrosus*, Pill Sedge, *Carex pilulifera*, Heath Bedstraw, *Galium saxatile*, and Heath Speedwell, *Veronica officinalis*, as well as many species from other acid habitats. As the soil becomes more heathy and acid, Lousewort, *Pedicularis sylvatica*, appears and the milkwort here is usually Heath Milkwort, *Polygala serpyllifolia*. Where gentians occur they are usually Field Gentian, *Gentianella campestris*. In the grassy/heathy interface ground where grazing is discouraged, usually because of the presence of Furze, Bitter-vetch, *Lathyrus linifolius*, and Moonwort, *Botrychium lunaria*, can be found occasionally. These three species are suffering the same fate as the heathy-ground violets. A very distinctive grass, Mat-grass, *Nardus stricta*, and Heath Wood-rush, *Luzula multiflora*, are much commoner than first appears, usually because they have their upper parts browsed off. Very often these areas can have surprisingly large numbers of species present, but the intensity of grazing prevents them from flowering. Field botany here is often a hands and knees job, searching for ground that has – for whatever reason – not been grazed. Usually the nearby roadside verge is more productive and easier to work. There are unusual areas where some of this type of ground can be accessed more easily. One such is the Curragh of Kildare and to a lesser extent on the Great Heath of Maryborough (Portlaoise). Although the area is best known for horse-racing, it is a huge expanse of open sheep pasture. The gravelly soils here are deep and heavily leached and upland acid-grassland species such as Mat-grass, Purple Moor-grass and Heath Rush occur in large patches. In other nearby areas of the Curragh, where soils are formed into low, ungrazed gravel ridges, many species from more lime-rich conditions occur. It is when we are presented with unusual combinations of species growing at close quarters in unlikely situations that we are given the opportunity to gain a better under-standing of the real habitat and environmental preferences of individual species.

Wet Grassland and Marshy Ground

Rainwater that gets into a runnel, stream or small river moves on, taking with it silt, soil chemicals and finely-powdered sandy gravel. Depending on topography, the water may move at different speeds – swift in the upper sections of rivers, sluggish in the lower courses. On flatter and more level ground the river may meander and be joined by tributaries as it winds its way towards the sea. These areas are often subject to flooding and the flood plains are often rich in nutrients brought down from higher ground. The water table can be fairly close to the surface and there are often drains positioned to take off the excess water that may have accumulated in winter or been deposited by sudden floods. Because these areas are very fertile – and despite their propensity to flooding – they are often used for summer grazing. Grass grows lushly here.

The extent of flooding in these areas can often be visualised from the local bridges. Examine the tall emergent grasses or the lower branches of the willows and alders that fringe the riverside. If water has lingered for any length of time, there will be mud stains on the stems of some of the taller grasses, especially Reed Canary-grass, *Phalaris arundinacea*. This species is very tolerant of fluctuating water levels and these muddy markers give an indication of the height of flooding. Now visualise the river valley flooded to that height. To the sides of the valley it is usually possible to spot a corresponding line of debris, leaves, twigs and more domestic rubbish forming a drift-line on the ground where the flood plain meets the rising land. All the land below this mark may be episodically inundated. This is reflected in the flora. However, within a flood plain there

MARSH

Marshlands flourish in the absence of intense grazing, revealing an amazing range of species. However, with no grazing, willow scrub gradually encroaches.

are many variations in the local flora, which relate to local topography, land-use history and the nature of the surrounding soils.

River valleys were and still are managed for grassland production and grazing. Hundreds of years of grazing have maintained a dense, lush sward composed in the main of common grass species along with a few low-growing perennial herbs. Taller plants do not do well in well-maintained pastures. In less intensely-grazed river valleys things are more interesting, botanically.

The botanical boundaries between marsh, meadow and flood plain are not always clear. The term meadow is applied to land that has been traditionally used for grazing and the production of hay, but often refers particularly to low-lying grassland near rivers and lakes. Marshes are usually too wet for normal agriculture and often remain waterlogged even in summer. There are considerable overlaps here indicating the relative balance of grasses versus so-called 'flowering' plants. This contrast is very evident in drumlin country. At the top of a slope there may be almost acid grassland. Further down the vegetation becomes more mixed and near the base of the slope in the area that floods in winter, there is a band of

Marshy ground is best visited in late spring before most of its plants have been grazed by cattle.

mixed vegetation comprising sedges, rushes and various taller broad-leaved species. Similar progressive alterations in the species mix can be observed on ground sloping down to a river.

A few large widespread species are particularly characteristic of flooded river valleys. The most obvious are Yellow Iris, *Iris pseudacorus*, Soft Rush, *Juncus effusus*, and Reed Canary-grass. Bare patches where water lingers usually have Creeping Bent, *Agrostis stolonifera*, and Great Willowherb, *Epilobium hirsutum*. A large sedge, Lesser Pond-sedge, *Carex acutiformis*, often indicates the presence of former pools or even ox-bows (wet

areas left behind where the river changed its course or was diverted). These are all fairly large nutrient-demanding species with well-developed rooting systems that can track the fluctuating water levels in the soil. They are often accompanied by Meadowsweet, *Filipendula ulmaria*, and Purple Loosestrife, *Lythrum salicaria*. These can tolerate some short-term flooding and usually occur in fairly strong stands, visible from a distance. Although water seldom moves through these sections other than during flooding episodes, these former river lines lie substantially nearer the water table and often hold additional species. Branched

(LEFT TO RIGHT): SOFT RUSH, MEADOWSWEET AND LOOSESTRIFE

Soft Rush, Meadowsweet and Purple Loosestrife are all tall species of marshy ground, all well able to tolerate fluctuating water levels because of their deep rooting systems.

Bur-reed, *Sparganium erectum*, Reed Sweet-grass, *Glyceria maxima*, and a number of less robust species will hang on here on this slightly lower land, even though open water is largely a thing of the past in these situations. Species that still occur on the nearby riverbanks will often be concentrated in these areas, now well away from the main watercourse. Where grazing continues, the floors of these areas are often covered with Creeping Buttercup, *Ranunculus repens*, and Silverweed, *Potentilla anserina*, especially where floodwater has persisted and retarded the growth of grasses. Species that develop early in the year are at a slight advantage in that they may have matured before the full impact of summer grazing takes effect. Some sedges occur here, notably Brown Sedge,

Carex disticha, and Hairy Sedge, *Carex hirta*, both of which can tolerate some grazing.

Sloping ground leading down to the river will often have Bulbous Buttercup, *Ranunculus bulbosus,* on the dry, lime-rich, well-aerated soils on the higher ground. Lower down, there is often a profusion of Meadow Buttercup, *Ranunculus acris*, and then at the wettest areas, Creeping Buttercup dominates.

Where there is a good supply of water near the surface, growth is normally quite high. Perennials with high-nutrient demands do well here. Low-growing wetland species cannot compete with the larger plants and usually get crowded or shaded out. These areas are usually grazed and scrub invasion is curtailed. Continued grazing is necessary to maintain them in an open state and, where it is abandoned, these areas can become colonised very rapidly by willows and alder. The substantial trees that fringe our rivers are very strong once they are established but are much more vulnerable to trampling and grazing when they are seedlings. When cattle are removed, there is a period when herbaceous perennials such as the larger willowherbs, docks, nettles and other nutrient-demanding species begin to take hold. Hemp-agrimony, *Eupatorium cannabinum*, often present in small stands, can become very dominant, especially when water trickles down from higher ground. Scrambling up through these can be found Hedge Bindweed, *Calystegia sepium*, and Woody Nightshade, *Solanum dulcamara*. When left alone for several years, these species can take over large stretches of abandoned riverside grassland, turning it into an impenetrable wall of dense vegetation.

Even within an individual apparently homogenous stretch of riverside grassland there are many variations in micro-topography of great significance to local plant distribution and biodiversity. Over time the water-deposited sands and silt have imparted a general levelling character to the terrain, but land drains and dips dictated by underlying topography, excavated pools, small quarries and disused features such as water-powered mills all contribute to the topographical mixture. In order to drive a water wheel, a head of water pressure had to be created. The river water was intercepted at a mill-race,

diverted into a channel at a relatively high point and routed to the mill. These mills are largely abandoned by now but are still prominent features in the landscape and often explain the occurrence of wet-ground species in unusual situations. Where these mill-races have fallen into disuse and leaked over the years, water has been directed and released into areas that would otherwise be dry.

MEADOW BUTTERCUP

Where grazing has been reduced or delayed, many marshlands can put on an impressive show early in the year. A few weeks later, when the cattle arrive, things will look very different.

Furthermore the areas occupied by the water storage areas and the lines of intercepted water leading to them still keep the ground water levels close enough to the surface to maintain a wet grassland flora.

Drains and other dips in the land where water accumulates or comes close to the surface usually give other wetland plants a place to grow. In these situations or even where water flushing down the

slopes of the river valley slows down when it hits the level ground, more marshy ground develops. Depending on the degree of grazing, these areas can be very rich in species or not so interesting. Dips of less than 10 cm can make a big difference to the distribution of wet-ground plants in these areas. A drain, even one that runs dry in summer, can have many extra species growing along its line. Light grazing here can be quite beneficial, especially to low-growing species. Marshy ground, more consistently damp even in summer but not necessarily with any open water, has many extra species. Devil's-bit Scabious, *Succisa pratensis*, and Cuckoo Flower, *Cardamine pratensis* (*pratensis* = growing in meadows), are aptly named, as are Common Marsh Bedstraw, *Galium palustre*, Marsh Thistle, *Cirsium palustre*, and Marsh Horsetail, *Equisetum palustre* (*palustre* = growing in marshes) and obviously Water Mint, *Mentha aquatica*.

Where the ground is a little lower, especially near drains, the wetland flora usually fares better. These plants are neither aquatics nor even emergents. They grow by the drain-sides because the ground is nearer the water. The main species here are true marsh plants. They usually cannot cope with grazing and at the same time need plenty of water. Where there are extensive stretches of this type of land the flora can be surprisingly colourful in early summer. Ragged Robin, *Lychnis flos-cuculi*, Marsh Marigold, *Caltha palustris*, Lesser Spearwort, *Ranunculus flammula*, Common Spotted-orchid, *Dactylorhiza fuchsii*, Angelica, *Angelica sylvestris*, Marsh Woundwort, *Stachys palustris*, and Square-stalked St John's-wort, *Hypericum tetrapterum*, are all good and widespread indicators of marshy ground. The mix of species is determined here not only by water availability and grazing regimes but also by the nature of the soil. In the fringe of vegetation in the

ORCHIDS

Wherever they occur, the presence of orchids indicates that there is still hope. Many species have had their geographical ranges drastically reduced and are still declining. Orchids as a group have been severely reduced by the combined impact of drainage and subsequent grazing.

MARSH WOUNDWORT

Marsh Woundwort has a powerful presence in all sorts of wet and flooded areas, even extending onto the edges of roadside drains.

(LEFT TO RIGHT): ANGELICA, SNEEZEWORT AND TUFTED VETCH WITH GREATER BIRD'S-FOOT TREFOIL

Angelica, Sneezewort and the combination of Tufted Vetch and Greater Bird's-foot Trefoil are typical of slightly base-poor conditions in wetlands in the drumlin belt of Cavan and Monaghan. In these areas all these species can even appear on roadside embankments where the main roads have cut through the drumlins.

poorly-drained slightly acid soils of the drumlin regions and in areas of high rainfall, Sneezewort, *Achillea ptarmica*, Greater Bird's-foot Trefoil, *Lotus pedunculatus*, Tufted Vetch, *Vicia cracca*, and Marsh Ragwort, *Senecio aquaticus*, form a substantial bar around lakes. In really wet areas these species can occur even on wet roadsides with other species of rush such as Soft Rush, which is widespread and Compact Rush, *Juncus conglomeratus*.

One of the major meadowland casualties of new agricultural methods in river valleys is Common Meadow-rue, *Thalictrum flavum*. This was once a widespread species, often forming large stands in the flood plain. It is a tall, non-woody plant, very susceptible to grazing and is now usually only found on the edges of rivers, either in

the zone of emergent vegetation on the riverbank or in wet scrub nearby where grazing is restricted. It still may be found on lime-rich soils adjoining lakes that are likely to flood. A more frequent associate, Common Valerian, *Valeriana officinalis*, can often do well in similar ground with other tall species.

Attempts to drain the lands of Ireland have met with varying degrees of failure. However, the deep arterial drainage schemes of the twentieth century were far more successful and were to have a profoundly modifying effect on riverside habitats. Not only did they alleviate sporadic flooding but they increased the throughput of water in river valleys. Wetlands in the immediate vicinity became dry. The upcast material was often deposited on the banks of the rivers either as prominent ridges of soil and rock or was distributed over the land. The much smaller areas that were irrigated by springs were less affected as their waters usually came, literally, from other sources. It is still possible using aerial photographs to detect features in the landscape where water once flowed but are now dry even in winter and hold no wetland species. An examination of the soil in these areas, especially where the sward is a little more open, will often reveal a soil that contains many particles of sandy material mixed with more humus-rich soil, indicating the former extent of alluvial deposition.

WATER-CRESS

Water-cress can clog up drains and cattle pools. When the drains are cleared, it reappears quickly along with a variety of short-lived annual wetland species.

This has been an ongoing feature in the transformation of the landscape. It is not so evident in areas where the water table is consistently near the surface, particularly in areas with broken topography where there are plenty of depressions in the landscape for wetland species. However, in level areas where there is a good covering of soil, wetlands are much rarer. Land drainage is a major factor but the naturally free-draining character of many soils is also contributory. Deep-rooting plants can resist for a few years as the water table gradually falls but the shallow-rooted smaller species die off fairly quickly. One area where this is most pronounced is in north Co. Dublin (Fingal). When Nathaniel Colgan wrote his Flora in 1904, he gave localities for all the rarer species he had encountered, including Sneezewort. It resembles a sturdy ragwort in stature but with the yellow ray-florets replaced by white ones. Colgan considered it to be a plant of damp pastures, marshy ground, gravelly places and cultivated land in peaty and sandy soil and he deemed it to be frequent and locally abundant in the county. A five-year survey of the flora of Co. Dublin 90 years later found only two plants in the north of the county in a dug-out drain and a further colony on the fringes of the Dublin Mountains. This indicates the local collapse of a conspicuous easily-recorded species that is still quite common elsewhere in Ireland.

Some soils are less permeable than others. These are usually called gleys. They are generally of sticky, bluish soil, finely particled and arrest the rate of water loss. They have often formed in low-lying areas and are sometimes able to retain a rudimentary wet-ground flora. These areas of impeded drainage are sometimes more easily seen in early winter in cereal-growing areas after the crop has been removed. Here rainwater can be seen lingering, sometimes for weeks, in these low-lying areas. Sometimes these areas flood in winter and, depending on the fall of the land, can even remain moist in summer. In pastureland they are often excavated further to provide watering holes for cattle, at which stage their botanical interest decreases significantly. Drainage operations affect the flora directly by literally cutting off the water supply. They also bring about land-use changes. Land that was previously suitable only for summer grazing can now be grazed earlier. The surviving flora is likely to be eaten before it has set its seed.

Bare Mud Habitats

Grazing by cattle in areas that are flooded in winter introduces a new structural element into wet grasslands. The land drains leading into streams and rivers are periodically excavated to improve water flow. Quickly-colonising species get started and gradually clog up the drains. They are then dug out again and the colonisation process resumes. There are a number of species which, therefore, go through a phase of colonisation and consolidation and are then set back for a few years before re-establishing themselves. The most regularly-occurring of these on good soils are Brooklime, *Veronica beccabunga*, and two common species of water-cress, Narrow-fruited Water-cress, *Nasturtium microphyllum*, and Water-cress, *Nasturtium officinale*. These are perennial species and they produce plenty of seed from which new plants will germinate.

Other plants are also found in these churned-up muddy areas, which are maintained in an open state by trampling livestock and in an elevated

REDSHANK

Redshank, usually a plant of weedy arable ground, occurs in natural habitats on lakeshores and also on bare muddy ground near lakes and rivers.

nutrient-rich state by their dung. These species are usually annuals and must complete their life cycle before summer comes and the mud hardens. One of the best exponents of this strategy is Marsh Yellow-cress, *Rorippa palustris*. It has divided pinnate leaves, small yellow flowers and stumpy fruits and has seeds that remain viable for long periods in the soil. Two wet-ground speedwells, Blue Water-speedwell, *Veronica anagallis-aquatica*, and Pink Water-speedwell, *Veronica catenata*, also turn up on muddy ground. The first of these is usually taller and is really a species of open drains, where it can become quite lush. Both grow, however, ephemerally, in muddy ground near rivers and lakes. If the bare nutrient-rich mud has been exposed, either by water failing to drain away or by cattle churning up the sward, some other species can appear, especially Celery-leaved Crowfoot, *Ranunculus scleratus*, and its relative, terrestrial forms of Thread-leaved Water-crowfoot, *Ranunculus tricophyllus*. The latter species is usually a proper submerged aquatic, which puts its flowering heads up above the water in summer. However, it can flower on bare almost dry mud, where the water in which it grew has disappeared suddenly. Two yellow-flowered species from the Daisy family flower later in the year, well into autumn. These are the Nodding Bur-marigold, *Bidens cernua,* and Trifid Bur-marigold, *Bidens tripartita*. They also occur in nutrient-rich, muddy ground, often in abundance. Despite being large plants, they are not very competitive and usually grow on the wettest mud where cattle sometimes cannot reach. However, the wet boundaries of these muddy areas fluctuate with the season and sometimes these species are stranded suddenly on dry ground. In the south Midlands a small dock, Golden Dock, *Rumex maritimus,* occurs on good soils near small lakes and pools in the draw-down zone, especially on these muddy grounds. It is a very distinctive species, with fruits with many appendages and golden-yellow leaves. It has been recorded rarely in the past and in terms of its habitat and lifestyle is clearly an extreme version of the limited window-of-opportunity group of muddy-ground colonists. On slightly more acid ground Water-pepper, *Persicaria hydropiper*, and Small Water-pepper, *Persicaria minor*, are to be found, especially in the north and west along with Marsh Cudweed, *Gnaphalium uliginosum*, and Bristle Club-rush, *Isolepis setacea*. Several of these species can sometimes be found growing together on the muddy margins of small lakes and sluggish rivers elsewhere. Where water levels have been regulated these species have now become rarer. Their natural preference was to live in the draw-down zone of lakes, rivers, reservoirs and muddy wetlands, growing best in late summer as the season advanced and water levels fell. These are rarer now as diversity and its associated randomness is progressively stripped from the countryside.

The Burren

The importance of the spectacularly colourful flora of the Burren region of north Co. Clare has long been recognised. Richard Heaton, a clergyman with an interest in botany, reported his findings to William How, author of one of the first books on plants and distribution, *Phytologia Britannica*, sometime before 1650. The two best-known Burren plants reported were Mountain Avens, *Dryas octopetala*, and Spring Gentian, *Gentiana verna* – species that botanical tourists have been flocking to see ever since. They can hardly be missed, as both species are in full flower and clearly visible from roadsides in the Burren spring, where the striking and unusual blue of the Gentian contrasts with the bright white petals of the Mountain Avens.

The Burren has many different plant communities, habitat types and rare or interesting species. Access is refreshingly less restricted than in many parts of Ireland and the vegetation is in a remarkably pure condition. In the course of a short walk a visitor may encounter species better known from cooler upland mainland Europe and from the warmer habitats further to the south, finding a few plants from the colder alpine regions and then seeing species that are thoroughly at home here in our softer climate. Some of the most interesting species occupy different habitat types but most of these occur in close proximity. That is part of the delight of the Burren. It should be remembered also that many habitats exist in the Burren that also occur elsewhere. The area has its share of agricultural, coastal and wooded flora. However, the main interest centres on the flora of the almost bare limestone pavement and the wetlands.

The flora of the exposed limestone bedrock is most unusual in Ireland, where so much of the countryside is covered with various forms of glacial till, bog or heathland. Much of the exposed rock of Ireland is of siliceous or 'acid' rocks. The contrasting bare limestone rocks of the Burren warm up early in the year and retain their heat. Their porous character, augmented by chemical decomposition by slightly acidic rainfall, results in the rapid loss of rainwater that passes directly downwards through the cracks. Surface erosion continues, soils form slowly and new microhabitats develop. Larger and deeper-rooting

Mountain Avens

The dense layers of Mountain Avens' white flowers, contrasting with its dark green leaf mats, form an enduring image in the Burren spring. Mountain Avens was one of the first species to be formally recorded from Ireland. It is a plant of upland ground elsewhere in the country but in the Burren it can grow down to sea level. In summer the flowers produce fruit crowned with feathery plumes resembling the seed heads of Clematis. Heaton remarked thus about 1650, stating: 'In the mountains betwixt Gort and Galloway. It makes a pretty shew in the winter with his rough heads like *Viorna*.'

nutrient-demanding plants cannot grow well on the thin, dry soils. The shallow soils and almost bare rock surfaces are occupied by short-lived annuals and longer-lived perennials. However, in the grykes (deep clefts between the flatter pavement areas) longer-lasting and even woody plants grow. Sometimes Hazel, *Corylus avellana*, Spindle, *Euonymus europaeus*, and other woody species survive, pinned back by wind and grazing. They can create a shaded habitat with a typical woodland flora beneath. Frost is a rarity and the climate is relatively mild. Alpine plants do well, being favoured by the free-draining stony soil, where the surrounding rock has been fragmented to the point where it forms a level 'scree', and many can thrive even near to sea level.

These life strategies have enabled different species to occupy different niches. Many have managed to spread throughout Ireland from these very natural-looking habitats. Others are tightly confined to the areas of exposed limestone, both within the Burren proper or extending to similar ground well beyond its boundaries. Short-lived annuals such as Hairy Bitter-cress, *Cardamine hirsuta*, Wall Speedwell, *Veronica arvensis*, and Rue-leaved Saxifrage, *Saxifraga tridactylites*, are more familiar as urban plants on walls and open gravelly ground. They grow rapidly in early spring and shed their seeds by early summer.

In the crevices on the pavement, Rusty-back Fern, *Ceterach officinarum*, forms huge tufts very different from the much neater-looking plant of limestone walls throughout lowland Ireland. Other ferns more often found on walls include Maidenhair Spleenwort, *Asplenium trichomanes*, and Wall-rue,

HAIRY BITTER-CRESS

Hairy Bitter-cress can form dense, short-lived colonies on very shallow soils on the Burren's natural limestone pavement. Small annual species must complete their growth cycle and set their seed long before the severe drought conditions of high summer set in. This abbreviated lifestyle coupled with the ability to produce large quantities of seeds also equips many such species to become garden weeds, where they successfully colonise bare, open soils that have been treated with herbicides.

RUE-LEAVED SAXIFRAGE

An annual species unlike most of the other Irish saxifrages, Rue-leaved Saxifrage also flowers early in the year, growing on the shallowest of soils but also in arid coastal grassland. This ability has stood it in good stead, allowing it to spread throughout Ireland where it often germinates in the moss-mats that develop on the tops of old limestone walls and the untrodden sections of urban pavements.

Asplenium ruta-muraria. These are not the plants that visiting botanists come to see, but they illustrate a life strategy that has enabled them to colonise built-up areas. However, the spectacular Maidenhair Fern itself, *Adiantum capillus-veneris*, widespread throughout the Burren, has not transferred to urban habitats. It is a species of much warmer climates and thrives in the frost-free environs of the west. This species can be found in many places in the Burren, where its fronds protrude from shaded rock crevices and can sometimes be spotted bobbing in the wind on damp or shaded roadside rock exposures. The other ferns with which it grows are clearly better able to cope with frost outside the climatic refuge.

There are many interesting species exhibiting distributions that challenge us to explain them. One of the best-known geographical contrasts is that between the Dense-flowered Orchid, *Neotinea maculata*, and Spring Gentian. The former is a species of the Mediterranean area and not known from Britain (though recently found on the Isle of Man). The latter is usually classified as an arctic-alpine but is not strictly so, as it is found in the north Pennines in Britain but occurs on relative low ground in Europe and barely makes it inside the Arctic Circle. Pyramidal Bugle, *Ajuga pyramidalis*, is a well-known boreal-montane plant that grows near sea level in the Burren and on the Aran Islands, then on Rathlin and northern Scotland. In contrast, Hoary Rock-rose, *Helianthemum oelandicum* (better known as *H. canum*), a species sometimes locally abundant even on rocky Burren roadsides, is from sunnier ground in southern Europe although it extends northward as far as the island of Öland off the south-east coast of Sweden, as its name suggests. Öland was one of the early research-grounds of Linnaeus, a limestone island very different from the adjoining mainland with a

DENSE-FLOWERED ORCHID

This inconspicuous little orchid is thinly scattered in the Burren in short grassland and has been found recently in a number of favoured sites beyond its traditional boundaries. It has also been discovered on the Isle of Man. It is one of the many biogeographical puzzles that present in the west of Ireland – in this case a species with a largely Mediterranean distribution but unknown in mainland Britain.

SHRUBBY CINQUEFOIL

Shrubby Cinquefoil is best known by now as a durable low garden shrub, appearing not only in its usual yellow-petalled form but also occurring in a variety of white- and orange-blossomed cultivars in mass plantings on urban roundabouts. It looks far more in keeping with its surroundings where it grows naturally at the upper flood levels of the Burren lakes.

very rich flora. Here he also found a significant site for another famous Burren plant, Shrubby Cinquefoil, *Potentilla fruticosa*. There are many other examples where species with wildly differing broad-scale distribution types may be found growing in close proximity. Some of these, occurring on the interface of different distribution types, serve as examples of species at their geographical extremes and as such are believed to have potential as indicators of climate change. They most certainly have great significance as indicators of grassland-management practice.

The grasslands in the Burren range from the heavily-grazed areas, usually on deeper soils, to the much more skeletal soils where the rarest species live. The latter are the key areas meriting conservation action. Though classified as grasslands, most of the species present are not in fact grasses. There are, however, some grasses that are significantly associated with Burren conditions, the chief of which is Blue Moor-grass, *Sesleria caerulea*, which forms strong tufts on the bare limestone pavement and produces unusually-coloured bluish flower heads. Setting aside the heavily-farmed areas, the grasslands themselves form a wonderful array of types, ranging from lime-rich to lime-poor, almost heathy grassland. Various schemes of classification

THYME BROOMRAPE

Various species of broomrape parasitise the roots of other plants, garnering their nourishment from the endeavours of their hosts. Thyme Broomrape is nearly always clearly parasitic on the roots of Wild Thyme. In the Burren it usually grows in very short grassland, scree slopes and on sand dunes but also occurs in a few select habitats elsewhere in Ireland. The current scientific name, *Orobanche alba*, may seem inappropriate but an older name, *O. rubra*, is more convincing. The Belfast botanist John Templeton discovered it on Cave Hill before it had been detected in Britain.

Well-known for its frequent and justified appearances in tourist brochures, Bloody Crane's-bill grows abundantly in the Burren and on rocky limestone ground further afield. It occurs elsewhere in isolated colonies around the Irish coast, extending as a native on the east coast cliffs as far north as Howth and Lambay Island and to Donegal in the west. In common with many attractive species, it has been taken into cultivation and has subsequently escaped into areas well beyond its natural range.

have attempted to identify the main gradients of vegetation variation and these are broadly related to soil depth, grazing practice and sward management. Thin, lightly-grazed terrain, rarely if ever fertilised, has the greatest range of rare and significant species and therefore has the highest conservation value. Scrub re-encroachment is now a feature of some parts of the Burren. Where grazing has relaxed, Hazel, Blackthorn, *Prunus spinosa*, and Bracken, *Pteridium aquilinum*, can spread rapidly from existing colonies. However, there are other areas with relatively species-poor grassland communities where scrub has not yet invaded. This tendency will have implications for open short grassland and heathland habitats, especially in areas where scrub can establish a firm roothold.

At first glance the sand dunes of the Burren coast seem very similar to those of many other areas. Bird's-foot Trefoil, *Lotus corniculatus*, is common and with it are Lady's Bedstraw, *Galium verum*, and a small white-flowered related species, Squinancywort, *Asperula cynanchica*. Orchids are very obvious here, especially Early-purple Orchid, *Orchis mascula*, Pyramidal Orchid, *Anacamptis pyramidalis*, and Fragrant Orchid, *Gymnadenia*

SAXIFRAGES

The dense, flowering masses of various saxifrages replicate the impression of a true alpine landscape. In the Burren, many usually upland species of rocky habitats can grow commonly almost at sea level on rocky terrain and thin grassland.

conopsea. Bee Orchid, *Ophrys apifera,* grows well and sometimes abundantly. These species extend from the sandhills onto the adjoining grasslands. Once the shallow soils are encountered, the marvellous mossy rocky grassland takes over. This is justifiably the habitat of the tourist posters. Mountain Avens is widespread and so are Spring Gentian, Hoary Rock-rose, Irish Eyebright, *Euphrasia salisburgensis,* Slender St John's-wort, *Hypericum pulchrum,* and Thyme, *Thymus*

serpyllum. Growing often as a parasite on Thyme can be found the stems of Thyme Broomrape, *Orobanche alba,* both on the shallow soils and in fixed dunes nearby. Despite its name, it usually has reddish flowers. Intermingled with these are the large strong pink flowers of Bloody Crane's-bill, *Geranium sanguineum,* and Madder, *Rubia peregrina,* and, here and there, Fly Orchid, *Ophrys insectifera,* Spring Sandwort, *Minuartia verna,* Irish Saxifrage, *Saxifraga rosacea* (especially nearer the sea), and Mossy Saxifrage, *S. hypnoides*. Elsewhere on the shallow soils, Mouse-eared-hawkweed, *Pilosella officinarum*, and Mountain Everlasting, *Antennaria dioica*, form large mats. Like the saxifrages, these are perennials and form substantial vegetative clumps that can withstand arid conditions.

Some of these species are not by any means restricted to the Burren but are far more easily encountered here than in most parts of Ireland. Fly Orchid is also found in fens. Both Madder and Bloody Crane's-bill are to be found on steep cliffs around the coast. Later in the year, Harebell, *Campanula rotundifolia*, launches into bloom with an exuberance seldom seen elsewhere in Ireland. Its blue nodding flowers define nicely the areas where grazing has had minimal impact. In contrast, Dropwort, *Filipendula vulgaris*, a plant of calcareous grassland in Britain, is a species that is widespread in the Burren proper but exceedingly rare outside it in Ireland. Its growth form indicates a plant that is ill-equipped to cope with grazing, a factor that affects many other herbaceous perennial species of similar stature.

Various plants have been recorded by botanists in the past but not seen for many years. One such was Arctic Sandwort, *Arenaria norvegica*, discovered, new to Ireland, in 1961. It is a species from Norway, Sweden, Iceland and Scotland. It was not seen for many years since, despite determined searches. Recently a visiting botanist re-discovered the species in a potentially new site in the Burren. It remains to be seen whether other native colonies of this species can be found. It may seem surprising that such discoveries can still be made in areas as well worked as the Burren. However, many plants are in flower only for a few weeks and can easily be missed, especially annuals and small delicate perennials.

There is amazing diversity in the flora, often over short distances due to the amount of variation in the almost bare-rock microhabitats. Ground that apparently comprises bare rock can have narrow fissures through which roots of certain species can grow downwards. In the grykes shallow soils form, down into which livestock cannot reach to browse. As the soil becomes more leached, usually on the highest ground, Ling, *Calluna vulgaris*, appears. Growing in these areas are other species usually associated with dry, very lime-poor habitats. The most obvious of these is Wood Sage, *Teucrium scorodonia*, which grows where the bare limestone is fragmented, often with Burnet Rose, *Rosa spinosissima*. On soils nearby Carline Thistle, *Carlina vulgaris* and Yellow-wort, *Blackstonia perfoliata*, flourish, and Salad Burnet, *Poterium sanguisorba*, grows in circumstances that challenge our preconceptions as to what constitutes a lime-loving and a lime-hating species. In crevices on the limestone pavement the reddish-flowers of Dark-red Helleborine, *Epipactis atrorubens*, appear, especially on higher ground, and it extends in some places onto a type of heathland where the leaching process is more extreme. Here Mountain Avens is still present in quantity along with Blue Moor-grass, Crowberry, *Empetrum nigrum*, and Golden-rod, *Solidago virguaea*. In some places on these higher areas, Bearberry, *Arctostaphylos uva-ursi*, also occurs. These species reinforce the feeling of naturalness and remoteness of the upland parts of the Burren and are thought to possibly represent a form of natural climax vegetation.

Turloughs are a particularly unusual feature of limestone landscapes. These low-lying areas flood both in winter and after sustained rainfall in summer. The number of species that can cope with these rapidly-alternating conditions is limited. They are often grazed and produce 'lawns' of

DROPWORT

Less well-known than many of its Burren associates, Dropwort is almost unknown elsewhere in Ireland. It is a close relative of the much commoner Meadowsweet. It is more widespread in Britain, where some of its limestone-grassland colonies have been lost through lack of grazing. Appropriate grazing levels are difficult to maintain for many grassland species – too much and the plants are eaten to the point of extinction, too little and the grassland reverts to scrub.

NORTHERN BEDSTRAW

A relation of the ubiquitous trailing Goose-grass, the more free-standing Northern Bedstraw is common in limestone grassland on the upper parts of lakeshores in the Burren, especially where the sloping bedrock protrudes. It extends well beyond the Burren, occupying similar rocky ground around the larger midland lakes but can also occupy drier ground.

short, closed vegetation usually with no woody vegetation in their lower parts. Where water lingers in their lower sections the grassy growth is inhibited and the ensuing muddy ground is colonised by a number of annual nutrient-demanding species, including species familiar from areas where natural rotting plant materials gather, such as on the drift-lines of larger lakeshores. Here grow various knotweeds such as the familiar Redshank, *Persicaria maculosa*, Small water-pepper, *P. minor*, Amphibious Bistort, *P. amphibia*, and even Water-pepper, *P. hydropiper*, which is usually a plant of more acid ground. Areas that are not permanently muddy or churned up by cattle are often dominated by a pure sward of Silverweed, *Potentilla anserina*, another plant from coastal drift-lines. When grazing has not been too severe various species of Yellow-cress (*Rorippa*) can grow and fruit but must do so quickly, as they are easily browsed by cattle. Marsh Yellow-cress, *Rorippa palustris*, is a widespread species in Ireland on muddy ground by rivers and wetlands cut up by cattle, but a second closely-related species, Northern Yellow-cress, *Rorippa islandica*, has been recognised in recent years from a number of Irish turloughs. Contemporary research has demonstrated that even common species such as Creeping Buttercup, *Ranunculus repens*, have leaf forms that become progressively more dissected in the most inundated zones.

At the upper levels of the turloughs the flora is very different and in some ways resembles that of dune slacks. At the upper drift-line a distinct band of violets can be seen, sometimes in great abundance in late spring. This is usually the Fen Violet, also known as the Turlough Violet, *Viola persicifolia*. Other violets can occur here, such as Heath Violet, *Viola canina*, and the much more widespread Common Dog-violet, *Viola riviniana*.

In some of the turloughs another very rare plant in Britain, Water Germander, *Teucrium scordium*, grows. This is the plant that is so obvious on the shores of Lough Ree but so rare elsewhere in Ireland. The upper limit of flooding has been traditionally defined by the presence of a moss, *Cinclidotus fontinaloides*, that can sometimes even be found growing on walls well above the apparent upper drift-lines' encroachment.

Although much is made of the aridness of the Burren, there is a number of large lakes as well as many smaller ones. These can flood extensively in winter and the more substantial ones do not dry out in summer. Many of these lakes are surrounded by a band of fen vegetation – typically formed on lime-rich peat fringed by more marly substrates at the upper margins. These eventually give way to communities where the ground water influence is lessened and more influenced by rainwater and comes to resemble in some ways the flora of raised bog margins.

Water bodies intermediate in the character of their flooding occur also. Many of these are therefore shallow and thus warm and subject to drying out around the margins. This is the favoured ground of the yellow-flowered Shrubby Cinquefoil, which is more familiar as a garden shrub in a variety of colour forms. Here it is truly native and extends a little beyond the Burren to Lough Corrib and to East Mayo. It is known from the Lake District and Upper Teesdale and also from the Pyrenees, the Maritime Alps, south-east Sweden and further afield. On out-jutting bedrock in these occasionally flooding zones Northern Bedstraw, *Galium boreale*, also grows. It often occurs with another close relative, Limestone Bedstraw, *Galium sterneri*. This species occurs throughout the Burren and closely resembles another bedstraw, Heath Bedstraw, *Galium saxatile*, that is much commoner throughout Ireland, particularly on acid substrates.

A visit to the Burren at any time of the year is always stimulating and challenging. There are many similar habitats (limestone and short lime-rich grassland over rock) in other parts of the west. Elements of the Burren flora extend far beyond the traditional boundary area in the north of Clare. The Aran Islands, though part of Co. Galway, have conventionally been included as part of the Burren complex and many of the best Burren plants can be found here, but there are contradictions. For instance, Purple Milk-vetch, *Astragalus danicus*, grows here in its only known Irish sites, and it forms a biogeographical puzzle. It is mainly a plant of the east of Britain, though it also occurs on the Isle of Man and the Hebrides. How can it be here on the western side of Ireland on Inishmore and Inishmaan but not on apparently similar ground in the Burren? This is the type of conundrum frequently encountered by plant geographers. Is there something unusual about the Aran Islands' environment that has not yet been recognised? Alternatively, is it a case of a species that was formerly more widespread having died out in other areas and persisting in sites favoured through combinations of historical and environmental factors yet to be appreciated?

The Burren is an amazing natural forum where many different species from different geographical backgrounds grow together. They each have their individual ecological preferences but can find expression here in conditions that in such benign combinations occur very rarely elsewhere in Ireland. In many other areas quality habitats are under constant pressure. Some species survive, but only just. Various habitats struggle on in a degraded condition, testaments to what was once present. However, in the best parts of the Burren, both habitats and their associated species are freed from the constraints of severe grazing and fertiliser application. The plants do well here because they can and because they are allowed to.

Recently, more appropriate, relevant and practical nature conservation measures have been introduced. Innovative agricultural schemes are in place, providing opportunities to maintain the amazing botanical diversity by funding measures to protect habitats that truly deserve protection. Maintaining the rich Burren flora is now engaging the national authorities and the public. The character of grazing – when it takes place and at what level of intensity – has been identified as a vital element in maintaining the open character of the vegetation. Ensuring that these habitats are managed in order to maintain them in their optimal condition by devising management strategies to do so are parts of the next challenge for nature conservation in Ireland.

Further Reading

Aalen, F.H.A., Whelan, K. & Stout, M. 1997. *Atlas of the Irish Rural Landscape.* Cork University Press.

Allen, D.E. & Hatfield, G. 2004. *Medicinal Plants in Folk Tradition. An Ethnobotany of Britain & Ireland.* Portland, Cambridge: Timber Press.

Braithwaite, M.E., Ellis, R.W. & Preston, C.D. 2006. *Change in the British Flora, 1987–2004.* London: BSBI.

Collins, T. 1985. *Floreat Hibernia. A Bio-bibliography of Robert Lloyd Praeger 1865–1953.* Royal Dublin Society.

Curtis, T. & McGough, N. *The Irish Red Data Book.* vol 1. *Vascular Plants.* Dublin: Stationery Office.

Feehan, J. & O'Donovan, G. 1996. *The Bogs of Ireland.* Dublin.

Fossitt, J. 2000. *A Guide to Habitats in Ireland.* Kilkenny: The Heritage Council.

Mitchell, F. & Ryan, M. 2001. *Reading the Irish Landscape.* Dublin: Town House.

Praeger, R.L. 1937. *The Way that I went.* Dublin: Hodges Figgis. Various subsequent editions.

Rodwell, J.S. (ed.) 1998. *British Plant Communities.* Volumes 1–5. Cambridge University Press.

Stearn, W. 1992. *Botanical Latin.* 4th edn. Devon: David & Charles.

Tansley, A. 1968. *Britain's Green Mantle.* 2nd edn. London: George Allen & Unwin.

Threlkeld, C. 1726. *Synopsis Stirpium Hibernicarum.* Dublin. A facsimile edition was published in 1988 by Boethius Press, Kilkenny, with a modern introduction and many interesting commentaries by E. Charles Nelson and a glossary of Irish plant names by Donal Synnott.

Viney, M. *Ireland.* 2003. Belfast: The Blackstaff Press.

White, J. (ed.) 1982. *Studies on Irish Vegetation.* Royal Dublin Society.

Biology and Environment, Proceedings of the Royal Irish Academy, is an essential source of information presenting the results of contemporary environmental research.

Identification

Curtis, T. & Thompson, R. 2009. *The Orchids of Ireland.* National Museums Northern Ireland.

Fitter, R. & Fitter, A. 1984. *Collins Guide to the Grasses, Sedges and Rushes of Britain and Northern Europe.* London: Collins.

Garrard, I. & Streeter, D. 1998. *The Wildflowers of the British Isles.* Midsummer Books.

Sayers, B. & Sex, S. 2008. *Ireland's Wild Orchids. A field guide.* Dublin: VS Publishing.

Sell, P. & Murrell, G. 1996 (onwards). *Flora of Great Britain and Ireland.* Volumes 1–5, of which 3 vols have so far appeared. Cambridge University Press.

Stace, C. 2010. *New Flora of the British Isles.* 3rd edn. Cambridge University Press.

Webb, D.A. *An Irish Flora.* Dundalgan Press. Various editions 1943–96. A new edition is in active preparation, edited by T. Curtis & J. Parnell.

Overviews of Distribution

Colgan, N. & Scully, R. 1898. *Contributions towards a Cybele Hibernica.* Dublin: Hodges, Figgis & Co.

Praeger, R.Ll. 1901. *Irish Topographical Botany.* Dublin: Royal Irish Academy.

1934. *The Botanist in Ireland.* Dublin: Hodges, Figgis & Co.

Preston, C., Pearman, D. & Dines, T. *New Atlas of the British and Irish Flora.* Oxford University Press.

Reynolds, S. 2002. *A Catalogue of the Alien Plants in Ireland.* Dublin: National Botanic Gardens.

Scannell, M.J.P. & Synnott, D.M. 1897. *Census Catalogue of the Flora of Ireland.* 2nd edn. Dublin: Stationery Office.

County Floras

County Floras are summaries of the knowledge of the history, distribution and habitats of the different plant species within a county. They represent the outcome of many decades of work by experienced field botanists. They provide first-hand information and are a powerful instrument in helping new botanists to become familiar with the whereabouts of species and their habitat preferences. County Floras often offer interpretations of the distribution of species. They are not identification guides. Many of the older Floras are long out of print, though some have been recently re-published or revised.

Akeroyd, J. (ed.) 1996. *The Wild Plants of Sherkin, Cape Clear and adjacent Islands of West Cork.* Cork: Sherkin Island Marine Station.

Booth, E. 1979. *The Flora of County Carlow.* Royal Dublin Society.

Brunker, J.P. 1950. *Flora of the County Wicklow.* Dundalk: Dundalgan Press (W. Tempest) Ltd.

Colgan, N. 1904. *Flora of the County Dublin.* Dublin: Hodges, Figgis & Co.

Dublin Naturalists' Field Club. 1998. *Flora of County Dublin.* Dublin: DNFC.

Feehan, J. 2010. *The Wildflowers of Offaly.* Tullamore: Offaly County Council.

Green, P. 2008. *Flora of County Waterford.* Dublin: OPW & National Botanic Gardens.

Hackney, P. 1992. *Stewart and Corry's Flora of the North-east of Ireland.* Belfast: Institute of Irish Studies.

Hart, H. 1898. *Flora of the County Donegal.* Dublin: Sealy, Bryers & Walker.

McNeill, I. 2010. *The Flora of County Tyrone.* Holywood: NMNI.

O'Mahony, T. *Wildflowers of Cork City and County.* Cork: The Collins Press.

Reilly, P. 2001. *The Flora of County Cavan.* Dublin: National Botanic Gardens,

Scully, R.W. 1916. *Flora of County Kerry.* Dublin: Hodges, Figgis & Co.

Webb, D.A., & Scannell, M. 1983. *Flora of Connemara and the Burren.* Royal Dublin Society & Cambridge University Press.

Wyse Jackson, P. & Sheehy Skeffington, M. 1984. *Flora of Inner Dublin.* Royal Dublin Society.

Contacts

The Dublin Naturalists' Field Club (DNFC) was founded in 1886 and currently arranges outings for members on a weekly to fortnightly basis, mainly in Dublin, Meath, Kildare and Wicklow with additional excursions elsewhere in Ireland. Details of activities may be found at www.dnfc.net. Membership is open to everyone interested in Irish natural history. Membership fees are very modest.

A similar society was founded even earlier in Belfast and welcomes naturalists in the same spirit as the Dublin group. See www.bnfc.org.uk.

The Botanical Society of the British Isles maintains the network of botanical recorders in Britain and Ireland. It publishes guides to the identification of difficult plant groups and a journal, and organises geographical mapping schemes that record and chart the distribution of the different species of plant living in the wild in Britain and Ireland. Again, membership is open to all. See www.bsbi.org.uk.

Acknowledgments

A series of lucky chances brought me into contact with the Dublin Naturalists' Field Club (DNFC) forty years ago. At that stage the Club had recently published *A Supplement to Colgan's Flora of the County Dublin*, updating the base-line study that Nathaniel Colgan had produced in 1904. As a result, I came into contact with many of the senior field botanists of the time, such as J.P. Brunker and Howard Hudson, who had learnt their craft and learnt it well from a previous generation. Years later I was to be associated with a further revision of the same Flora. In the course of my extended connection with the DNFC, I worked with many fine field botanists and was inducted into the living tradition of field botany and recording. To all of them, many no longer with us, I owe far more than I can now realise.

The outstanding person who set the standard for most of the current crop of field botanists was and is Maura Scannell, instilling confidence, plucking items of highly-relevant knowledge from obscurity and providing constant support within a unique Gaelic cocktail. As a result of her endeavours, a new generation of Irish field botanists came into being, the individuals learning from each other and in their time grafting new botanists onto an ancient, gnarled and much-ramified tree of environmental knowledge.

An apprenticeship with the plant group of the Field Club brought me later into contact with Con Breen and Donal Synnott, Dr Mary Carson, Aedine Mangan and the late Gerry Sheehan, all of whom provided direct field experience, books or lifts to places I could not have then known to have existed. I can remember with great precision the first day I realised the connection between plants and place. A field trip by car had been organised but there were too few seats. An alternative excursion was promptly arranged, a leader deputised (F.A.L. Gardner) and we, the seatless ones, were brought to the Glenasmole Waterworks where I saw my first 'rare' plants – a cluster of sedges and orchids, butterworts and Lesser Clubmoss – in what we now know to be a flush issuing from a petrifying spring. That *ad hoc* serendipity has been a feature of the DNFC's activity, connecting the known and the unknown in a unique spirit that is as necessary and relevant today at it was when the club was founded in 1886. That spirit of ecological enquiry was to be reactivated many years later whilst under the supervision of Dr D. Kelly.

The genesis of the current project arose out of a series of meetings between myself, Carsten Krieger and Fergal Tobin of Gill & Macmillan, and the end product I suspect represents a significant and startling departure from Fergal's original concept. However, he persisted with the venture as it grew in some novel directions. Carsten had independently been photographing Irish plants in their natural habitats. About the same time I had led a series of field trips under the aegis of the DNFC, exploring the species and habitats of the Dublin coast, drawing together observations that had been made in the course of habitat inventory work organised by Hans Visser and Debbie Tiernan of Fingal County Council and supported by the Heritage Council. These trips had flagged up the need for a simple book that would provide an accessible first step for those concerned with landscape protection, habitat management and their combined relationships to plant and habitat conservation. Many of our members became engaged with the latter projects, especially Con Breen, Dr David Nash, Dr Peter Wyse Jackson, Katy Duff, Melinda Lyons, Pat Lenihan, P.J. Walls, Sylvia Reynolds and Gerry Sharkey, each contributing individually to the ongoing process of making collectively obvious that which had been previously obscure.

The Botanical Society of the British Isles (BSBI) has consistently supported Irish field botanists for many years. The fusion of field work and data handling resulted in the production of the *New Atlas of the British & Irish Flora* in 2002. It is from this work that the distribution map of Dark-red Helleborine has been adapted.

As the project matured, as copy-editor Tess Tattersall was charged with the unenviable task of reducing an excessively long manuscript to a more readable size, excising the repetitious and arcane, whilst ensuring that the remaining elements joined up in logical sequence. In addition she was tasked with extracting written responses from me to various perfectly reasonable queries and has succeeded where many others have failed.

My interest in nature, in Dublin and Ireland would not have been possible without the help of my mother, Mary, father, Edward Doogue, and my aunt, Mae Doogue, who somehow found the resources in far more financially austere times to acquire on my behalf books on nature, geography and history and who brought direction and enlightenment into the life of a schoolboy in the Finglas of the 1950s.

Finally, I would like to thank my many past pupils from Scoil Mhuire, Marino, for giving me an opportunity to try out my various new discoveries, to demonstrate the fruits of my weekend field trips, to succeed as a teacher and to fail. In these days of regulation and homogenisation of education it was a pleasure and an experience to have spent so many years defending a type of learning that placed pupils before plans and put direct contact with the diverse and varied phenomenon that we call nature where it should be – in the field.

Declan Doogue

First and foremost I would like to thank Ina, Jonah and Lucy for their support and tolerating my absence when I had to go flower hunting in a far flung corner of Ireland again. A special thanks goes to my son Jonah, who pointed out every weed in West Clare to me and insisted I had to make a picture of it. A huge thank you goes to my agent Paul Feldstein for his tireless work. A big thank you also to Fergal Tobin and all the staff at Gill & Macmillan for taking on this project and making it a joy to work on. And last but not least I would like to thank Declan for some very inspiring, interesting and enjoyable field trips. Your knowledge and passion are truly amazing.

Carsten Krieger

Index

Sundew, 22, *260*
  Great (*Drosera anglica*), 254, 260
  Oblong-leaved (*Drosera intermedia*), 260, *261*
  Round-leaved (*Drosera rotundifolia*), *23*, 244, 253, *253*, 258
Sweet-briar (*Rosa rubiginosa*), 171–2, 194, 272
  Small-flowered (*Rosa micrantha*), 172
  Small-leaved (*Rosa agrestis*), 172, 194
Sweet-grass, Reed (*Glyceria maxima*), 154, 210–13, 223, 280
Swine's Cress, Lesser (*Lepidium didymum*) (*Coronopus didymus*), 67
Sycamore (*Acer pseudoplatanus*), 58, *59*, 106, 164, 183

Teasel, *129*
Thale Cress (*Arabidopsis thaliana*), 47, 48
Thistle
  Carline (*Carlina vulgaris*), *104*, 105, 268, 298
  Creeping (*Cirsium arvense*), 97
  Marsh (*Cirsium palustre*), 282, *282*
  Meadow (*Cirsium dissectum*), 235
  Slender (*Carduus tenuiflorus*), 65
  Sow-thistle, Perennial (*Sonchus arvensis*), *96*, 97, 140
  Spear, *63*
Threlkeld, Caleb, 13–14, 61, 79, 147, 173
Thrift (*Armeria maritima*), *41*, 113, *113*, *146*, 147, 150
Thyme, Wild (*Thymus praecox*), *101*, *103*, 105, 270, *273*
Thyme Broomrape (*Orobanche alba*), *295*, 297
Toadflax, Ivy-leaved (*Cymbalaria muralis*), *72*, *78*, 81
Toothwort (*Lathraea squamaria*), 192–4
Tormentil (*Potentilla erecta*), 197, *234*, 235, 241, 259, 268
Traveller's Joy (*Clematis vitalba*), *172*, 172–3
Tree Mallow, *142*
Trefoil
  Bird's-foot Trefoil (*Lotus corniculatus*), 54, 86, *86*, 101, 268, 274–5, 296
  Bird's-foot Trefoil, Greater (*Lotus pedunculatus*), 124, 285, *285*
  Bird's-foot Trefoil, Hairy (*Lotus subbiflorus*), 274
  Hop (*Trifolium campestre*), 102
  Lesser (*Trifolium dubium*), 57
Tussock-sedge, Greater (*Carex paniculata*), 202
Tutsan (*Hypericum androsaemum*), 173, *173*
Twayblade
  Common (*Neottia ovata*), 124, *124*
  Lesser (*Neottia cordata*), 258

Valerian
  Common (*Valeriana officinalis*), 154, *155*, 201, 285
  Red (*Centranthus ruber*), *3*, 80–1
Vetch
  Bitter-vetch (*Lathyrus linifolius*), 276
  Bush (*Vicia sepium*), *180*, 181, 192
  Kidney (*Anthyllis vulneraria*), *101*, 102, *102*, 245, 246, 268, *271*
  Purple Milk-vetch (*Astragalus danicus*), 301
  Tufted (*Vicia cracca*), 285, *285*

Vetchling, Meadow (*Lathyrus pratensis*), 267, *267*
Violet, *191*, 301
  Dog-violet, Common (*Viola riviniana*), 105, 178, 187, 192, 301
  Dog-violet, Heath (*Viola canina*), 105, 178, 276
  Dog-violet, Pale (*Viola lactea*), 276
  Fen (Turlough Violet) (*Viola persicifolia*), 301
  Hairy (*Viola hirta*), 267
  Heath (*Viola canina*), 301
  Marsh (*Viola palustris*), 244, 259
  Wood (*Viola reichenbachiana*), 178, 187–9
Viper's-bugloss (*Echium vulgare*), 104, *104*

Wall Barley (*Hordeum murinum*), 61
Wallflower (*Erysimum cherii*), 71, 76–7
Wall Pennywort (Navelwort) (*Umbilicus rupestris*), 14, *14*, 74, *74*
Wall Pepper *see* Biting Stonecrop
Wall-rue (*Asplenium ruta-muraria*), 79, 291–3
Wall Speedwell (*Veronica arvensis*), 73, 291
Water Avens (*Geum rivale*), 202, *202*
Water-cress (*Nasturtium officinale*), 286, 287
  Narrow-fruited (*Nasturtium microphyllum*), 287
Watercress, Fool's (*Apium nodiflorum*), 213
Water-crowfoot, *207*, 209, 210
  Brackish (*R. baudottii*), 209
  Common (*R. aquatalis*), 209
  Fan-leaved (*Ranunculus circinatus*), 154
  Ivy-leaved (*Ranunculus hederaceus*), 210
  Pond (*Ranunculus peltatus*), 209
  River (*R. fluitans*), 209
  Stream (*Ranunculus penicillatus*), 209
  Thread-leaved (*Ranunculus tricophyllus*), 210
Water-dropwort, Parsley (*Oenanthe lachenalii*), 115, 233
Water Fern (*Azolla filiculoides*), 156, 223
Water Germander (*Teucrium scordium*), 222, 301
Water Horsetail (*Equisetum fluviatile*), 157, 224
Water-lily
  White (*Nymphaea alba*), 215–17, *217*
  Yellow (*Nuphar lutea*), 156, *208*, 210, 222
Water-milfoil, 210
  Alternate (*Myriophyllum alterniflorum*), 206, 217
  Spiked (*Myriophyllum spicatum*), 210
  Whorled (*Myriophyllum verticillatum*), 210
Water Mint (*Mentha aquatica*), *36*, 124, *124*, 235, 282
Water-moss
  Alpine (*Fontinalis squamosa*), 207
  Greater (*Fontinalis antipyretica*), 207
Water-pepper (*Persicaria hydropiper*), 219, 288, 301
  Small (*Persicaria minor*), 219, 288, 301
Water-plantain (*Alisma plantago-aquatica*), 154, 224, *226*
  Lesser (*Baldellia ranunculoides*), 224
  Narrow-leaved (*Alisma lanceolatum*), 224
Water-speedwell
  Blue (*Veronica anagallis-aquatica*), 213, 288

Pink (*Veronica catenata*), 288
Waterweed, Curly (*Lagarosiphon major*), 222
Weasel-snout, Yellow (*Lamiastrum galeobdolon*), 192
Whins *see* Furze
Whitebeam, Irish (*Sorbus hibernica*), 171, 186–7
Whitlow-grass, Spring (*Erophila verna*), 73
Whorl-grass (*Catabrosa aquatica*), 213
Willow, 127, 171, *174*, 195, 203
  Almond (*Salix triandra*), 203
  Crack-willow (*Salix fragilis*), 203
  Creeping (*Salix repens*), 127, *128*
  Dwarf (*Salix herbacea*), 245
  Eared (*Salix aurita*), 127, 167, 171, 244
  Goat (*Salix caprea*), 171, 186
  Grey (*Salix cinerea*), 127, 171, 201
  Purple (*Salix purpurea*), 203
  White (*Salix alba*), *174*, 203
Willowherb, 70
  American (*Epilobium ciliatum*), 70
  Broad-leaved (*Epilobium montanum*), 70
  Great (*Epilobium hirsutum*), 90, 127, *216*, 236, *236*, 279
  Hoary (*Epilobium parviflorum*), 90, 127
  Rosebay (*Chamerion angustifolium*) (*Epilobium angustifolium*), 68, 70, 246, 257
  Small-flowered (*Epilobium roseum*), 70
  Square-stalked (*Epilobium tetragonum*), 70
Wintergreen, 127
  Round-leaved (*Pyrola rotundifolia*), 127
Wood Anemone (*Anemone nemorosa*), *188*, 189, *191*
Wood Avens (*Geum urbanum*), *3*, 181, 192
Woodbine (*Lonicera periclymenum*), 172
Wood Melick (*Melica uniflora*), 192
Woodruff (*Asperula odorata*), *187*, 189
Wood-rush (*Luzula sylvatica*), 197, *197*
  Field (*Luzula campestris*), 102, 268
  Heath (*Luzula multiflora*), 276
Wood Sage (*Teucrium scorodonia*), 89, 197, 275, 298
Wood Sanicle (*Sanicula europaea*), *187*, 189
Wood-sorrel (*Oxalis acetosella*), 198–9, *199*
Wood Speedwell (*Veronica montana*), *186*, 189
Wood Violet (*Viola reichenbachiana*), 178, 187–9
Woody Nightshade (*Solanum dulcamara*), *139*, 139–40, 173, *175*, 201, 281
Wormwood, Sea (*Artemisia maritima*), 147
Woundwort
  Hedge (*Stachys sylvatica*), 181
  Marsh (*Stachys palustris*), 282, *284*
Wych Elm (*Ulmus glabra*), 186

Yarrow (*Achillea millefolium*), 57
Yellow-cress (*Rorippa*), 301
  Marsh (*Rorippa palustris*), 288, 301
  Northern (*Rorippa islandica*), 301
Yellow Flag (Yellow Iris) (*Iris pseudacorus*), 30, *31*, 140, *152*, 154, 201, 279
Yellow-rattle, *270*
Yellow-wort (*Blackstonia perfoliata*), 268, 298
Yew (*Taxus baccata*), 183, *183*, 195